B2948.R64 1974
0 0068 00029993 0
Rosen, Stanley/G. W. F. Hegel;an intro
Whitworth College Library

15

D1554535

G. W. F. HEGEL

G. W. F. HEGEL

An Introduction to the Science of Wisdom

Stanley Rosen

New Haven and London Yale University Press

1974

Library of Congress catalog card number: 73-86916
International standard book number: 0-300-01688-3

Designed by John O. C. McCrillis
and set in Baskerville type.
Printed in the United States of America by
The Vail-Ballou Press, Binghamton, New York.

Published in Great Britain, Europe, and Africa by
Yale University Press, Ltd., London.
Distributed in Latin America by Kaiman & Polon,
Inc., New York City; in Australasia and Southeast
Asia by John Wiley & Sons Australasia Pty. Ltd.,
Sydney; in India by UBS Publishers' Distributors Pvt.,
Ltd., Delhi; in Japan by John Weatherhill, Inc., Tokyo.

This book is dedicated to
Gaston Fessard, S. J., and Alexandre Kojève

Une idée forte communique un peu de sa force au contradicteur. Participant à la valeur universelle des esprits, elle s'insère, se greffe en l'esprit de celui qu'elle réfute, au milieu d'idées adjacentes, à l'aide desquelles, reprenant quelque avantage, il la complète, la rectifie; si bien que la sentence finale est en quelque sort l'oeuvre des deux personnes qui discutaient. C'est aux idées qui ne sont pas, à proprement parler, des idées, aux idées qui, ne tenant à rien, ne trouvent aucun point d'appui, aucun rameau fraternel dans l'esprit de l'adversaire, que celui-ci, aux prises avec le pur vide, ne trouve rien à répondre.

Marcel Proust, *A la recherche du temps perdu*

Contents

Preface

Intentions

This book is intended primarily for the English-speaking philosopher with little or no knowledge of Hegel. In addition, I allow myself the hope that certain sections may prove of interest to the more specialized reader. I have tried to write a coherent account of Hegel's teaching that is both comprehensive and technically precise. As the reader will see, the effort to fulfill this intention has led me to present material which is sometimes more difficult than that normally to be found in works of an introductory nature. My excuse is Hegel's teaching itself. An oversimplified account of that teaching would be no account at all. The inclusion of technical formulations, however, is scarcely inappropriate to a philosophical essay. I have done everything in my power to lead the serious student into the heart of Hegel's logical doctrine in a series of precise steps.

These steps combine material of a historical and analytical nature, including an occasional remark about the post-Hegelian situation. They do not include an exhaustive summary of Hegel's corpus, published and unpublished. Such summaries tend to be either too inaccurate for competent instruction or are themselves so cryptic as to require a commentary. Instead, I prefer to analyze in greater detail a small number of Hegelian texts which are crucial to any effort to grasp his teaching. The majority of these texts are drawn from the *Phenomenology of Spirit* and the *Science of Logic,* although my analyses are based upon, and refer to, all of Hegel's major works. Furthermore, I avoid almost entirely discussions of Hegel's life and (with the exception of the introductory section of the first chapter) "the spirit of his time." A concise analysis of Hegel's relation to the teachings of his predecessors is another matter. Many references to the history of philosophy are obviously unavoidable in any discussion of Hegel.

It is my deep conviction that Hegel cannot be properly understood without careful analysis of his relation to Greek philosophy. A detailed study of certain central issues in Plato and Aristotle, such as the internal structure of form, the nature of thinking, and the connected roles of negation and contradiction, will considerably facilitate the approach to Hegel's dialectico-speculative logic. In the case of the moderns, the student of Hegel must pay special attention to Fichte (and in that way, as will become evident, to Kant). In an introduction, despite all intentions of thoroughness, one has to compromise in deciding which issues to include and which may be safely omitted. I have tried to supply the indispensable historical background, and so to indicate the direction in which the reader must go if he wishes to deepen his understanding of Hegel's critical assimilation of his predecessors.

I should say a word here about the secondary literature. There is a large number of extremely good books, monographs, and articles on Hegel. I have made very great efforts to read as widely as possible in this literature. The student will find an introductory guide to scholarly studies on Hegel in my notes and selective bibliography. In view of the great difficulty associated with the analysis and criticism of Hegel himself, as well as the intended audience of this volume, I have felt myself to be justified in making the absolute minimum of references to other scholars in my text. Needless to say, this should not be construed as an expression of independence on my part. My major debts are reflected in my notes. The bibliography is not intended to be complete or even to record the extent of my reading, but to indicate a fair number of valuable works on Hegel or on themes closely connected to the study of Hegel.

One more preliminary comment. It would be extremely unwise to attempt an introduction to Hegel, at any level of complexity, by speaking exclusively or predominantly in his idiom. I see no need to burden the student with an excessive amount of awkward English translations of Hegel's terminology, or efforts to duplicate in English his peculiar style, which mixes the austere and the baroque in a way that cannot be readily accepted by those who have been accustomed to the English manner of doing philosophy. But I trust that this need to make Hegel speak English has not resulted in any distortion of the technical elements of his teaching. Certainly there is no Hegelian reason why it should. The claim to absolute wisdom, grounded in the universality of the concept, can scarcely be valid if it is to be expressed in German only.

The Structure of This Work

Before describing in detail the structure of the present study, I should like to formulate briefly the central theoretical assumption which has governed its composition. There is no point to studying Hegel, and in fact one is not studying Hegel, unless one enters very soon into the complexities of his logic. Hegel is first and foremost a logician and not a philosopher of history, a political thinker, a theologian, or a *Lebensphilosoph.* Of course, as a logician, he is all of these and more. This is because Hegel accepts the Greek conception of philosophy as the attempt to give a *logos* or discursive account of the Whole. Regardless of all questions concerning the relationships of Hegel's books within the system, I venture to assert that none of his writings or lectures can be read in a proper manner without a grasp of the main tenets of his logic. This is surely supported, if it is not finally proved, by the organization of the *Encyclopedia,* for all its sketchiness the only comprehensive plan of what the system looks like as an articulated whole.

The *Encyclopedia* apart, it is not necessary, nor for that matter would it be sufficient, to begin one's study of Hegel by mastering the central passages of the *Science of Logic.* On the contrary, and in keeping with Hegel's notion of the "circularity" of wisdom, we cannot understand what Hegel means by "logic" except by constant reference to such major themes as history, religion, or self-consciousness. It should be borne in mind that Hegel's logic is not the logic of Russell, Gentzen, and Tarski. Neither is his science of wisdom the espistemology or ontology of contemporary philosophers. But Hegel himself begins, as a mature thinker, from a radical criticism of the logic, epistemology, and ontology of his predecessors and contemporaries. In my opinion, his criticisms are equally pertinent to the major schools of our own time. As the reader will see, Hegel does not "reject" formal logic or mathematics; instead, he provides us with a meta-critique of the philosophical presuppositions of those who accept logic as the prototype, or even the sum, of philosophical reason. On all counts, it seems to me that an attempt to explain Hegel as a logician is both accurate in itself and appropriate to the contemporary philosophical taste.

In describing the organization of the present volume, I should first say a word about the historical situation which gives rise to Hegel. Whereas philosophy has been traditionally understood as the love or pursuit of wisdom, Hegel claims to be wise, and so to possess wisdom, in a comprehensive and completely discursive sense. This claim goes altogether beyond that of other figures in the history of philosophy, as for example Aristotle, one of Hegel's models. Aristotle evidently claims to be wise in the sense of possessing the "first philosophy" or (as it has come to be known) "metaphysics." But an essential ingredient in Aristotle's "wisdom" is the knowledge that a genuinely comprehensive wisdom or "science" is impossible. Stated simply, such a science is impossible because the "principles" of the separate sciences are discontinuous. There is no "science of science" or deduction of all principles from one first principle which certifies itself.

When the influence of Aristotle declined or was rejected at the beginning of the modern era, perhaps the most important philosophical tendency was to substitute "scientific method" (in a sense modeled after mathematics and the empirical or experimental sciences) for wisdom in the older sense. Whereas it is impossible to know "everything," we do know the method by which anything whatsoever can be known. Such is the claim, implicit or explicit, which underlies the origins of modern (and much of contemporary) philosophy. However, this claim is subject to two serious internal defects. First, "everything," or the things to be known, are now understood as spatio-temporal, and therefore historical, phenomena. The question as to the essence of things is tacitly answered by identifying it with the mathematical elements of scientific method. As soon as we begin to question the status of these mathematical elements, a distinction arises between "essences" and "appearances" which is, if not the same, certainly as profound or comprehensive as the so-called classical dualism of eternity and temporality. The second defect follows immediately: even the mathematical essences are now interpreted as "concepts" or "ideas" not in the Platonic but in the Cartesian sense. And this raises the problem of subjectivism.

The turn to mathematically oriented scientific method is inseparable from a rejection of Platonic dualism, and so too of Aristotelian physics (which contains this dualism in its denial that matter can be studied with mathematical precision), on behalf of the new view that "numbers" are contained within the phenomena of spatio-temporal experience. This is not to suggest that these numbers are understood as literally present within, and as themselves, extended bodies, as a kind of materialistic version of Pythagoreanism. The presence of numbers within the phenomena is due to the inseparable link between the phenomena and the enumerator or mathematical scientist. What "appears" must appear to an intellect. The power of the intellect to count and measure the phenomena means that numbers or mathematical essences must be *within* the intellect, whether or not they are also in some sense within the phenomena. Since we do not wish to resurrect the ghostly or metaphysical realm of eternal and separate essences, it follows that mathematical essences must be constructed or produced by the intellect. And since the intellect is itself a resident in the spatio-temporal world, it, together with its products, must be historical rather than eternal.

If we try to avoid this "historicizing" of mathematical actuality by retaining the separation of intellect from spatio-temporal phenomena, the problem of dualism is obviously insoluble. Not merely is a comprehensive science, one which includes self-knowledge, impossible, but there is no guarantee that "what appears" to a separate intellect is not itself the surface or illusory mask of some hidden world of "things in themselves." Or to put the same point from the opposite perspective, an intellect which is separate from both eternity (in the Platonic sense) and temporality (the domain of phenomena), would seem to be subject to no restrictions whatsoever with respect to the "essences" it can produce. Instead of mathematical essence, we have poems: philosophy enters into the path of "creativity." The net result is a history of the creations of the intellect or the human spirit.

The scientific revolution against the Platonic-Aristotelian tradition thus accomplishes a pyrrhic victory. Dualism is retained, and a dualism in which both members are understood as historical processes. In the terminology of modern philosophy, the subject-object relation cannot be captured by mathematical equations because the subject itself, and therefore the process by which the subject-object relation is posed, is inaccessible to any stable, structural description. Since the intellect, and hence self-consciousness, is not numbers or ratios of numbers, but the processes by which numbers are produced and ordered in significant relations or ratios, it is impossible to give a scientific account of the intellect, and therefore of the significance of science. Science can "objectify" itself only *by forgetting its subjective origins.* We make it an article of faith that whatever cannot be captured in mathematical equations is illusory or unimportant. This requires us to reject ourselves, the creators of science, as unscientific, or else to attempt the self-destructive reconstitution of ourselves into objects of science, all the while claiming that at long last we are on the road to "scientific" self-understanding.

This is the process which Hegel sets himself to overcome, not in the sense of rejecting it but rather of completing it by working out its defects or internal contradictions. In other words, Hegel defines the process by which we acquire wisdom as identical with the historical experience of Western man, that is, with the history of philosophy (understood to include the history of science, or the explanation of the significance of science). Hegel advocates neither a return to the ancient world, whether in its pagan or Christian form, nor a straightforward rejection of antiquity on behalf of a resolute modernism. The comprehensive science of wisdom, as understood by

Hegel, must include both eternity and temporality: both Platonic forms and modern phenomena, as it were.

Putting to one side questions of historical difference, Hegel in effect contends that modern science suffers from the same destructive dualism as does Platonism. The distinction between mathematical laws and their phenomenal instances is equivalent, when properly analyzed, to the Platonic distinction between separated Ideas and the instances of genesis. (This criticism applies equally to the so-called late Platonic doctrine of genera and species, which remain eternal forms of temporal instances.) A consequence of this fact is that modern science suffers from the Platonic incapacity to explain rationally the scientist, that is, to articulate a doctrine of self-consciousness, or perhaps more accurately, to transform self-consciousness into self-knowledge, thereby fulfilling the injunction of the Delphic Oracle.

The classical distinction between knower and known is the ancestor of the modern distinction between subject and object. This distinction, which underlies the subject-predicate distinction of grammar and logic, is present even within mathematics, although in such a way as to render the subjective component mute. Whereas this is intelligible and unobjectionable within the technical domain of mathematics, it proves to be a fatal characteristic if mathematics is employed as the paradigm of rational thinking and so of "philosophical method." This effort generates paradoxes, antinomies, and contradictions which, when we discover them, we regard as constituting the boundaries of intelligibility. They are intrinsic to the methods of rationalism, hence characteristic of the intellect if not of the world "in itself." This boundary of the intelligible corresponds to the Christian doctrine of the *nihil* from which God created the world and which thus stands between God and the world. In religious language, Hegel attempts to understand the *nihil* and so to assimilate it into the world, or in other words, to render God fully intelligible by overcoming the barrier between Him and the world.

In this light, Hegel's greatest innovation is to develop a new doctrine of contradiction and negativity, the core of his "dialectic," which attempts to resolve the *aporiai* of classical rationalism at a higher, more comprehensive, and so genuinely rational level. The crucial step in this new doctrine is to distinguish between form and the *process of formation.* A mathematically oriented analysis of phenomena proceeds by means of finite, self-identical, separately knowable or at least separately manipulable elements, which are treated as self-evident even though no thought is given to the "self" for which they are ostensibly evident.

In Hegel's new doctrine (not totally new, of course), the "self" which forms mathematical elements is not itself a form but *pure negative activity.* This conception of activity arises from a combining of features belonging to several previous philosophical and religious doctrines: the pure "thought thinking itself" of Aristotle, the forming or form-creating divine intellect of Christian Neo-Platonism, the self-caused god or substance of Spinoza, the transformation of Kant's synthetic unity of apperception into the Absolute Ego of Fichte and Schelling. Hegel attempts to explain the in-itself manifest presence of the Absolute not as an individual ego but as the Divine Spirit which manifests itself in the self-conscious and conceptual activities of the individual (in a way similar to the presence of Spinoza's attribute of thought within the modes of finite intellects). This deduction begins from the previously mentioned self-contradictory character of mathematical rationalism itself.

Put briefly, Hegel attempts to show that the contradictions of formal or discursive analysis (which he calls, following his contemporaries, *reflection*) are responsible for oscillations within the ostensibly stable elements or properties of forms themselves. These oscillations, which transform formal elements into each other or identify what is different as they differentiate what is identical, are the manifestation of the pure negative activity of Spirit or the Absolute. In order to understand Hegel's doctrine of the Absolute, and so his dialectic, or in other words to understand exactly what Hegel means by "wisdom" (or the "science of wisdom"), it is necessary to understand his analysis of the history of philosophy.

Hegel's own thought is not simply one of many discontinuous "theories" or "systems" conceived by the mind of man, which can be studied in relative isolation from the others with perhaps a bow to "the climate of opinion of the time." Hegel insists that his science of wisdom is the *logical* conclusion or culmination of Western philosophy taken as a whole. The contradictions of discursive analysis are therefore present as a dialectical structure within the history of philosophy.

For this reason, namely, since divine history manifests itself as human history, one could say that Hegel's science of wisdom is a philosophy of history. But such an expression is seriously misleading unless we understand accurately that the philosophy of history is for Hegel a dialectico-logical process, turning upon the dialectic of the subject and the object, which in turn reveals itself as the Whole or totality of human experience, differing in different ages with respect to its essential features, but always marked by internal contradictions which lead to the transformation of each stage into the next, until the final or Hegelian resolution is accomplished. The study of history, or of Hegel's philosophy of history, *is* the study of Hegel's doctrine of contradiction, and therefore of his conception of pure negative activity, or of the dialectic of the subject and the object as the posing of the Whole. In order to study Hegel, therefore, we have to attend to each of these crucial elements in his teaching.

This necessity has determined the structure of the present volume. We begin in as simple a manner as possible, with a sketch of Hegel's plan as expressed primarily in terms of religion, history, and politics. Hegel's intention of reconciling ancients and moderns is then illustrated in terms of his general understanding of the history of philosophy. Hegel sees himself as standing to Kant, Fichte, and Schelling in a way analogous to Aristotle's relation to Parmenides, Heraclitus, and Plato. The need to reconcile ancients and moderns leads in turn to a discussion of Hegel's conception of the *completion* of history, and so to what Hegel means by "the Whole" (and thus "the Absolute"). Next we turn to an analysis of the dialectic of subject and object, the indispensable precondition for the transition from Hegel as philosopher of history to Hegel as dialectical logician. Since Hegel's logic is explicitly understood by him as an overcoming of the *aporiai* of Greek ontology, we study next the indispensable minimum of topics from Plato and Aristotle, in order to follow with some precision the development of Hegel's central doctrines of negativity and contradiction. These doctrines are a "synthesis" of Greek themes and Hegel's critical assimilation of the dialectic of Fichte. Fichte's dialectic proceeds from an understanding of the intrinsic limitations of discursive or analytic thinking, called *reflection*. We study briefly the status of reflection in Locke, in order to see how Hegel assimilates the empiricist as well as the Idealist tradition (stemming from Spinoza) of modern philosophy, and then consider the principal technical steps in the Fichtean analysis of reflection. Only then is it possible to combine these elements into a grasp of Hegel's dialectic.

When that has been accomplished, we are in a position to go on to a variety of special topics in Hegel's system. We consider first the relation between logic and phenomenology in Hegel's teaching, and why it is not possible to understand accurately the *Phenomenology of Spirit* without a knowledge of the main points of the *Science of Logic*. This is shown with respect to the related issues of the connection between eternity and temporality and what Hegel calls "the inverted world." The most famous Hegelian themes of the unhappy consciousness are considered next, including the dialectic of the master and slave and Hegel's doctrine of alienation. Next we turn to a detailed study of the Enlightenment, or the working out of the logical *aporiai* of classical rationalism in the form of modern nihilism. After a summary consideration of Hegel's conception of "the Absolute," which is also a summary of what has gone before, with special attention to the problem of "method," we conclude with the sketch of a general criticism of Hegel's teaching.

I am extremely grateful to the Earhart Foundation of Ann Arbor, Michigan, and to the Institute for the Arts and Humanistic Studies of Pennsylvania State University, both of which provided essential financial assistance and release from my teaching duties for the period needed to complete this study. My special thanks for help in various ways to James Edie of Northwestern University; to Carl Hausman, Thomas Magner, Stanley Paulson, and Stanley Weintraub of Pennsylvania State University; to the members of the Philosophical Seminar at Heidelberg University, and especially to Dieter Henrich; to Otto Pöggeler, director of the Hegel-Archiv at Bochum University; to Jane Isay and Cynthia Brodhead of Yale University Press, as well as to their reader; and in particular to my students, one of whom, Robert Rethy, prepared all references to English translations of Hegel and typed the final version of the bibliography.

S. R.

Institute for the Arts and Humanistic Studies
University Park, Pennsylvania
March 1973

G. W. F. HEGEL

1 Introduction: Philosophy and History

The Quarrel between Ancients and Moderns

Georg Wilhelm Friedrich Hegel was born in 1770 and died in 1831. He was educated at Tübingen, in theology and philosophy, and spent the greater part of his life as a teacher, primarily as a professor of philosophy at the University of Berlin, although he held a variety of other positions, including posts at the universities of Jena and Heidelberg. Much has been made of Hegel's personal life, although it consists largely in study and writing, or, as he would himself have added, in fulfilling his duties as a civil servant under the Prussian government. One might venture to say that few philosophers have been subjected to so minute a documentation, ranging from close analysis of his schoolboy notebooks to every draft of his unpublished university lectures. There can be no doubt that the careful editing of Hegel's unpublished manuscripts of his mature years, starting perhaps with the Jena writings, has added an essential dimension to our understanding of his thought. I am considerably more skeptical about the results of the exhaustive study of his youthful notes and essays. We have been told by students of extreme competence and industry that the young Hegel was a pious Christian, an atheist, a Greek humanist, a citizen of the Enlightenment, a violent partisan of the French Revolution, and a putative arch-conservative. Of course, the same quarrels exist with respect to Hegel's mature writings. But since the earlier material is as ambiguous as the later, its imperfect form and the youth of the author argue strongly against our placing too much confidence in its hermeneutic illumination.[1] Therefore I have chosen to pass on to the Hegel of 1801 and thereafter.

1. It seems to me clearly inappropriate to base the study of a philosopher's ripe teaching on impressions garnered from the study of fragments composed by a boy scarcely out of his teens. Further, it is at least arguable how much a thinker's mature doctrines have been conditioned by youthful experiences. Without exaggerating in the opposite direction, I

Hegel's life encompasses the greatest decades of German spiritual activity. It would be tedious to remind the reader of more than a handful of Hegel's extraordinary contemporaries, many of them known to him personally, and some from his schooldays at Tübingen: Kant, Fichte, Schelling, Schiller, Hölderlin, Goethe—there is almost no end to the list of distinguished names. Any effort to order the activity of this period in terms of intellectual or spiritual "movements" would be equally fruitless and seriously misleading. Names like "Enlightenment," "Neo-Classicism," or "Romanticism" are at once too complex to be meaningful without careful analysis and too simple to serve as categories for the classification of genius. The same difficulties arise with respect to the most important historical event of Hegel's lifetime, and one which is frequently used as a touchstone in interpreting his thought: the French Revolution. It is easy enough to say that this event defines the end of one age and the beginning of another. One might utter generalities about the political emancipation of the common man, the age of revolution, or the birth of radical ideology from the ashes of traditional political philosophy. Apart from their intrinsic questionableness, however, none of these slogans would throw a clear light on Hegel's own understanding of the French Revolution.

This is of course not to imply that the individuals and events just mentioned are tangential to the study of Hegel's philosophy. The problem is just the opposite. One can scarcely conceive of a major figure or episode in the course of Western

---

suggest merely that an excessive concern with autobiography runs the risk of obscuring the philosophical independence of a man's thought. This is not intended to deny the interest and value of intellectual biography or historical studies of groups of thinkers. For that matter, some extremely good books have been written to defend what strike me as erroneous theses about the significance of Hegel's early writings. There is now an excellent book in English on Hegel's early life: H. Harris, *Hegel's Development: Toward the Sunlight* (Oxford, Clarendon Press, 1971). Still extremely interesting, despite its dubious thesis, is G. Lukács, *Der junge Hegel,* in *Werke,* Vol. 8 (Neuwied and Berlin, Luchterhand, 1967). See also A. T. B. Peperzak, *Le jeune Hegel et la vision morale du monde* (The Hague, M. Nijhoff, 1960; rev. ed. 1969).

civilization (with the possible exception of the Middle Ages) which does not contribute its share to the richness of Hegel's thought. Hegel's science of wisdom could be defined in a preliminary way as a logical meditation on the history of the human race (primarily, to be sure, the history of European man). It would therefore be a serious error for us to take our bearings simply in terms of the events of Hegel's lifetime. Indeed, it would be impossible to do so. If we consider only the extreme formulations for the sake of initial clarity, there are perhaps two main attitudes toward the French Revolution. Some regard it as the end of European civilization, and others as the dawn of heaven upon earth. These attitudes are related to a question which, when properly defined, expresses what I take to be an accurate description of Hegel's central concern: the quarrel between the ancients and the moderns. This phrase referred originally to a dispute concerning the relative merits of classical and modern art, especially poetry. In a deeper sense, it may be understood (as it was by the greatest of those who participated in it) to designate the philosophical and scientific revolution against the ancient world which characterizes the sixteenth and seventeenth centuries in Europe.[2]

The quarrel of the moderns against the ancients was continued into the eighteenth century; but following upon the French Revolution, especially in Germany, one finds efforts to reconcile the two great epochs by uniting the best of each. Prior to Hegel himself, perhaps the outstanding example of this effort at reconciliation is the teaching of Kant. In this chapter I shall first present an introductory sketch of the sense in which Hegel's thought is an attempt to resolve the quarrel between the ancients and the moderns. This sketch will also introduce us to Hegel as a philosopher of history, perhaps the way in which he is most frequently presented to beginners. We shall see how such a conception of Hegel is intrinsically unintelligible unless it directs us almost at once to Hegel's logic. I shall then argue the point in greater technical detail by means of a comparison of Hegel's attitudes toward the Pre-Socratics

2. A good study of this important subject: R. F. Jones, *Ancients and Moderns* (Saint Louis, Washington University Studies, 1961).

and toward Kant. This restatement should also indicate the needed connection between discussions of Hegel's philosophy of history and his logic.

The Religious Significance of Modernity

The founders of the modern epoch regularly describe themselves as engaged in the discovery of new ways, orders, or methods.[3] These new ways are so comprehensive or fundamental as to entail the rejection of the old ways. Unfortunately, it is not simply obvious in each case that the new way constitutes an improvement over the old. No competent observer would question the superiority of Galileo's mechanics to that of Aristotle. The same cannot be said, however, about the relative merits of the ethical and political teachings of Aristotle on the one hand and of Machiavelli or Hobbes on the other. Furthermore, it is impossible to separate progress in mathematics, science, and technology from political, religious, or philosophical developments. It is no accident that the fathers of modern science were outspoken enemies of previous "metaphysical" philosophies (if they were sometimes not averse to new metaphysical theories of their own) or returned to the mathematical aspects of Platonism in such a way as to reject the Aristotelian doctrines of their scientific predecessors.[4] Especially if we take our bearings by Descartes, the so-called father of modern philosophy, we easily discern that modernity originates in the belief, implicit or explicit, that intellectual progress requires the discovery of one true (because certain) method, applicable in all fields of study. The paradigm of this method is mathematics: not simply the geometry and arithmetic which underlie Platonic rationalism, but the coordination of these two in algebra or in abstract symbols which are neither

3. For some representative passages, together with a discussion in terms of Descartes, see my essay, "A Central Ambiguity in Descartes," in *Cartesian Essays,* ed. B. Magnus and J. B. Wilbur (The Hague, M. Nijhoff, 1969), pp. 17–35.

4. For the necessary background in the philosophical presuppositions of modern science, cf. A. Koyré, *From the Closed World to the Infinite Universe* (New York, Harper and Row, 1958); and E. J. Dijksterhuis, *The Mechanization of the World Picture* (Oxford, Clarendon Press, 1961).

numbers nor theoretical bodies but the elements of "pure" thought.[5]

My reference to Platonism should suggest to the reader that the modern revolution is by no means a complete rejection of the past. A detailed analysis of the modern epoch would reveal a continuity of development in many crucial ways. For example, the conception of *renaissance,* which designates the circumstances underlying the birth of the modern age, itself refers to the rebirth or rejuvenation of antiquity in its Christian as well as its Greek form.[6] So too the belief in the efficacy of a universal method based upon mathematical reasoning is obviously a consequence of the Greek understanding of man as the "logical" animal. Nevertheless, if one places too much emphasis upon the continuity of historical development, the very phenomenon that we set out to understand, the difference between antiquity and modernity, itself disappears. For the same reason, it is not possible to grasp adequately the essence of the modern spirit as due to a "secularizing" of Christianity.[7] A secularized Christianity is no longer Christian: one must then explain the factors underlying the *loss* of Christianity, or of Christian vitality as an other-worldly faith. But this amounts to an explanation of modernity as a revolution against Christianity. Modern mathematical science, whatever its debt to the past, originates in the rejection of Aristotelian astronomy and physics. More fundamentally, it rests upon a new conception of number as applicable to sublunar motions without the sacrifice of its theoretical status, and, finally, to a radically new conception of that theoretical status itself. The modern "spirit" rests similarly upon the rejection of ancient teachings concerning the eternal order of nature or the subordination of man to an all-powerful God. With every due qualification, this new spirit

5. There is a thorough discussion of this point in J. Klein, *Greek Mathematical Thought and the Origin of Algebra* (Cambridge, Mass., MIT Press, 1968).

6. See K. Burdach, *Reformation, Renaissance, Humanismus* (Darmstadt, Wissenschaftliche Buchgesellschaft, 1963; 1st ed., 1925).

7. Cf. H. Blumenberg, *Die Legitimität der Neuzeit* (Frankfurt, Suhrkamp Verlag, 1966).

is accurately described by Descartes in the injunction that man use the new science to become master and possessor of nature.[8]

Not the least of the difficulties involved in the effort to grasp the significance of the origins of modernity lies in understanding the religious implications of Descartes' injunction to man. This may be expressed in a way which will prepare us for a crucial difficulty in Hegel's own teaching. At first glance, it seems evident that man cannot acquire mastery and possession over nature without usurping the titles of the previous owner. Whatever prudential rhetoric Descartes may have employed to conceal his intentions, he and his progeny were widely held to be atheists, at least until the beginnings of this century, and by readers of the highest capacity. On second thought, however, another interpretation seems to be possible. As Hegel was fond of reminding us, God himself confirms the prophecy of Satan after Adam has eaten the forbidden fruit. "Look, Adam has become like one of us, and knows what is good and evil."[9] Adam's divine status is not rescinded by his expulsion from Paradise; one could say that the likeness must be transformed into an identity by the sweat of labor. In Hegelian language, the story of the Garden of Eden is a prefiguration of the connection between self-consciousness and knowledge. Man discovers himself, and therefore his future, not in knowledge of mathematics but in the knowledge of good and evil, or as we may say, in the significance of mathematics. This discovery is of a potentiality which must be actualized not by the labor of the body (modern physics) but by that of the concept or spirit.[10] Whereas mathematical physics is for Descartes evidently a tool of the anti-Christian pride of the philosophers, or a "passion of

8. *Discours de la méthode,* ed. E. Gilson (Paris, J. Vrin, 1947), pp. 61 f. Cf. Gilson's note on Francis Bacon, p. 446.

9. *Berliner Schriften* (Hamburg, Felix Meiner Verlag, 1956), p. 187; *Vorlesungen über die Philosophie der Religion* (Hamburg, Felix Meiner Verlag, 1966), Vol. 1, pt. 2, p. 31.

10. Thus Hegel corrects the Bible's explicit formulation of the story of Eden. The Bible makes man like a god or already divine by the simple fact of eating the forbidden fruit. This is to overlook the significance of labor. Cf. *Philosophie der Religion,* Vol. 2, pt. 1, p. 87.

the soul,"[11] it is for Hegel a product of reason or the "ruling" part of the soul, to use the language of Plato's *Republic*. From this standpoint, the mastery and possession of nature is not a consequence of atheism but of God's providence (which Hegel calls the theme of world-history). As a result of this providence, man returns to God, thanks to his own conceptual labor, or fulfills the promise of his divinity as present within God, even though as himself. Man is "one of us" (in God's words) and so no longer merely "like one of us."

Let us put to one side the question of Descartes' precise intentions. The fact is that there are alternative interpretations of the significance of the modern revolution. According to the first, man follows the governance of God and undergoes an initial discovery which is at the same time an "alienation" or separation from one's essential being; but this alienation is the necessary condition for the comprehensive because comprehending reconciliation with the divine essence. In the case of the second interpretation, it makes no sense to speak of atheism, if for no other reason than that man has himself become a god. For the same reason, it would be extremely difficult, if not quite impossible, to call the process of reconciliation a "secularization-process." We might do better to refer to it as the sacralization of secular history, a process which shows that the history of man is the same as the history of the content of Absolute Spirit or God.[12] But this is not the same as to say that Hegel accepts an orthodox Christian eschatology, or that he is a traditionally Christian philosopher of history. At the completion of history, man understands the unity of the divine and human natures: "The truth is that there is only one Reason, and only one Spirit."[13] The unity of man and God leaves it at best unclear whether the traditional, separate, or transcendent

11. One of Descartes' most important works, too often neglected even by scholars, is entitled *Les passions de l'âme*. For a discussion of philosophical pride, see my *Nihilism* (New Haven, Yale University Press, 1969), pp. 63 ff.

12. *Philosophie der Religion*, Vol. 1, pt. 1, p. 278. All translations are my own. References to English editions are for the convenience of the reader.

13. Ibid., Vol. 2, pt. 3, pp. 134–37.

God of Christianity is still present in Hegel's science of wisdom.

We shall return in various ways to this problem. Suffice it here to say that, whereas Hegel insists upon religious self-consciousness as the root of Spirit, "the foundation of all actuality," [14] he submits Christianity (the ostensibly true religion) to an interpretation so rationalistic as to evoke the often overpowering conviction that we are once more in the presence of the pride of the philosophers. I note here only that Hegel takes sin, in conjunction with the story of Eden, to refer to incompleteness qua absence of rational knowledge, and that according to him, man is immortal only in knowing eternity by conceptual thinking.[15] These doctrines may remind many of Socrates rather than of Jesus. When we remember, too, that for Hegel religion contains only an image or representation of truth, which is adequately stated only in logic or discursive reason, then Hegel's deviation from orthodoxy should be evident. As a teacher of mine once remarked, if Hegel was a Christian, he belonged to a sect of which he was the only member.

One would not go too far in suggesting that Descartes marks the beginning of the modern age, or its philosophical articulation, whereas Hegel marks its end. I have tried to indicate that there is an ambiguity at the beginning and the end of this age concerning the significance of religion. This ambiguity is inseparable from the question of the significance of the modern age, taken in its most characteristic sense as a revolution against antiquity. Again making all due allowance for ambiguity, this much seems clear. Whereas neither Descartes nor Hegel is a representative of antiquity, it is impossible to say of Hegel that he is an unqualified modern. I myself cannot doubt Descartes' credentials as a philosophical citizen of the age he did so much to found. In the present context, beyond what has already been said, I must limit myself to mentioning that Descartes scorned history in general and the "wisdom of the ancients" (except in certain branches of mathematics) in partic-

14. Ibid., Vol. 1, pt. 1, p. 140.
15. Ibid., Vol. 1, pt. 3, pp. 111 ff., 124, 129.

ular.[16] One function of the famous Cartesian "universal" doubt, introduced by the hypothesis that the world has been created by an evil genius (by Satan rather than by God), is to liberate the human mind from every vestige of ancient doctrine.[17] True enough, Descartes subsequently invokes the notion of God to guarantee the truth of his clear and distinct ideas. But this has nothing to do with an allegiance to Christianity; the god of the philosophers has never been an enemy of veracity nor a resident of a specific historical epoch. In the case of Hegel, however, every effort is made to preserve the wisdom of the ancients. If this wisdom is transformed in its ascent to a higher level, it nevertheless transforms by its presence the character of modern wisdom as well. In other words, Hegelian wisdom is a reconciliation of ancient and modern wisdom, and therefore neither ancient nor modern but the (intended) perfection of both, or the discursive account of the completion of history in its essential sense as the human manifestation of Absolute Spirit or God.

According to Hegel, man can never return to the Garden of Eden; Paradise is for beasts, not for human spirits.[18] In slightly different terms, wisdom is acquired by a turn inward, a process of education which is also a "recollection," not of separate Platonic Ideas, but of the concrete historical experience of the human race.[19] It is true that "turning inward" is a "turning around," again in the Platonic sense of "turning away" from appearances to the essential actualities.[20] But this

16. *Discours de la méthode,* pp. 6, 13, 19. Cf. *Meditationes,* in *Oeuvres,* ed. Adam-Tannery (Paris, J. Vrin, 1947–57), 7 : 17.

17. *Meditationes,* pp. 18 ff.

18. *Vorlesungen über die Philosophie der Weltgeschichte* (Hamburg, Felix Meiner Verlag, 1968), p. 728.

19. *Phänomenologie des Geistes* (Hamburg, Felix Meiner Verlag, 1952), pp. 563 f. *Phenomenology of Mind,* trans. J. B. Baillie (New York, Harper and Row, 1967), pp. 807 f; *Enzyklopädie* (1830), ed. Nicolin-Pöggeler (Hamburg, Felix Meiner Verlag, 1969), p. 4. W. Wallace's translation of the first part of the *Enzyklopädie, The Logic of Hegel* (Oxford, Clarendon Press, 1892), hereafter referred to as *Encyclopedia–Wallace,* does not contain Hegel's *Vorrede.*

20. *Republic* 7.518d3 ff. For Hegel, "actuality" includes appearances as well as essence.

is to say that, in the deepest sense of the term (not to be confused with its contemporary political usage), Hegel is a conservative rather than a revolutionary. This is so especially because the turn to essence is necessary in order to "conserve" appearances or (in the old Greek phrase) to "save the phenomena." Hegel conserves human experience, ancient and modern alike. His anti-Cartesianism is expressed by this conservatism, but equally well in his conception that nature is mastered by spirit rather than by physics. Hegel's reconciliation of the quarrel between the ancients and the moderns is at the same time a sacralizing of human history, which is accomplished by rejecting the Greek view that nature or the heavenly beings are higher than man and his productions.[21] "Nature" is for Hegel still "extension" or "externality," albeit in the ultimate sense of the externalization of Absolute Spirit. In other words, it is still the "nature" of Kant; like Kant, Hegel places "purposiveness" in Spirit (or the transcendental ego). In this sense, Hegel's reconciliation of antiquity and modernity is, like Kant's, Christian rather than Greek. But it is Greek rather than Christian in making purpose accessible to conceptual intelligence.

In this way Hegel completes the reconciliation between God and man in the eternal present of wisdom as accessible to and in a certain sense "produced by" the spirit of the finite, historical individual. If I may now return to the example with which I began this discussion, the French Revolution is for Hegel neither simply good nor bad, neither the end of one age nor the beginning of another. It is instead a penultimate expression of modern man's effort to acquire freedom by jettisoning the past. This effort is bad in that the past cannot be jettisoned without invoking barbarism and terror. But the effort is good

21. Hegel frequently remarks that human spirit in its manifestations is higher than nature. This follows from the general position that the end or purpose is exhibited by the Absolute in man, not in nature. Cf. *Enzyklopädie*, p. 199 (par. 245). *Hegel's Philosophy of Nature,* trans. A. V. Miller with a foreword by J. N. Findlay (Oxford, Clarendon Press, 1970), p. 4 f. This translation of Part Two of the *Enzyklopädie* will be cited as *Encyclopedia–Miller*.

as an instance of "the cunning of reason" or the process by which man acquires self-consciousness, and therefore freedom, through the experience of his own suffering. The terror purifies revolutionary man, or transforms him into the rational citizen of Napoleonic Europe.[22]

An adequate discussion of Hegel's attitude toward the French Revolution would encompass his entire teaching, even if presented in terms of the philosophy of history. I have, however, already indicated that for Hegel, the essential content of human and divine history is the same. We can grasp the significance of human history only by "recapturing" conceptually (in a way not totally unrelated to Proust's recapture of "lost time") the logical pattern of its development. This means that the necessity of moving within the activity of thinking from one category to another, or of rendering conceptual knowledge progressively more concrete, has its practical counterpart in the necessary development of human history. In both cases, however, the development is not linear but characterized by contradiction. Stated simply, the preservation of previous degrees of significance includes as transitional stages the negation of these degrees of significance. The incompleteness of each degree threatens it with contradiction or annihilation by its opposite, until the contradicting degrees are assimilated into a third and higher level of development. In the language of history, we preserve the sense of each epoch, but in a way which shows the incompleteness of each epoch, or its intrinsically self-contradictory nature, when taken in isolation. In the language of logic, the procession of categories is the activity of thinking itself, or of the motion from one conceptual moment to its opposite and thence to an assimilation of the opposed moments at a higher, more concrete level. In logic as in history, progress occurs thanks to "the force of the negative." The effort to remain at a preliminary, more abstract level cannot be sustained and transforms itself, by a negation or internal criticism, into the next level.

22. This formulation is based upon Hegel's analysis of the French Revolution in the *Phänomenologie*. In later years, Hegel modified this analysis, and the Napoleonic was replaced by the Prussian state.

Thus the comprehension of history is structurally identical with the process of thinking the Absolute. Such a comprehension or process requires us, in Hegel's striking phrase, to "exhibit" or think God "as he is in his eternal essence, prior to the creation of nature and a finite spirit." [23] Hegel, one could say, starts from the central Christian teaching that God does not merely reveal his Word to mankind, but actually enters into human history in the person of Jesus Christ. Christ is for Hegel the representation of the harmony between the eternal and the temporal or divine and human realms. In this harmony, the divine and human preserve their respective integrity while sharing an essential identity. This identity is one of life in the deepest and most comprehensive sense: of Absolute Spirit as the activity which manifests itself in every finite mode of creation, without thereby limiting itself to any single mode or form. The religious representation of the unity of life in God and man is to be found in the Book of Genesis, where God shapes man's body from dust but breathes life or soul into his still inanimate flesh. In Hegelian language, this means that the creation of individual mortals is not also a creation *ex nihilo* of the human soul or spirit.

The finite spirit of man is "the breath of God" or a mode in the Absolute. But the "life" common to mode and Absolute, let me repeat, is not a specific or detached form. It is the "principle" of activity, again, not in a geometrical or algebraic sense, but as the itself living "fountain of life." This means that God or the Absolute is present within man as his own spiritual activity. Therefore, God is coeval with human history, understood as the expression of human spiritual activity. We must rephrase the orthodox conception of divine revelation accordingly: God reveals himself *to himself,* in and through the medium (or audience) of man. Man understands God by understanding himself, and he does this by first grasping (or "recap-

23. *Wissenschaft der Logik* (Leipzig, Felix Meiner Verlag, 1951), 1 : 31; *Hegel's Science of Logic,* trans. A. V. Miller (London, George Allen and Unwin; New York, Humanities Press, 1969), p. 50. Hereafter cited as *Logic.*

turing") the significance of the totality of human history. This doctrine, of course, has nothing to do with "mysticism." The "identity-within-difference" or harmony of God and man is the logical foundation for the total conceptualization of the activity of the Absolute. Hegel is first and foremost a logician, although it should be clear by now that his logic includes content as well as form.

We are not quite ready to enter into a technical discussion of Hegel's logic. But this must be said immediately: in order to know anything at all, in the genuine or scientific sense of "knowledge" (as opposed to contingent statements of probability), one must know *everything*. Needless to say, this means knowing everything that is knowable or capable of rigorous logical definition. In conventional language, to know is to know the essence of something. But essences are not radically detached from each other; their very accessibility to discourse, and especially to logical analysis, shows already that they are related to each other in a way corresponding to the scientific ideal of a complete explanation, as for example in the "unified field" theory of physics. Stated with utmost simplicity, formal logic itself functions upon the assumption that there are universal principles of explanation, related systematically in a way which corresponds to, or is perhaps even the same as, the "logical structure of the world." Hegel's science of wisdom may be understood as a radical reinterpretation of the universalistic implications of formal logic. The key to the reinterpretation is the thesis that forms (and so too formal principles of deduction) are the expression of a more universal spiritual activity, which is not itself a form but the source or *formation-process* by which the world "takes shape."

The understanding of the identity-within-difference between God and man is then the reverse of irrationalism or of transrationalism. Hegel, so to speak, takes literally the motto of the Enlightenment: *sapere aude* ("dare to know"). It goes without saying that this places a great strain upon the interpreter, but it would be cowardly to do less than follow the lead of Hegel as best we can. As Hegel made clear from the beginning of his career, the central task of philosophy is to overcome the separation between belief and knowledge,[24] or to take seriously the biblical injunction that God is known by his works. I trust it is already evident that there is no simple starting point for the study of Hegel. More specifically, Hegel cannot be properly understood with reference only to the events of his lifetime. It is true that, according to Hegel, everyone is a resident of his own age and can no more leave it than shed his own skin.[25] But it is also true that Hegel regarded his own age as decisive in the sense that the revelation of essential truth had been completed in it and completely understood by himself.[26] As we should now surmise, the understanding of Hegel's own age is necessarily an understanding of history altogether, and so of God as well as man. This is what I meant by saying that Hegel intends his science of wisdom as a resolution to the quarrel between the ancients and the moderns.

The Logical Structure of the History of Philosophy

Having introduced Hegel in his most familiar role, as a philosopher of history, I shall now develop some of the more difficult implications of my preliminary discussion in terms of Hegel's treatment of the history of philosophy. My analysis turns upon the connection between Hegel's criticism of Kant and of the Eleatics. This will suggest how for Hegel, to begin with modern German philosophy is necessarily to begin with the origins of Greek thought. Although I shall be dealing with passages from a variety of sources, especially important for what follows are Hegel's early essay "The Relation of Skepticism to Philosophy," and the section on Zeno in the *Lectures on the History of Philosophy*.[27]

24. *Glauben und Wissen* is the title of an important early essay published by Hegel in 1802.

25. *Grundlinien der Philosophie des Rechts* (Hamburg, Felix Meiner Verlag, 1955), p. 16. *Hegel's Philosophy of Right,* trans. with notes by T. M. Knox (New York, Oxford University Press, 1969), p. 11.

26. *Die Vernunft in der Geschichte* (Hamburg, Felix Meiner Verlag, 1955), p. 30.

27. "Verhältnis des Skeptizismus zur Philosophie, Darstellung seiner verschiedenen Modifikationen, und Vergleichung des Neuesten mit dem

I alluded above to the relation between Hegel's rationalism and the Kantian doctrine of purposiveness. One could also say that Hegel begins from a revision of the Kantian distinction between understanding (*Verstand*) and reason (*Vernunft*). This distinction is implicit in the development of modern philosophy from Descartes onward. The immediate certitude of the Cartesian *cogito* shows it to be the ancestral characteristic of "reason" in the various senses concerned with self-consciousness, whereas Descartes' definition of "reason" (*ratio*) as "ordering and measuring" (*ordo et mensura*) is the proximate ancestor of "understanding" in the sense of discursive, analytical thinking. This latter sense evidently originates in the Platonic doctrine of *diaeresis,* or dividing and collecting in accordance with kinds, which is itself governed by the principle of contradiction. Thinking as immediate certitude can also be found in the Platonic dialogues, but not in the same sense as it is in Descartes. The approximate Platonic counterpart to the thinking which exhibits itself as self-consciousness is to be found in the mythical accounts of the soul, and especially those dealing with Eros, recollection, or existence prior to incarnation. As is perhaps most obvious in the case of Eros, the principle of contradiction does not govern this kind of thinking. As Diotima says in the *Symposium,* Eros is continuously discontinuous or neither mortal nor immortal; it waxes and wanes, lives and dies, and can be defined only as the desire for what it lacks.[28]

In Plato, the attempt to think the Whole leads invariably to logical contradictions, so long, that is, as it is carried out by discursive analysis. The restrictions imposed upon logical analysis by the principle of contradiction force Plato, as it seems, to have recourse to mythical accounts of the Whole, whether in the cosmological or human senses of this difficult

alter" (1802), in *Jenaer kritischen Schriften,* ed. Buchner-Pöggeler, in *Gesammelte Werke* (Hamburg, Felix Meiner Verlag, 1968), Vol. 4; *Vorlesungen über die Geschichte der Philosophie,* in *Sämtlichte Werke* (hereafter *SW*), ed. H. Glockner (Stuttgart, F. Frommanns Verlag, 1959), Vol. 17.

28. *Symposium* 202d–203e.

term. In Descartes there are no myths; instead, the effort is made to carry through the conceptual grasp of the Whole by means of the techniques of discursive analysis, albeit in a radically improved form. One might suggest that Descartes supposes himself to avoid contradiction by identifying the Whole with his *method,* instead of with a class or ontological entity. Even if the instances of Being are endless, the universal and homogeneous method enables us to know them all seriatim. I shall return in a later chapter to the notion of the Whole. Here it will suffice to say that, on the basis of modern mathematical rationalism, the horizon of cognitive intelligibility is defined by the principle of contradiction. Interestingly enough, the great deficiency of the Cartesian philosophy concerns the soul, or the phenomenon of self-consciousness, which the Cartesian *cogito* seems to call so forcefully to the center of the stage. Self-consciousness is not amenable to conceptual analysis; the soul cannot understand itself by employing the techniques which are ostensibly guaranteed to explain everything whatsoever. One might infer from this that the soul is unintelligible, or not a "thing," and hence not an object for analysis. This was approximately the inference of Kant.

The transition from Descartes to Kant in the present context is represented by the triumph of Newtonian mechanics. Modern science yields necessary or certain knowledge of the body, but if that knowledge is applied to the mind or soul, the result is a loss of freedom, and even further, of self-consciousness or subjectivity. Either mind is reduced to corporeal motion or passion, or else it is "raised" to an identity with the eternal order which is at the same time a rejection of individual human identity. Modern philosophy is marked by a dualism of body and soul, thought and extension, nature and grace, or noumena and phenomena: in other words, by the failure of human intelligence to give a rational, coherent, and comprehensive account of experience. Modern philosophy fails to overcome the skepticism of the British empiricists. For us, the decisive case is the failure of Kant to overcome Hume's skepticism concerning self-consciousness or personal identity. The ego is the source of every unification, and therefore of causality. If the ego cannot be grasped conceptually, then rational thought dissolves. In order to overcome this radical defect, Kant initiated the "Copernican Revolution" which has its essence in the doctrine of the transcendental ego. But there is still a disjunction between the activity of the transcendental ego, or the "synthetic unity of apperception," and the phenomenon of self-consciousness or personal identity. Kant in effect grants Hume's point that no discursive knowledge of the self is accessible to man.

Just as in the case of Locke and Hume, the Kantian version of the *ego cogitans* is conscious of the consequence of its cogitations but not of itself. The synthetic unity of apperception is an empty or logical thesis. Instead of explaining self-consciousness, it defines the horizon of intelligibility as accessible to the analytical techniques of the discursive understanding. It is true that no object can be posed for analysis except with respect to a subject. But the subject knows itself merely as the "I think" which accompanies the posing of the object. Any effort by the self to think itself objectively or analytically leads to the reification or objectification of the subject by itself. The self is accessible to analytical understanding only as a phenomenon. We shall study the details of this situation more closely in a subsequent chapter. Here, let us concentrate upon the absence in Kant of an "intellectual intuition" providing us with the noumenal or true nature of the self. The immediate certitude of the Cartesian *cogito* is evidently even more radically sundered from conceptual certainty in Kant than it is in Descartes.

Kant and his immediate successors make the "spontaneity" of the ego intelligible, not in terms of analytical knowledge of the world of subjects and objects, but rather via the conscience.[29] The laws of understanding lead to the domain of Newtonian mechanism. Conscience, however, leads to the moral law; or the sense of personal dignity leads to an obliga-

29. The immediate influence on Kant in this respect is Rousseau. Cf. *Émile* (Paris, Garnier, 1924), p. 336; the conscience never deceives us; sentiments are in touch with the nature of things. Reason judges or combines sensations, and is subject to error (pp. 316, 341).

tion to the laws of *practical* reason, which preserves human freedom and the significance of life precisely because these have nothing to do with discursive or theoretical understanding. In a reversal of the classical or traditional perspective (still accepted by Descartes), theoretical understanding is restricted to phenomena and does not apply to things as they are in themselves. Any effort to understand the first principles of experience by means of the discursive understanding leads directly to the paralogisms and antinomies of the pure reason. In other words, the principle of contradiction defines the horizon of theoretical or analytical intelligibility. Kant grounds contradiction in the function of human intelligence, whereas he preserves the consistency or freedom from contradiction of the (phenomenal) world about which one thinks. Kant admits that men are drawn to the thinking of contradictions, or to engaging in the effort to resolve the paralogisms and antinomies of pure reason, by a kind of innate necessity. Thus Hegel says that it is one of Kant's greatest services to have raised the status of dialectic (the thinking of contradictions) to a necessary activity of reason. But Kant could not grasp the significance of his own accomplishment because of his failure to overcome the standpoint of Hume.[30]

Kant imprisons man in knowledge of the phenomenal world, thanks fundamentally to his acceptance of the principle of contradiction. He therefore separates man from Being or God.[31] This is the ultimate consequence of the distinction between understanding and reason, a distinction which is for Hegel equivalent as it stands to the triumph of modern Skepticism. Simply put, modern Skepticism is a consequence of deficiencies in the modern doctrine of self-consciousness which, if not corrected, lead to nihilism and the loss of consciousness. Hegel's purification of the modern epoch requires the development of his dialectico-speculative logic, which includes as an essential component the techniques and results of ancient Skepticism.[32]

30. *Logik*, 1 : 38; 2 : 431 ff. *Logic*, pp. 56, 777 ff.

31. *Enzyklopädie* p. 78 (par. 51). *Encyclopedia–Wallace*, p. 107 f.

32. Cf. *Enzyklopädie*, pp. 102 f. (par. 81), 111 (par. 89). *Encyclopedia–*

In general terms, the superiority of ancient to modern Skepticism is this: ancient Skepticism doubts sense perception and not the cognitive capacity of reason. It thus serves the valuable function of dissolving the common-sense understanding of the world. Of course, ancient Skepticism is governed by the principle of contradiction. But this amounts to the assertion that reason possesses the "negative" capacity to discover the locus of contradiction in the phenomenal world. Reason criticizes an understanding which has not yet attained to the level of genuinely conceptual thinking. The destructive analysis of common sense by ancient Skepticism is thus a positive accomplishment of reason. Modern Skepticism, on the other hand, doubts reason while accepting the ultimate validity of sense perception. At the same time, it exempts physics, astronomy, and analytical thinking (*Verstand*) from doubt. These decisions, joined to the validation of sense-perception, result in dogmatism. Hegel means by this that the finite sphere of understanding (in effect, the world of empirical science, or the method of the scientist), despite its relation of opposition to reason, is posed as the Absolute: as the arbiter of rationality and knowledge. In slightly different terms, the principle of contradiction, which governs the domain of understanding, is arbitrarily asserted to be valid for reason as well. Since the exercise of reason leads to the posing of contradictory assertions as both true, reason is rejected as "unreasonable." Again, the repudiation of the Absolute qua reason as unknowable, whereas the logic and mathematics of understanding are accepted as unquestionably valid, makes these laws the effective Absolute.

The consequence of rendering the understanding absolute is the separation of Being from Thinking (which I capitalize to indicate their comprehensiveness). Whereas the classical doctrine, as initially exemplified in the famous dictum of Parmenides, poses the sameness of Being and Thinking, modern philosophy encloses man in a restricted concept of thinking

---

Wallace pp. 147 f., 169 f. Hegel's remark on the superfluousness of Skepticism as an introduction to science refers to an independent Skepticism of the empirical, unscientific mind: pp. 101 ff. (par. 78), *Encyclopedia–Wallace*, pp. 141 ff.

which renders Being inaccessible. Kant is thus still an empiricist, albeit one who makes almost explicit the subjective character of experience; again, we see that he has not surpassed Hume.[33] If experience is subjective and Being (in the classical sense) is inaccessible, then the critical philosophy of Kant produces an Idealism which is indistinguishable from nihilism. The positive form of the nihilism in which pre-Hegelian thought culminates may be illustrated by the assertion of Fichte that Being is a secondary or derivative concept, one which, in opposition to pure activity, negates freedom or conceals the Absolute.[34] The understanding interferes with the apprehension of the Absolute, and reason is incapable of providing us with a conceptual grasp of the Absolute. If we look beyond Hegel's own direct knowledge of the Fichtean teaching, it is still quite intelligible on Hegelian grounds that Fichte's later philosophy, the culmination of the modern doctrine of self-consciousness, advocates the destruction of the finite ego or of self-consciousness in an effort to attain the Absolute. This reference to the late Fichte, however, goes beyond the limits of the present discussion. Let me summarize the issue just sketched as follows. Modern philosophy prior to Hegel terminates in a crisis with respect to form. On the one hand, modern philosophy cannot rid itself of the classical conception that Being and Knowing are united in their actuality by a common formal structure. On the other hand, the manifest difference between formal structure and self-consciousness leads to the following contradiction: self-consciousness is immediately knowable but not knowable conceptually or analytically. The contradiction is resolved by interpreting "knowledge" in the first case in noncognitive or purely negative ways. The first principles and foundations of knowledge are then unknowable.

33. "Verhältnis des Skeptizismus," esp. pp. 204–08, 215, 219, 222 f.

34. Cf. "Zweite Einleitung in die Wissenschaftslehre," in *Erste und Zweite Einleitung in die Wissenschaftslehre,* ed. F. Medicus (Hamburg, Felix Meiner Verlag, 1954), p. 85. *Science of Knowledge, with the First and Second Introductions,* trans. Peter Heath and John Lachs (New York, Appleton Century Crofts, 1970), p. 69.

This is the situation in his own time which Hegel sets out to rectify. As I indicated above, his procedure is not simply to move forward but to take a giant step backward to Greek philosophy in preparation for his own assimilative solution. To give the pertinent example, Hegel in a way stands to Kant and Fichte as Plato stands to Eleaticism. Thus, in the *Lectures on the History of Philosophy,* Hegel discusses Eleatic logic in the form of a comparison between Zeno and Kant.[35] In Zeno, we see the beginning of dialectic as the pure excitation of thinking in concepts (296; 239). That is, the *aporiai,* or proofs of the simultaneous validity of contradictory theses, are the first expressions of reason's capacity to grasp the conceptual truth which underlies common-sense interpretations of sense perception. Reason sees that its contradictions reside in the consciousness of sense experience or appearance. The One alone is true. However, although this dichotomy between the One and the many or appearances is a true conclusion of reason, the One in itself cannot be known. Reason discovers its own limitations. As we might say, to give an account is to enter into the domain of the many, and so to terminate in contradiction or silence.

Approximately as in Kant, reason discovers the role of contradiction in dialectic but is unable to perform the "absolute reflection" by which it sees that the truth is the contradiction *as a whole.* For the Eleatics, then, the One is true but in the strict sense unknowable, whereas appearances are false but knowable. For Kant, it is also the case that we know only appearances, whereas the world in itself (= the One) is the absolute truth (342; 277). But Kant does not make appearances the locus of contradiction, since knowledge is for him consistent in the sense of obeying the principle of contradiction. Hegel is here interpreting Kant's restriction of knowledge to appearance as an implicit admission of the falseness or con-

35. *SW,* 17 : 296 ff. *Hegel's Lectures on the History of Philosophy,* trans. E. S. Haldane and F. H. Simson, 3 vols. (London, Routledge and Kegan Paul, 1892–96), 1 : 239 ff. Numbers in parentheses in the text refer *first* to the German edition cited above, n. 27, *second* to volume 1 of the translation.

tradictory nature of knowledge (since it is detached from the essence or Absolute). Thus Hegel observes: "In Kant, it is the spiritual that ruins the world; for Zeno, the world is the appearing in and for itself, untrue" (343; 277). Zeno's dialectic is subjective because it shows the contradictory nature of our consciousness (even though it does not grasp the implications of this demonstration). In a different but related sense, Kant's dialectic is also subjective, because it shows the contradictory nature of consciousness in attempting to think the unity of the world of appearances, even though it excludes contradiction from the world as an object of empirico-scientific knowledge. Just as Kant prepares the way for Hegel via Fichte and Schelling, so Zeno prepares the way for Plato via Heraclitus. This corresponds to the movement from subjective to objective dialectic (344; 278 f.).

"Heraclitus now grasps the Absolute itself as this process" of contradiction. He grasps the Absolute, and not just human consciousness, as dialectic itself: "In Heraclitus we first meet with the philosophical Idea in its speculative form: the common-sense 'reasoning' (*Raisonnement*) of Parmenides and Zeno is abstract understanding. . . . Here we see land; [36] there is no sentence of Heraclitus that I have not taken up into my logic" (344; 279). For Heraclitus, the world in itself, and hence reason as true or comprehensive thinking, is dialectical. Heraclitus grasps the fundamental Hegelian conception that the Whole, and so each of its parts, is a harmony of opposites, or in modern terminology, that non-*P* is an essential ingredient in the logical structure of *P*.[37] One could perhaps say that Heraclitus brings to life the essentially geometrical dialectic of the Eleatics. But his identity of *P* and non-*P*, or of life and death, is self-cancelling, because he lacks a third or mediating dimension in which identical opposites are preserved. Plato's doctrine of the community of forms is an attempt to provide this

36. The same metaphor is used in conjunction with Descartes: *SW*, 19 : 328; *Lectures on the History of Philosophy*, 3 : 217.

37. For a discussion of contradiction relevant to this issue and to contemporary logic, cf. E. Toms, *Being, Negation, and Logic* (Oxford, Basil Blackwell, 1962).

third dimension, but it is still too closely determined by geometrical modes of thought, and in addition, it lacks the moment of self-consciousness which is essential for the genuine fulfillment of the Parmenidean reference to the sameness of Being and Thinking. With respect to Heraclitus, it is still not seen that, since *P* is itself the negation of non-*P*, the identity of opposites is a negative affirmation or a comparative structure ("the negation of negation") in which the first moment, ostensibly positive, is at once negative, and the second moment, ostensibly negative, is at once positive.

In this historical sketch, we have come to the center of the most difficult notions in Hegel's logic. These will require a separate and precise exposition later in our study. Their early appearance is intentional, however, as it shows the sense in which Hegel's completion of modern philosophy is at the same time a return to the debates within classical thought. The Hegelian doctrine of consciousness is "the identity of identity and non-identity," or the bond [38] that holds together opposites in the very activity of opposing them or holding them apart. Heraclitus identifies thoughts with the total process of thinking but has no means to hold them apart within the same process. Therefore, thinking is negated or erased by itself as a process (407; 320). As I have already indicated, the Platonic synthesis of the Eleatics and Heraclitus fails because of the unselfconscious nature of the community of forms. The effort to transform the bond between *P* and non-*P* into thinking or mind leads to Aristotle, Neo-Platonism, and finally to Hegel. Hegel is able to correct Kant and Fichte by the process of correcting Plato and Aristotle. In other words, the Hegelian science of wisdom incorporates elements from the ancients as well as moderns, or resolves their quarrel by showing the role each has to play in the truth as a Whole.[39]

Earlier in this chapter, I remarked that there is no simple

38. See F. Chiereghin, *Hegel e la Metafisica Classica* (Padua, CEDAM, 1966) for an interesting discussion of the Platonic influence on Hegel in connection with this term.

39. "Das Wahre ist das Ganze"; *Phänomenologie*, p. 21; *Phenomenology*, p. 81.

starting point for the study of Hegel. Nevertheless, some starting points are simpler than others. In this chapter, I have been discussing Hegel first as a philosopher of history and then as a historian of philosophy. The difficulty with such a procedure is that one must somehow make evident from the outset Hegel's peculiar conception of "history." Hegel's science of wisdom is a *system* in the etymological sense of the term: everything "stands together" or is interconnected. A similar remark can be made about his key term "Absolute." The "Absolute" is free because it is the complete or the Whole, and this means that it explains itself or is the first principle of a system. The study of the system qua pattern of interconnectedness (which is not just a pattern but a spiritual or intellectual activity) is the study of logic. We may therefore say that history unfolds or reveals itself in a logical or systematic manner. In the next chapter, we must consider the notion of history more systematically.

A Note on "Phenomenology"

In view of the widespread contemporary use of the term "phenomenology," it is important to distinguish between Hegel's use of the term and those uses which come after him.* If we disregard the merely fashionable, and hence meaningless, uses, the term "phenomenology" in its present-day sense is derived from Husserl. To say this is by no means to reduce the whole issue to simplicity. In the first place, it might be argued that Husserl himself changed his conception of the meaning of phenomenology. But whether or not this is true, there can be no doubt that Husserl's use, as modified by Heidegger, has given rise to a second understanding; it is this second understanding which predominates among contemporary philosophers. I shall say only a few words on this complex subject.

The essential task is to distinguish between Hegelian and Husserlian, or early Husserlian, versions of phenomenology. For Hegel, phenomenology is the science of the Absolute as experienced. This means that the phenomena have an internal

* I am indebted to my colleague, Professor Thomas Seebohm, for a number of suggestions in the preparation of this note.

order or structure which is not the same as their structure *as* phenomena. At least for the Husserl of the *Ideas, Formal and Transcendental Logic,* and *Cartesian Meditations,* phenomenology is the science of pure essences, and of the transcendental subjectivity in which these essences are constituted. Husserl's phenomenology is rooted in Plato, Kant, and modern mathematics. His essences are mathematical in the sense of possessing no teleological order, no hierarchical structure which is the presence of divine totality in and through the phenomena. Each essence is self-identical, or obedient to the laws of finite (nondialectical) logic. If I may so put it, each essence is an absolute expression of the Absolute, and not a dialectical element in the gradually to be completed self-exhibition of a totally visible Absolute.

Hegel's *logos* is intended as a complete account of the phenomena, whereas for Husserl, this is impossible. Phenomenology is for Husserl a method with an infinite subject matter. The *logos* is epistemology, and therefore, from a Hegelian perspective, detached or alienated from the essences it describes. In other words, the Husserlian method is an instance of what Hegel calls "reflection," using this term in its Fichtean sense. The alienation of method from essence is visible in the difference between transcendental subjectivity, which Husserl conceived in a way as the consciousness of the spatio-temporal continuum, and the essences as geometrical crystallizations of transcendental spatio-temporality. (Husserl distinguishes between exact or mathematical essences, which I call here "geometrical," and morphological essences, or inexact types, like the essence of the medieval town. The latter cannot be treated formally or mathematically, but from a Hegelian standpoint, they remain distinct products of reflection, or imperfect approximations to mathematical essences.) An essence is timeless, yet constituted in and of time. We see here a vestige of the old Aristotelian situation. As mind actualizes in form, it disappears. As mind attempts to reflect upon itself apart from its formal actualizations, it is totally empty of content, a mere abstract continuum of flow which is inexplicably conscious or capable of becoming conscious in the noetic act. There is in

Husserl no doctrine of self-consciousness in the sense of the German Idealists or Hegel, but only a logical analysis of the abstract process which underlies the sequence or flow of essence-actualizations, each element of which is no longer anything like the abstract flow of the substratum itself.

In sum, Platonic Ideas are stripped of their hierarchical or teleological attributes, transformed into Aristotelian forms which actualize in the Kantian transcendental ego instead of the Aristotelian or Greek *nous,* and subject to analysis by a method which is in principle that of mathematical *ratio* or the reflection of *Verstand.* There is in Husserl no sense of dialectic, no overcoming of the paradoxes of finite logic, no idea of completeness, no account of Spirit as Absolute, no explanation of consciousness or self-consciousness, and therefore no account of the relation between subjectivity and the constituted content of subjectivity. Or so it would be claimed by Hegel. In the last analysis, Husserl's transcendental Absolute is the *nunc stans* of the inner time-consciousness from which the unit of the hyletic field and the unit of the ego-pole are constituted in the same way. As in the case of Kant's "I think . . ." there is no ego apart from the activity of cognition.

2 The Completion of World-History

History and Historicity

The philosophy of history is for Hegel concerned with world-history, or the gradual unfolding of the universal significance of the human spirit. It is "the thinking contemplation" of history from a universal viewpoint, not in an abstract sense but as "Spirit which is eternally by itself and for which there is no past. (Or it is the Idea)." Such a history is fundamentally political.[1] The universal or Absolute Spirit takes on concrete form through the activities of world-historical individuals like Caesar and Napoleon, in the various peoples (almost "families") who themselves acquire concrete actuality in states. The rational governance of the world by Absolute Spirit is thus visible in the state as the harmony of the universal and particular: an "individual" in Hegel's special terminology. The individuality of the state is itself rendered concrete within the free citizen, and his freedom in turn by obedience to the law, or more precisely, by duty to ethical objectivity. The citizen is objectively free, not as an abstract, finite, private, subjective and so merely moral person, who follows his feelings, his conscience, or his "good heart," but rather as a person who finds his individual satisfaction in the fulfilling of universal ends.[2] As Hegel strikingly puts it, the individual has a right not to superficial happiness but to the fulfillment of morality (in the political sense of "ethics") within the community. Hegel calls this fulfillment "satisfaction." This is his version of Kant's criticism of eudaimonism or the view that the end of the individual's life is a right to happiness. Satisfaction is both higher and deeper than happiness: it is transindividual, or the transformation of merely individual gratification (which is body-oriented) into spiritual perfection.[3] "World-historical in-

1. *Die Vernunft in der Geschichte,* pp. 15, 22, 25.

2. *Philosophie des Rechts,* pp. 124 f. (par. 139), 133 f. (par. 140); *Philosophy of Right,* pp. 92 f., 98 f.

3. *Die Vernunft in der Geschichte,* pp. 92 f., 107 f.

dividuals, who have pursued such ends, have indeed satisfied themselves but they did not act with a will to be happy." [4] In general, Hegel's political philosophy unites the Aristotelian doctrine of the political essence of ethics and the Kantian-Fichtean doctrine of the state as itself a world-historical individual. Of course, Hegel achieves the goal of world-history in the here and now, instead of removing it to the infinitely distant future, or to the domain of "what ought to be," as do Kant and Fichte (who are to this extent still Platonists). In addition, the assimilation of politics into the philosophy of history is a consequence of the identification between the individual and the universal Spirit. Whereas Aristotle distinguishes, so to speak, between the mind of man and the mind of God, and hence between man's practical and theoretical perfections, Hegel unites them in the concrete actuality of world-history. The virtue of the state is thus identical with the satisfaction of mankind—not of every man, but of the human spirit, which has achieved Absolute Spirit in Hegel's own time.

This is not to say that Hegel simply condemns private desire or selfish gratification. He observes that modern man has the right to insist upon subjective gratification. In the tradition of such modern philosophers as Machiavelli and Hobbes, he recognizes desire as the "engine" of world-history (thereby uniting the Platonic Eros with the directedness of historical development). The spirit first knows itself as subjective feeling. When feeling is localized externally or given an objective status, spirit divides itself into an inner and an outer world. We become alienated from ourselves or regard our true self as contained in the object outside us, which we desire to assimilate. Desire is thus fundamentally desire for myself, or for my interior essence, from which I have become detached. The struggle to satisfy my desires leads to the development of individual consciousness. Since others desire the same things, this struggle is also the origin of the family, the state, and in general, of world-history.[5] The struggle to satisfy private desires is

4. Ibid., p. 93.

5. Ibid., pp. 56, 85, 102. Cf. *Philosophie des Rechts,* p. 112 (par. 124);

thus an initially unconscious sign of the cunning of reason, or as Hegel puts it, of the use of natural tools to conquer nature.[6] Selfishness is a sign of the rule of reason over the world (again a Kantian idea in more developed form).[7] And this in turn means that the real end of desire is satisfaction in the Hegelian sense of "the good": actual freedom in the ethical citizen, who recovers his lost interior essence in the comprehension of the significance of human life. We desire not "this" or "that" but the "absolute end" of world-history.[8] We desire the good (that is, "we" taken collectively), and we satisfy this desire in the state. The state is not a tyrant but renders accessible the good to all citizens in ways compatible with their particular natures. In his way, Hegel accepts the Socratic (and especially Aristotelian) notion of man as by "nature" (Hegel would say "by his spirit") a political being.

The highest human satisfaction, however, is in thinking, and so in philosophy or the science of wisdom, which is "thinking about thinking." The desire for the good culminates in the love of wisdom; again, Hegel retains the classical Greek notion, albeit wedding it to the modern doctrine of desire. In religious language, world-history is understood as a theodicy or justification of God's will. We justify God by reconciling ourselves to evil, that is, to the actual world, or to "the present." But this reconciliation in turn depends upon knowledge of God's "presence" within the actual or historical present.[9] It depends upon "science" in the Hegelian sense of systematic, conceptual,

---

Philosophy of Right, p. 84: the mark of modernity is the right of the individual to be satisfied.

6. *Philosophie der Weltgeschichte,* p. 544.

7. This theme, which originates in the doctrines of Machiavelli, Hobbes, and the other founders of modern political philosophy, is incorporated into German philosophy of history by Kant. See his essay of 1784, *Idee zu einer allgemeinen Geschichte in weltbürgerlicher Absicht,* in *Werke, Akademie Textausgabe,* (Berlin, Walter de Gruyter, 1968), Vol. 8.

8. *Philosophie des Rechts,* p. 116 (par. 129); *Philosophy of Right,* p. 86.

9. *Die Vernunft in der Geschichte,* p. 77; *Philosophie der Weltgeschichte,* p. 938.

discursive wisdom. It is mere chatter to speak of God's rule in some "beyond" in the sense either of a transcendent heaven or as the "open future" of human history.[10] Hegel regularly criticizes the Kantian doctrine that man fulfills his moral obligation in the categorical imperative or obedience to universal moral laws as an expression of the pure will. The pure will is for Hegel empty of content, negative, and so it separates man from the reality of his existence and ethical significance in historical or political actions (which negate the negativity of will). For Kant, man acquires significance from the possession of a good will. For Hegel, man is fundamentally what he does.[11] Kant's doctrine of morality expresses the conception of the primacy of the subject or "person" in contrast to the objective state or union of subject and object in the citizen. It substitutes "what ought to be" for what is, and thereby makes impossible human satisfaction or the justification of God's behavior toward mankind.[12] To insist upon a pure will is thus to make this world, and human beings as they are, worthless.

Science justifies God, or explains the necessity of contingency (and so evil), by explaining the present as the "end" of history in the sense of its fulfillment. Contingent history does not cease, but its significance is fully revealed. Therefore the principle of reason employed by the genuinely philosophical historian (of whom Hegel is the first) is the spiritual "totality of all viewpoints." [13] As Hegel says, he knows the Whole.[14] The Christian revelation makes it possible for men to see the eternal truth, but Hegel is the first to develop or explain it philosophically.[15] Science and the justification of God thus depend upon the complete manifestation of theoretical truth within practice. Nevertheless, within practice, it is theory or science which affords genuine satisfaction. The fulfillment of history, the actualization of the rational state, ethical satisfaction, and

10. *Die Vernunft in der Geschichte*, p. 41.

11. Ibid., p. 66.

12. *Philosophie des Rechts*, pp. 102 (par. 108), 111 (par. 124), 289 (par. 343); *Philosophy of Right* pp. 76, 83, 216 f.

13. *Die Vernunft in der Geschichte*, p. 32.

14. Ibid., p. 30.

15. Ibid., pp. 45–47.

the justification of, or reconciliation with, God, all depend upon man's capaciy to identify with the World-Spirit in "the excitation of its activity," which is "to know itself absolutely." [16] Activity, and so contingency, continue, but there cannot be anything radically new, no degree of essential satisfaction still to be obtained in some historical or transcendent future.[17] The fulfillment of the individual in the state is thus the only genuine expression of his freedom; this in turn depends upon the rationality and so the ethical nature of the state. But since the state is itself a "citizen" of world-history, and since the truth of world-history is finally accessible to the scientific thinker alone, it is obvious that Hegel cannot be primarily a political philosopher, and certainly not a "philosopher of the future." Neither can he be primarily a religious thinker, since the end of human or world-history, namely, freedom as the substance of Spirit, God, or the Idea, is contained in its purest or highest form in the *Science of Logic*.[18]

In the previous chapter I said that Hegel is primarily a logician. Of course, this does not mean that, in order to understand history, we must subject it to "logical analysis" in the formalist sense of that expression. Logic in the Hegelian sense is the study of *Logos* or the Word of God, revealing itself as the fundamental course of human history. This raises the possibility of a misunderstanding. Hegel is not a *historicist,* if by that term we mean someone who equates reality, truth, or being with the process of history experienced by man as a contingent, radically temporal instance of that process. Nevertheless, Hegel conceives of God or the Absolute as activity which, even though eternal and necessary, exhibits its essential nature in human history. Hegel escapes historicism by his insistence upon the completeness and complete accessibility to human intelligence of the divine exhibition. In other words,

16. *Philosophie des Rechts,* p. 293 (par. 352); *Philosophy of Right,* p. 219.

17. *Philosophie des Rechts,* pp. 296 f (pars. 358–60); cf. pp. 16 f.; *Philosophy of Right,* pp. 222 f; cf. 12 f.; *Die Vernunft in der Geschichte,* p. 181.

18. *Die Vernunft in der Geschichte,* pp. 53, 55.

satisfaction, the reconciliation with God, and wisdom are all equivalent to the completion of history and cannot be rendered compatible with an unending sequence of contingent historical events.

A more serious source of confusion, however, arises from Hegel's evident role as precursor of the contemporary doctrine of the *historicity* of Being (or in Hegel's term, the Whole). We may understand "historicity" to designate the process or activity by which Being emerges from an unknown or at least conceptually inaccessible source. Such a Being is not an eternal order in the classical sense, but changes its essential shape, or what counts as order, in accordance with a pulsation-process of emergence, in such a way as to give rise to human history by "opening" or defining the horizons within which human history occurs. The process of the opening or defining of horizons is not itself history but historicity. How we see our history is thus a changing, arbitrary "gift" from an unknowable but possibly experienceable "source." I cannot enter here into an adequate discussion of post-Hegelian doctrines of historicity.[19] Because of their contemporary popularity, however, it is necessary to refer to them in order to distinguish them from Hegel's own teaching. For our purposes, the crucial difference is as follows. Hegel is a rationalist, of however peculiar a kind, who adheres to the classical program of giving a logical explanation of the totality of things, or the Whole. The pulsation-process of the emergence of Being is for Hegel altogether intelligible. One might argue whether Hegel's conception of the intelligibility of the Absolute leads him to forget the "ontological difference" between the Absolute and its finite manifestations. Those who assert such a criticism, in any case, merely underline the difference between Hegelian and post-Hegelian ontologies. The latter, even as influenced by Hegel, take their bearings by a rejection of his rationalist procedures and claims to

19. Cf. K. Löwith, *From Hegel to Nietzsche* (New York, Doubleday, 1967); and my *Nihilism*. H. Marcuse, *Hegels Ontologie und die Theorie der Geschichtlichkeit*, 2d. ed. (Frankfurt, Vittorio Klostermann, 1968), places an exaggerated emphasis upon the "historicistic" character of Hegel's teaching, but is interesting.

success. For these doctrines, wisdom, if possible at all, can be understood only as a kind of "learned ignorance" which defines the limits of reason, the inaccessibility of the pulsation-process and its source to logical explanation, and the need for a "new" kind of thinking, curiously like doctrines of intellectual intuition prevalent in Hegel's own time, and designed to "leap" over the restrictions of traditional rationalism.

The partisans of historicity must deny that history is essentially complete, or even that the very conception of completeness makes any sense. On this score, the historicistic thinker is curiously enough more like the Platonic rationalist (whom he severely criticizes) than is Hegel. This is because the contemporary and the ancient both agree that wisdom in the Hegelian sense is impossible. For both, the philosopher is "open to the Whole" as to something which he may prophesy or discern "through a glass darkly," but as that which, even though it is the condition of his thought, must forever elude it. Both deny, if not the fact of the identity-within-difference between God and man, certainly its complete intelligibility.

Whole and parts

The first step in our analysis of what Hegel means by the "completion" of history has led to the problem of historicity, because of the peculiar character of Hegel's identification of eternity and temporality within human historical experience. In order to distinguish precisely Hegel's dialectical rationalism from historicistic teachings, it will be necessary for us to consider the notion of "completeness" from a logical standpoint. In this section, I shall begin the logical discussion with a consideration of the traditional problem of the "whole and its parts." As usual, when "Whole" is capitalized, it will refer to the comprehensive totality of the Absolute. Since Hegel speaks more regularly of the Absolute than of the Whole (although he uses both terms), it may be well to justify my procedure by explaining the connection between the terms. To repeat: what Hegel means by "completeness" in history is the total manifestation of the Absolute, or in other words, the presence of scientific wisdom. Knowledge of the Absolute is the same as absolute existence (or in the Parmenidean phrase, of the sameness of Being and Thinking). Since the highest definition of the Absolute is *Spirit*,[20] and since Spirit, as the identity of identity and non-identity, encompasses the three spheres of nature, self-consciousness, and conceptual knowledge, or the community of world, man, and God, it is evident that the term *Absolute* functions in Hegel as does the term *Whole* in classical thought. There is, of course, this crucial difference: the classical rationalist does not identify the Whole with any of its parts, not even with the part that thinks the Whole. Hegel makes precisely this identification.[21] We now turn to the task of understanding why he does so, or in general, what he means by the previously cited assertion that "the true is the Whole."

When we speak of "the whole and its parts," we normally mean a collection of individuals which is itself an individual. For example, we might refer to the human body as the "whole" of its various organs, limbs, or elements. Or we could perhaps say that space, taken as a "whole," includes every one of its parts: this or that place, this or that stretch of space. The example of space is obviously trickier than that of body, because it seems to be impossible to perceive the whole of space, whereas we can grasp a whole human body with relative ease. In addition, space can be divided up into parts in more complicated ways than can a body, without damaging its integrity or wholeness. We can take "space" as a transitional example from particular or extended wholes to logical wholes, like the abstract "classes" or "sets" of mathematics. Even though it is in practice out of the question for us to perceive space as a whole, we can conceive or "grasp" it mentally, within the confines of a rigorously determinate definition. In the case of a class, which is itself by definition an entity inaccessible to sense-

20. *Enzyklopädie*, p. 314 (par. 384); *Hegel's Philosophy of Mind*, trans. W. Wallace and A. V. Miller, (London and New York, Oxford University Press, 1971), p. 18. This translation of Part Three of the *Enzyklopädie* will be cited as *Encyclopedia Wallace–Miller*.

21. Cf. *Enzyklopädie*, pp. 136 (par. 136), 138 (par. 139); *Encyclopedia–Wallace*, pp. 246 f., 252. Whereas the Whole appears in every part, this "appearance" must be raised to the level of self-consciousness, or to the conceptual understanding of the Whole.

perception, there is no way to grasp it except by mental or conceptual operations. We can perceive this or that apple, but no one could perceive the class of all apples in the way that he perceives individual apples, that is, parts of this whole. The crucial point, however, is this: whatever the difference between sense-perception and mental conception, the act by which we grasp a particular or a whole (in the sense of a class of all particulars of a given kind) is *in each case itself particular.* Of course we may be aware in general of our perceptual field and the many objects it encompasses, or of our stream of consciousness, alive with uncountable feelings, perceptions, and thoughts. But such awareness is at best the precondition for knowledge. The act of knowing, perceiving, or for that matter being aware of anything at all as that specific anything, requires us to focus our attention on it. Let us say that, in general terms, "attending to" is taking on the shape, or identifying with the structure of, a *this* rather than a *that.*

The problem of wholes and parts can be stated within the language of traditional (non-Hegelian) rationalist logic in the following general way. Every conceivable whole is a finite or determinate entity; it is conceivable because it has a specific form. To know a whole is always to know "this specific whole." But when philosophers talk about *the* Whole, they seem to be referring to something which has a self-contradictory nature and so which cannot be logically grasped at all. The Whole is on the one hand specific, since it refers not to this or that whole but to *all of them.* On the other hand, as the Whole of wholes, or "the class of all classes," it has no specificity whatsoever. Logic or rational discourse itself functions by the method of division and collection. Whether thinking and speaking are identical or merely inseparable, we cannot think logically except about entities of which we can speak, and to speak is to classify (implicitly or explicitly). But the classification-process is a specifying-process, and this means that one species is divided off from another by the very act in which we classify an individual as a member of a given species. When I say, "This is an apple," I am implicitly saying also, "and it is not a tangerine, a peach, etc.," or in general, "it is not anything else." One could claim (as Hegel in fact does) that the act of knowing an apple, if considered rigorously, is necessarily the act of knowing everything else from which the apple is by definition excluded. But this would seem to mean that, in order to know the apple, we must know not just the apple but *everything*. To know *everything*, however, is not the same as knowing the apple.

I repeat: to know the apple (or anything else) is to know this rather than that, and in this way rather than that, to grasp a scientific form, to analyze, divide, or separate out, even as one is gathering together. In the case of the Whole, however, this is manifestly impossible. Whether logical discourse is a perfect expression of how things are, or whether because we cannot know except by explaining logical discourse, the fact remains that we cannot give a logical account of the Whole. If to give an account is to specify, to separate out, to say something of something, then every ostensible account of the Whole would in fact be an account of *part* of the Whole. We might go a step farther and insist that there is no Whole, since "to be" is to be something, a this or a that, or a thing of this or that kind. This would leave us with a conception of reality as a manifold of kinds or species but with no common genus. We are then asked to conceive a discontinuous sequence of species, unrelated logically to common structure, yet related logically to the common structure of rational discourse itself. Logicians normally express the paradoxical character of the Whole by referring to the paradox of the class of all classes. This may be formulated in various ways. I shall first indicate a technical version and then restate the general idea in an informal way that is related to a conception of Greek philosophy. Let us first consider the class of all classes, symbolized as M. We then define UM as the class of all classes contained within M. For any class whatsoever, the cardinal number of that class is always smaller than the cardinal number of the class of classes contained within it. For example, if a given class C contains two elements, UC will contain 2^2 classes. Let the elements of C be a and b. Then the elements of UC will be: a, b, a and b (or C itself), and O (or the null-class). Since

M is the class of all classes, *UM* must be included within *M*. This would mean that the cardinal number of *UM* is smaller than (or equal to) the cardinal number of *M*. But we have just seen that the cardinal number of *UM* must be larger than the cardinal number of *M*. This is a brief sketch of *Cantor's paradox*. However, for our purposes, the paradox of the class of all classes may be stated in a simpler way. Either this class belongs to itself or it does not. If it does not, then the class is incomplete, lacking itself among its members. If it does belong to itself, then we construct another class, which includes both "all" classes and the former "class of all classes" (now demoted to membership within a more comprehensive class). In either of these cases, there is no Whole but only a manyness, whether static or infinitely expanding. One may also adjust one's logic in such a way as to exclude the class of all classes, but this is merely to grant that the Whole is inaccessible.

There is, however, a difference between the logical notion of a class of all classes and the philosophical notion of the Whole. The class of all classes is conceived from the outset by analogy with any of its members; that is, it is conceived from the outset as a finite, stable, and detached or self-identical structure. The very definition of a class, or more comprehensively, the nature of non-Hegelian logic (which defines a class in accordance with the principle of contradiction), makes it impossible from the outset that there should be a "class of all classes" in the sense of "the Whole." But it is possible to speak philosophically of the Whole in a way quite different from the logician's class of all classes. We might, for example, refer to the principles underlying the organization of all classes or parts. In this sense, the logician's definition of a class is already an assertion, even a reflexive definition of the Whole, except that it does not quite refer to itself as definition in the same sense that it refers to what it defines. To rephrase this slightly, the definition of a class is a formation-rule: the Whole is just whatever obeys that rule. The rule by which classes are formed cannot itself be a class. Yet it expresses the essence of any class whatsoever. If we could grasp the formation-rule completely, we would have grasped the Whole, and not just a part of the Whole. Even further, we would have grasped the Whole in such a way as to avoid completely the paradox of the class of all classes. For that matter, there might be an infinite process of class-formation. If we knew the workings of that process, then we would know the Whole, and in the genuine philosophical sense of knowing the Whole qua Whole, rather than qua its part or some selection of them.

But this example needs refinement. In the preceding paragraph, I referred to the formation-rule of a logician. Within the domain of logic itself, *no reference is made to the logician.* One could say that, in his own way, the non-Hegelian logician shares the Hegelian desire to describe "God" in his eternal essence, as he is prior to the creation of the finite spirit. However, the non-Hegelian conceives of "God" as a logical structure rather than as infinite Spirit, and so, strangely enough, as a class of all classes, thereby guaranteeing in advance the failure of his enterprise, taken as a "Whole." The crucial thesis of Hegel's logic is, however, that the class cannot be known apart from, or without also knowing, the logician. In Hegelian language, we cannot know the object of knowledge without knowing the subject whose object it is. The logician seems to proceed as though he and his audience were extraneous to logic itself. He condemns references to himself or to his thought-processes as *psychologism,* namely, the doctrine that classes, deductions, or in sum, truth, are functions of human perception and conception. The logician rightly rejects psychologism as a kind of relativism or historicism which destroys the very possibility of truth, of a genuinely logical "object" or domain of objectivity. But Hegel's thesis has nothing to do with psychologism.

The psychologistic doctrine makes truth relative to, because a product of, the individual thinker or the race of man as a finite, self-restricted species of intelligence, working in particular ways. According to psychologism in its most comprehensive form, men call "truth" what they grasp of the world, whereas to other thinking beings, the truth might be altogether different. The antipsychologistic logician insists upon the distinction between the logical "concept" as an objective form, and the process of "conception" by which the concept is "seen" or "grasped." However, this distinction cannot be enforced by self-forgetfulness. A radical analysis is required of the relation between concept and conception (or between Being and Thinking). Hegel attempts to supply us with such an analysis. According to Hegel, the truth in its comprehensive sense is a relation (of identity-within-difference) between the subject and object. We shall be concerned in the next chapter with the subject and object as the two sides of the relation constituting the Whole. For the present, let us restrict our attention to the relation *as* Whole. This relation is the Hegelian analogue to the previously mentioned formation-rule of the hypothetical or perfectly wise logician. In other words, it is the activity of the Absolute or divine and eternal truth, and in no sense relative to individuals or humans as distinct from animals or gods. Hegel thus goes even farther than Kant in asserting that the thinkable qua thinkable is the same for all thinking beings, including God. We can escape from psychologism only because the object is given to us within the knowing-process by the activity of the Absolute, or the process by which *everything is what it is.* He arrives at this knowledge by rejecting the traditional rationalist contention, going back to Plato, that "to know" is to know a determinate, finite, stable, detached form. We shall inspect Hegel's rejection of this aspect of Platonism in chapter 4. But it will be helpful to anticipate here the main lines of Hegel's argument. If to know and to be are always specific in the way just stated, then the mind can never know itself or the process of knowing as a living activity. The mind is not a specific form but a capacity to receive or produce all forms. Psychology "objectifies" the mind, but in so doing, it destroys or disregards the phenomenon of subjectivity. That is, it replaces the mind as a living unity of diverse activities by a discontinuous sequence of nonliving forms or formulae. Like the logician, the psychologist forgets about himself, and not simply as a contingent individual but as part of the Whole. Stated less crudely, he forgets subjectivity or self-consciousness as the medium within which forms and formulae are formulated.

It is important to underline that Hegel is not a "subjectivist." He does not claim that objects are in fact merely phantoms or products of the imagination. But neither does he claim that objects are only modes of subjectivity per se. Instead, he argues that we cannot know an object except by knowing that it is an object for a subject. We know nothing except what we know; "to be" and "to think" are coextensive, and even the same, provided we understand "same" in the special Hegelian sense of "identity-within-difference." What is the same here is the formation-process: subject and object preserve their identities or difference from each other within their identity. The subject cannot be known except in terms of its identity as subject *of* objects. There is no abstract subject, void of objects like an empty box waiting to be filled, or like Locke's *tabula rasa* waiting to be inscribed. Subject and object are correlative terms; they call each other into being, and they condition or define each other. One could say rather crudely that every "thing" is a subject or object. But the Absolute is not a "thing," whether in the sense of subject or object. The Absolute is the formation-process of subjects and objects. If we begin our scientific investigation by disregarding subjectivity, or by dedicating ourselves to the effort to objectify it, then we shall never understand subjectivity or objectivity, and the Whole or Absolute will be forever denied us.

Again we anticipate an issue that will be more closely analyzed in chapter 4, but it is necessary to indicate here that the difficulties of traditional logic concerning the Whole are also visible within its analysis of the part. Let us put to one side the question of the subject or knower and concentrate upon the form or object of knowledge. A complete analysis of a form is one which specifies, and in that sense counts, all of its essential elements. We may further assume that this has been done (although there are extraordinary difficulties concealed beneath this assumption). The question then arises: what about the *order* of the essential elements, which is in fact what we mean by this specific form? If the order of the constituting elements is itself an element, then we need one element more than the sum of the constituting elements in order to constitute the form. If the order of the elements is not itself an element, then no formal analysis of the specific form is possible: we can list its constituents or provide an image of the form in question. But the image is intelligible only if we already know the original; and in this case, there is no analytical equivalent to "knowing the original." In the first case, the form is more than itself; in the second, it seems to be equal to itself. In both cases, there is no analytical explanation of the unity of the form as unity, and hence of the form as form. The form as analyzed seems in each case to be less than itself, just as a unity is less than a "sum" of parts. The wholeness of the form, to restate this point, is equated with the "fact" of the co-presence of many formal elements. Since no explanation can be given which renders this co-presence necessary (for that would amount to a "deduction" of the elements from the unity of their order), it is not long before the co-presence is treated as contingent. The wholeness of the unity of a form gives way to the "allness" of the sum of the parts of a form, which in turn dissolves, either into the "invisible substance" of modern empiricism (which is in turn rejected as an illusion), or into the intention of the analyst. Again, either this intention is ignored, or it is itself analyzed into a contingent co-presence of formal elements. But this leads either to no explanation of parts as wholes, or to an infinite regress. Hegel's science of wisdom is an effort to escape from these self-destructive consequences of modern rationalism, which is itself a descendant of Platonic logic.

Logic and the End of History

Now let me return to the question of the end of history, understood as its completeness, or more fundamentally, to the connection between history and logic. Wisdom, in its purest form the science of logic, is conceptual or discursive knowledge of the Absolute. Since the Absolute is the formation-process of subjects and objects, wisdom is knowledge of the formation-process, and not the empirical knowledge of every product of that process. With respect to the example of historicity, Hegel claims to know and to have explained what the representatives of that school call "the origin of Being" as the pulsation-process of Being's emergence. There is for Hegel nothing "behind" that process, no hidden source or God from which Being emerges. Philosophies of historicity, seen in a Hegelian perspective, are a variation on the orthodox Christian doctrine of a creation *ex nihilo*. Hegel would object to them, precisely as he did to the orthodox Christians, that one must and can explain the *nihil* or Nothing, not as a separate source or dimension, however: for that would be to identify God as Nothing and to rob his creation of substance, or to make it "illusion" (*Schein*) in the sense of a phantom on the surface of Nothing. Instead, Nothing must be explained as an integral dimension of the activity of the Absolute understood as the formation-process.

We should notice another crucial difference in this connection between Hegelian logic and traditional rationalism. The non-Hegelian logician, however systematic his deductions, must always begin from axioms, definitions, deductive rules, and the like, which are not deduced from anything but given *ex nihilo,* in a way like God's creation of the world. Since the logician is not God, however, his deductive system is relative to its axioms, etc. The arbitrariness of this relativity is clear from the fact that we are free to change our axioms, etc., or in effect to contradict the initial logic of our choice. But even if this is not altogether true, or if there are certain "common axioms" for every deductive logic, it remains the case that they cannot themselves be deduced. The fact that we are forced to accept them if we wish to explain or argue at all does not alter the fact that our explanations rest upon an unexplained, and to that extent nonlogical or arbitrary foundation. In Hegel's logic, however, everything follows from the Absolute, which, as eternal or "circular" in the sense of complete self-perpetuating activity, *follows from itself.* It is important to see that the Absolute cannot be said to follow from Nothing, for this would reproduce the mystery of the Christian dogma of creation. On the contrary, Nothing is included within the Absolute. Since the Absolute reveals its nature fully in its products, as the Christian God does not, Hegel's logic is, or leads to, a presuppositionless and therefore circular or perfect science.

We can draw this chapter to a close by returning to the discussion of the opening pages in the light of our technical analysis of the Whole. Actuality or essential history is equivalent to the complete manifestation of the Absolute as formation-process. Man's essential possibilities have all been fulfilled or actualized when once he is able to grasp the Absolute, precisely because the Absolute is the essence of human possibility. No doubt there will be an unending stream of variations on these essential actualities, but they can be grasped, saved, or understood completely. Absolute knowledge thus makes human historical life for the first time genuinely significant. Far from doing away with contingency, Hegel preserves it as rational. In religious language, Hegel's eschatology insists that God and man have already been reconciled in the "eternal present" of completed history.[22] The stages of world-history correspond to the tripartite structure of the Christian God.[23] In antiquity, the Father alone manifests himself as creator of the world. With the coming of Christ, the Middle Ages begin, or the realm of the Son. "With the Reformation, however, the realm of the Spirit now begins, in which God as Spirit is actually known. Herewith the new, the last flag" of history is raised. Modernity has as its sole task "to win the form of freedom, of universality," namely, to complete the process described in Hegel's science of wisdom.[24] And again: "With this formal, absolute principle of freedom, we come to the last stage of history, to our world, to our day." [25] Modern men who are capable of thinking now recognize the objective content of the World-Spirit as their own. They understand the accomplishment of reconciliation, or the identity of their age with the heaven upon earth promised for heaven alone by orthodox Christianity.[26] Christ now dwells within each member of the

22. *Philosophie der Weltgeschichte,* p. 743.
23. Ibid., pp. 722, 734.
24. Ibid., p. 881.
25. Ibid., p. 920.
26. Ibid., p. 938.

(German or Prussian Lutheran) community as the intelligible Absolute Spirit.[27]

World-history is "spiritual actuality in its total circumference of interiority and exteriority." [28] In the closing paragraphs of the *Philosophy of Right,* Hegel summarizes the essential stages of world-history as they receive their final recapitulative development in the modern age, which is for Hegel dominated and defined by the Germanic people as the instrument of the Lutheran Reformation. The main result is the already noted overcoming of the separation between the realms of heaven and of earth, but now described in political language. The reconciliation between God and man is objectified within the state ("the image and actuality of reason"); it furnishes the "feeling and the representation" of truth in religion, and finally, in the science of wisdom. In this last and perfect objectification, man is provided with "the free conceptual knowledge of this truth as one and the same in its reciprocally completing manifestations, in the *state,* in *nature,* and in the *ideal world.*" [29] The content of essential history and logic is therefore the same. It should now be evident that one cannot understand Hegel's philosophy of history, nor his political and religious teaching, without understanding his logic.

27. Ibid., pp. 738, 822, 847.

28. *Philosophie des Rechts,* p. 288 (par. 341); *Philosophy of Right,* p. 216

29. Ibid., p. 297 (par. 360); p. 222.

3 Subject-Object

The Subject-Object Structure of Logic

Hegel's logic is a kind of synthesis of the philosophical and religious senses of the Greek word *Logos*. His *Logos* is not simply the rational discourse of man, but it is also the living and productive Word of God. One of Hegel's favorite scriptural texts, the Gospel according to Saint John, begins with the sentence: "In the beginning was the Word, and the Word was with God." Hegel takes this to mean that God's "creation" is in fact the intelligible manifestation of the divine Spirit which informs all things. In other words, the world is *present from the beginning;* the conception of a creation *ex nihilo* is valid, if at all, only at the level of religious representation, but not at the level of scientific knowledge. The logical significance of the Christian doctrine of the Trinity could then be restated in the following manner. The Father "poses" the world and is reflected within its essence as the Son; the separation implied by the notion of reflection is overcome within the Spirit or Holy Ghost. The Trinity is thus the paradigm for the crucial Hegelian conception of the overcoming of the separation between subject and object, an overcoming in which each retains its identity, or constitutes an "identity of identity and non-identity." We have already seen that the Absolute is Spirit, and that Spirit is the Whole. In the previous chapter, we studied the problem of the Whole with respect to both history and logic. In this chapter, we shall concentrate upon the Whole as subject and object. The connection between logic and history thus means that the process by which man overcomes alienation through an appropriation of the historical world is the same process by which he overcomes his separation from God or Absolute Spirit. The "reunion" of Father and Son within the Holy Ghost is the paradigmatic expression of the reunion of subject and object within the human spirit, which is a manifestation of Absolute Spirit.

Let me begin with an extremely simple formulation of the difficulty which Hegel sets himself to resolve. In order to obtain comprehensive knowledge, it is necessary to explain the possibility of knowledge, or the connection between the knower and what is known. The experience of consciousness suggests very strongly that there is a radical difference between the activity of thinking and the things about which we think. How is this difference overcome? If we go too far toward identifying thinking and the things about which we think, this surely makes nonsense of our experience. On the other hand, if we insist upon preserving the radical difference between thinking and being, not only will we fail to account for the accessibility of things to thinking, but we will be unable to think about, or to explain the fact that we "appear" to be thinking about, thinking itself. For Hegel as well as for Fichte and Schelling, these two extremes represent the deficiencies of Idealism and Realism respectively. As we may now express this, the Idealist fails to account for nature or *objectivity*, whereas the Realist cannot explain *subjectivity*. The problem, then, is to overcome the separation between the subject and the object, without dissolving their intrinsic characteristics. It should be evident from this elementary sketch that Hegel will reject any solution which transforms objects into "ideas" or "thoughts." We shall therefore have to distinguish carefully between a "subjective Idealism" which lacks an objective correlative, and the conception of Absolute Subjectivity or Spirit, which manifests itself as both subject and object. Nevertheless, we must say that the subject has precedence over the object to this extent: it makes no sense to refer to Absolute Objectivity, for then self-consciousness, thinking, and spirituality are excluded from the Absolute at the very outset. The attempt to explain the connection between the subject and the object is already an act of the subject.

As part of this preliminary sketch, it may be wise to comment briefly on a terminological point. We may be tempted to wonder whether the dilemma of the subject-object distinction is not forced upon us by the use of the terms themselves. Certain contemporary philosophers, for example Heidegger, claim to have by-passed the very framework of the subject-object distinction. Nevertheless, there is in Heidegger a curiously Hegelian presence of Being to itself in the thinking of man. Heidegger seems to have accomplished the absence of "subject" and "object" by adopting a version of the Hegelian Absolute as the identity of identity and non-identity. At the same time, there is also a suppression of subjectivity which reminds us of the late Fichte and, what is more pertinent to the present investigation, of the Greek thinkers whom Hegel both criticizes and assimilates. In general, the Greeks as well as Heidegger wish to think Being as it is, and not as it is reflected within, or perspectivally accessible to, a subject. The Greek conception of Being as the presence of form makes it impossible to think thinking or mind as that to which form is present. Heidegger, on the other hand, through his curious combination of Fichtean and Hegelian themes, makes the thinking of Being rather a thinking of the absence of Being, or of the "presence" of Being to itself in the concealed form of beings, primary among which is man. In short, Heidegger's thinking of Being rather a thinking of the absence of Being, as the *image* of Being, rather than of Being as it is "in and for itself" (to employ a Hegelian term). It would take us too far afield to pursue this suggestion concerning Heidegger, which I have raised here only to indicate why the possible objection against the language of "subjects" and "objects" does not allow us to by-pass the Hegelian analysis.[1] The problems intrinsic to the dualism of Being and Thinking are not resolved by a shift in terminology. At the same time, it is reasonable to guard against accepting unnecessary theoretical difficulties because of a careless use of language.

1. The connections between Heidegger, Hegel, and the late Fichte on the one hand, and the late Schelling on the other, may be studied with the help of two excellent books: W. Janke, *Fichte* (Berlin, Walter de Gruyter, 1970); W. Schulz, *Die Vollendung des deutschen Idealismus in der Spätphilosophie Schellings* (Stuttgart, W. Kohlhammer Verlag, 1955).

Aristotelian and Spinozist Elements in Hegel's Noetics

We turn now to a more detailed study of Hegel's reconciliation of the subject and object. At the beginning of this chapter, I invoked the Christian conception of the Trinity as the paradigm of Hegel's solution. It should have been evident in the very formulation of the paradigm that Hegel submits Christian doctrine to a special interpretation. A "logical" account of the Trinity is evidently based upon, or derives essential sustenance from, the rationalist tradition of Western philosophy. Crucial to Hegel's interpretation of the Trinity is the Aristotelian doctrine of the actualization of mind as the form of the thing thought. One could say briefly that Hegel's reconciliation of subject and object turns upon the "spiritualizing" or rendering self-conscious of the mind as the activity of actualizing form. According to Hegel, Aristotle has achieved the speculative but not the systematic level of thought.[2] The most important Aristotelian insight is for Hegel the conception of nature as spiritedness (*Lebendigkeit*). Nature is an organism whose continuity is derived from or expressed as its perfection of "thought thinking itself." Hegel understands this perfection as the pure negativity of subject.[3] That is, mind, as the activity which actualizes form, is not itself form. Since form is "presence" in the sense of the positive determination of this qua this, the formation-process itself, which brings about the presence of this or that positive determination, may be called "negative work."

According to the Hegelian interpretation, Aristotle surpasses Plato by making the activity of thinking superior to the separate form understood as the product of that activity.[4] Since Aristotle himself insists that the mind conforms to the

2. *Vorlesungen über die Geschichte der Philosophie, SW,* 18 : 298; cf. pp. 186, 340; *Lectures on the History of Philosophy* 2 : 117; cf. 2 : 17, 156.

3. *SW,* 18 : 330, 346; *Lectures on the History of Philosophy,* 2 : 147, 159; *Phänomenologie,* p. 22; *Phenomenology,* p. 83; *Enzyklopädie,* p. 312 (par. 379); *Encyclopedia Wallace–Miller,* p. 4.

4. *Enzyklopädie,* p. 437 (par. 552); cf. pp. 318 ff. (par. 389); *Encyclopedia Wallace-Miller,* pp. 288 f., cf. pp. 29 ff.

form in the act of knowing,[5] it is clear that Hegel's interpretation does not remain faithful to the Aristotelian intention. Nevertheless, it is possible to question the internal consistency of Aristotle's intention. The difficulty is evident from Aristotle's distinction between the two intellects in the *De Anima:* the separate, actualizing, and eternal intellect on the one hand, and on the other, the passive-receptive or potential intellect in which the form is actualized.[6] On the basis of this distinction, one could argue (as does Hegel) that the divine intellect, as the activity of actualizing forms, is itself always actual, but not as form, and so as *pure negativity* in the peculiarly Hegelian sense suggested by this quotation from a lecture note taken by Hegel's student, Boumann: "Mind is not an inert being but, on the contrary, absolutely restless being, pure activity, the negating or ideality of every fixed category of the abstractive intellect." [7]

The abstractive intellect (*Verstand*) is thus the Aristotelian potential intellect, which thinks the forms posed for it by the pure negative activity of the divine intellect. But there are two crucial deficiencies in the Aristotelian doctrine. First, Aristotle does not explain the relation between the divine and the potential intellects, although he does assert that both are present within the phenomenon of human thinking. Second, even if there were an explanation of this relation, there would still be no account of self-consciousness. Either the divine intellect is inaccessible to human thinking, or else its accessibility makes it impossible for man to think himself as a self-conscious individual. For to say that "thought thinks itself" as pure negativity would be for Aristotle to deny cognitive content to the divine activity. To put this in one last way, Aristotle's divine intelligence would seem to be detached or alienated from the human soul in which it carries out its work. Similarly, the essence of Being as form would seem to

5. *Metaphysics* Θ 1051b6 ff.; 1.1057a11. Cf. *De Anima* Γ 429a13.

6. *De Anima* Γ 430a22–25.

7. *Hegel's Philosophy of Mind,* trans. Wallace–Miller (Oxford, Clarendon Press, 1971), p. 3.

be detached from the form itself, since the essence of form is the same as the actualization of divine intelligence.

According to Aristotle, the forms of things are in both the things and the mind. The mind thus becomes the thing "somehow" by thinking its essence. In the comprehensive case, the cosmos has its being or presents itself within the perpetual thinking of the divine intellect, which thinks itself, and not the cosmos or the consequence of its "negative" intellectual activity. If we preserve the distinctness of essential forms, yet emphasize their "place" within the divine intellect, and conceive of the cosmos as an emanation or "procession" from divine thinking, the result is very close to Neo-Platonism. The Neo-Platonist, of course, defines the divine mind in which form actualizes as itself an emanation from the One, which is beyond both Being and Thinking. But the main point is that the forms are in the mind and assume the status of thoughts of the deity.[8] Especially under the influence of the Christian notion of a creator-God, there is a shift in emphasis from the forms, or beings, to the intellectual-spiritual activity of thinking. With respect to the forms, potentiality is made prior to actuality. As Gerhard Huber observes, Plotinus prepares a "dynamicizing of Being." [9] This may be understood in two related senses. First, Being is now conceived as a process rather than as a static eternal order. Second, the identity in actuality of Being and intellect means that the process of Being is the same as the life-pulse of God or divine intellect. At least by the time of Christian Neo-Platonism, God is no longer said simply to think the world, but also to be conscious of himself as thinking the world. Victorinus and Augustine revise the pagan Neo-Platonism in terms of the underlying

8. It should be observed that in Plotinus, despite the generating of forms by mind in the activity of thinking (*Enneads* 1.6.9.34; 6.7.10 ff.), the forms are prior to mind in their accessibility to thinking (5.9.7 ff.). The generation of forms is something like the Husserlian doctrine of "constitution."

9. *Das Sein und das Absolute* (Basel, Verlag für Recht und Gesellschaft AG, 1955), pp. 31 ff. Cf. K. Kremer, *Die neuplatonische Seinsphilosophie und ihre Wirkung auf Thomas von Aquin* (Leiden, E. J. Brill, 1966), pp. 70 ff.

unity of the Trinity; they assimilate the transcendence of the One into the divine intellect.[10] As we may express this, the triune God is an identity of identity and non-identity (that is, of himself as intellect and as the Ideas actualized by his intellect), but not yet in the sense which includes the created world as a dimension of eternity or the divine nature itself.

Let us distinguish within the Neo-Platonist tradition between its Aristotelian and its Christian dimensions. In the Aristotelian teaching, the world is present within the deity, which lacks self-consciousness. In the Christian teaching, God possesses self-consciousness but is separate from the world. The task which Hegel sets himself is to reconcile these two dimensions within Neo-Platonism by removing the deficiencies of each. In so doing, Hegel does not simply provide us with an improved version of Neo-Platonism. He has effected the fundamental synthesis of the Greek and Christian traditions which permits him to repair the defects of modern philosophy: dualism and the loss of self-consciousness. At bottom, there is no essential difference between Hegel's revision of Neo-Platonism and his perfection of modern philosophy in the sense that each completes the other. Hegel's approach to the task just described is already visible in his first philosophical publication, an analysis of the difference between the doctrines of Fichte and Schelling as these had developed by 1801.[11] In this essay, Hegel criticizes Fichte and states the superiority of Schelling's teaching with respect to the Absolute as the principle of subjectivity and objectivity. For our purposes, the main point of this essay can be stated in the following manner.

According to Hegel, Fichte's Absolute is pure subjectivity, an absolute ego or principle of consciousness which does not include objectivity. Therefore, the distinction between subject and object in Fichte's world is purely subjective. The domain

10. Huber, *Das Sein und das Absolute*, pp. 147 ff.

11. *Differenz des Fichte'schen und Schelling'schen Systems der Philosophie* (1801) in *Jenaer kritischen Schriften*. For a very good study of this important essay, see H. Girndt, *Die Differenz des Fichteschen und Hegelschen Systems in der Hegelschen "Differenzschrift"* (Bonn, H. Bouvier, 1965).

of objectivity, also called "nature" or the "non-ego," is a consequence of the inexplicable restriction upon subjectivity. This restriction takes place *within* subjectivity: I experience the outer world within my own subjective experience. The "outer" has objective meaning only within my subjectivity, yet it cannot be genuinely explained or assimilated by the "inner" or subjective dimension. Fichte's problem has its roots in the Cartesian conception of substance. According to Descartes, the term "substance" means what is absolutely independent and is truly applied to God alone. We may also use the term in the case of created substances, of which there are two: body and mind, defined respectively by the attributes of extension and thought. In addition to the dualism between body and mind, there is a separation between God and his created substances. Although Descartes claims that we can know something about God, he insists that this knowledge is not *adequate*. We need not consider the reasons underlying Descartes' doctrine of substance. Suffice it to say that it raises two difficulties. First, the ambiguous status of our knowledge of God makes it impossible (or at least doubtful) for God to serve as the unity of his two created substances. Second, we do not know substance itself, except via its attributes. The unity of the created substance is detached from its intelligible characteristic. Spinoza presents us with a somewhat simplified version of the same doctrine. Now thought and extension are attributes of one substance, namely, God. Furthermore, Spinoza attempts to overcome the dualism of his two (known) attributes by arguing that the order and connection of thoughts is the same as the order and connection of things.[12] But the "Cartesian" difficulties are not thereby removed.

One might understand Spinoza to mean that God, substance, or the Absolute, is precisely that "order and connection" which is common to the two domains of ego and non-ego, and so is not identical to either alone. Unfortunately, Spinoza's God or substance is lacking in subjectivity or life. This is not altered by the attribute of thought, since what thinks is the

12. *Ethics* 2, prop. 7. Cf. Descartes, *Principles,* 1 : li ff.

finite mode. Either God does not think at all, and we continue in the dualism of mind and body, or only God (as the essence of finite modes) thinks, in which case his thinking is impersonal or geometric: in effect the establishing of the mathematical relations between finite modes. The Spinozist "order and connection" is too much like the Platonic "community" to which I referred previously. In other words, the shortcomings of Spinozism are essentially the same as those of Neo-Platonism. Spinoza seems to combine God and the world in the manner of Aristotle. There is also a parallel between the way Aristotle relates divine and potential intellect and the Spinozist doctrine of the attribute of thought and its modes or finite minds. However, since God is substance rather than subjectivity, he lacks self-consciousness and thereby renders insubstantial or illusory the self-consciousness of mortals. As Hegel puts this, Spinoza's Absolute has no necessary connection with its modes. Finite modes are an external or illusory determination or negation, and so not a part of infinite substance. The finite is not reflected into substance because there is no interiority into which it could be received. Consequently, there is no "third dimension" or Spirit within which substance and its attributes can be unified.[13] According to Hegel, then, Spinoza is not a pantheist, as is widely supposed. He is an atheist, because he does not conceive of God as Spirit or subjectivity.[14] Let us call this his "Aristotelian" defect. But Spinoza is also an acosmist, because what he denies is the reality of the created world.[15] Let us call this Spinoza's "Christian" defect (because the separation of God as essence from the world as appearance deprives the latter of substantiality). Spinoza's God is not alive, and his creation is an illusion.

What Spinoza calls the "order and connection" of thoughts

13. *Logik*, 2 : 250, 337; cf. 1 : 396; *Logic*, pp. 610, 689 f; cf. 382 f.

14. *SW*, 19 : 408; cf. *Lectures on the History of Philosophy*, 3 : 282 (the translation does not fully correspond to the German text here).

15. *Enzyklopädie*, pp. 76 (par. 50), 455 (par. 573); *Encyclopedia–Wallace*, p. 106; *Encyclopedia Wallace–Miller*, p. 307. *SW*, 19 : 373; *Lectures on the History of Philosophy*, 3 : 280 ff.

and things is thus suspiciously like the "order and measurement" of the Cartesian definition of mathematical reason. In order to bring Spinoza's substance to life, we must reidentify the "order and connection" as Absolute Spirit, which is cognitively accessible in and as its (negative) activity of generating subjects and objects. We require a *logic of activity* which explains how structure is formed but which is not itself formal, objective, or quasi-geometrical. This does not require the suppression of mathematical logic or empirical science. Hegel leaves these untouched within their own domain. His own concern is with the analysis of thinking as the pure negative activity of Absolute Spirit. In religious language, man thinks rationally because God is thinking in man. As Hegel puts it in a later work, "God's self-knowledge is farther a self-consciousness in men." [16] One could therefore adopt the Neo-Platonist doctrine of creation as "emanation." Unlike the Neo-Platonists, however, Hegel contends that the unity of the Absolute is intelligible in the "wave-length" or pulse-beat of the emanative process of divine creation. Let us also note that it would be wrong to identify the divine activity *as* the pulse-beat; instead, we must say that it shows itself within its pulse-beat. The divine activity is always accessible in what it does, without objectifying itself or identifying itself as this or that deed. Nevertheless, as the itself living principle of life, or of the identity-within-difference of subject and object, the Absolute is accessible via its highest or most revealing instance: the individual, self-conscious, and discursively thinking human being.

Kant, Fichte, and Schelling: The Differenzschrift of 1801

This brings us to the situation, as Hegel understood it, in Kant and Fichte. Hegel accepted Fichte's doctrines as he knew them (roughly those elaborated between 1794 and 1797) to be the correct exposition, and in fact the completion, of the Kantian teaching. Our detour by way of Descartes and Spinoza was a necessary preparation for Hegel's discussion in 1801 of Fichte and Schelling. The Fichtean treatment of sub-

16. *Enzyklopädie*, p. 447 par. 564); *Encyclopedia Wallace–Miller*, p. 298.

ject-object (says Hegel) is just the Kantian dualism of ego and nature, with the latter understood as the non-ego or thing-in-itself. In Hegel's view, Kant never explained adequately his contention that the ego is activated, or begins the process of constructing the form or rational essence of the object, in response to a stimulus from the "outer" world of things-in-themselves. Fichte tried to overcome the Kantian dualism between phenomena and things-in-themselves, or between the ego and the non-ego, by incorporating the stimulus (Kant's "sensation") into the Absolute taken as subjectivity. But Fichte's "subjectivizing" of the non-ego failed to make it intelligible. As an unknown function of subjectivity, objectivity is at once subjective and nonsubjective: it is both within and external to subjectivity.

Fichte's Absolute is then an ego or subjective activity which works by differentiating itself into an empirical or finite ego (the human subject), already opposed to the non-ego (the natural or objective world). But the Absolute works in such a way as to render inaccessible to theoretical reason the *way* itself. Fichte goes only part-way toward rectifying the central defect of Spinozism. He transforms substance into subject, or the "order and connection" of thoughts and things into subjective activity. But Fichtean activity, like Heideggerian Being, "reveals" itself in a concealed manner. There can be no discursive, analytical, or reflective understanding of the activity, because the reflective understanding is already the concealment of the Absolute within the analytical opposition of subject-object. The Absolute always "positions" the finite ego as opposed and conditioned by the non-ego. To theorize in the sense of *Verstand* is to "reflect" in the sense of splitting apart the object from a reflecting subject. We can overcome the separation in reflection of subject from object only by means of an "intellectual intuition" (evidently related to Spinoza's "intellectual love of God") of the synthesis of subject and object. But the effort to describe this synthesis cognitively at once separates it into its thesis and antithesis. We see here the prototype of the Hegelian dialectic of subject and object. There are two main differences between Fichtean and Hegelian dialectic. The first has to do with history. For Fichte, the study of temporal objects may be called a "pragmatic history of the human spirit." But the finite world is historical in a Kantian sense, because it is other than the absolute activity which produces it, and whose "moments," separated in analysis, are in fact simultaneous. It is Schelling who identifies from the outset the finite and the infinite worlds; history and the Absolute are one and complete in the sense adopted by Hegel. The second and more important difference is that Hegel claims to grasp the complete structure of the dialectic of reflection, or to perform an "absolute reflection" which is a logical comprehension of the Absolute.[17]

According to the Hegel of 1801, Schelling is the first philosopher to have provided us with an adequate approach to the Absolute. The reader should remember that Hegel subsequently criticized Schelling severely for the inadequacies of his conception of the Absolute. Nevertheless, Hegel's early allegiance to Schelling (whether sincere or not) is of central importance to us for two reasons. The first I have already mentioned: Schelling connects the Fichtean dialectic of reflection to a conception of the historical development of Spirit.[18] The second reason must now be considered in some detail. We have seen that for Hegel, Fichte separated subject and object within an Absolute which is itself not just "subjectivity" but a subject which cannot account for objectivity. So far as Hegel is concerned, this amounts to the denial of genuine objectivity, or at least to the possibility of explaining its genesis (since the presence of objects is already a structural feature of every explanation). Objects are inexplicably present as opposed to subjects, yet both are said to be consequences of the activity of the Absolute. For Schelling, on the

17. Much work has been done in the past decade on the criticism of Hegel's interpretation of Fichte. In addition to the works previously cited by Janke and Girndt, see I. Görland, *Die Kantkritik des jungen Hegel* (Frankfurt, Vittorio Klostermann, 1966); and L. Siep, *Hegels Fichtekritik und die Wissenschaftslehre von 1804* (Freiburg and Munich, Verlag Karl Alber, 1970).

18. *System des transzendentalen Idealismus* (1800), introduction by W. Schulz (Hamburg, Felix Meiner Verlag, 1957), pp. 2 f.

contrary, subject and object must *each* be subject-object. Each must be the expression of an activity which already unites subjectivity and objectivity so as to preserve them even while identifying them. As Schelling interprets Fichte (and he is followed here by Hegel), Fichte no doubt intended to postulate an Absolute which is the source of both subject and object. He failed, however, by making his Absolute altogether subjective or by modeling it after the ego. We see here the Kantian failure, previously noted, to explain the external stimulus of sensation, upon which the categorial or discursive thinking of the ego is dependent. Schelling calls his Absolute "the identity of identity and non-identity." He means that the Absolute is neither pure subjectivity nor objectivity but "the point of indifference" between the two.[19] What we call "subjects arise from the preponderance of the subjective over the objective dimension in the given instance of absolute activity, whereas the reverse is true in the case of what we call "objects." Schelling thus preserves the sameness of Thinking and Being, which is indispensable for the intelligibility of anything whatsoever. For otherwise, as in empiricistic epistemologies, there would be no way to account for the correspondence of thoughts and beings. But to turn at once to Hegel's later criticism, Schelling's spiritualizing of Spinoza's "order and connection" is at the same time like an erasing of the articulations that define the intelligibility of what is ordered and connected. To say that the Absolute is "a point of indifference" is like turning on a light that makes everything invisible. In Hegel's famous phrase, Schelling's Absolute is "a night in which all cows are black." [20]

Hegel's ultimate intention is to preserve discursive science, the product of reflection, or the reciprocal definition of subject and object which provides us with the world of determinate beings. In the Hegelian interpretation, this is for Fichte impossible because of the unintelligibility of the ulti-

19. Cf. Schelling's essay of 1801, *Darstellung meines Systems der Philosophie,* in *Schriften von 1801–1804* (Darmstadt, Wissenschaftliche Buchgesellschaft, 1968), and Hegel's *Differenzschrift,* p. 64.

20. *Phänomenologie,* p. 19; *Phenomenology,* p. 79.

mate principle, and thus the way in which everything follows from it. Kant's successors criticized him for not giving a genuine "transcendental deduction" or logical account of how his categories (the way in which understanding thinks an object) follow systematically from the synthetic unity of apperception (an absolute, and absolutely intelligible, principle). Yet this is precisely what they themselves fail to do. To be sure, they construct "systems" of varying degrees of complexity, but in each case the absolute principle of the system is absolutely unintelligible. In short, we have not proceeded beyond the unknowable (or nonexistent) substance of modern philosophy. The essence is still separate from its appearances, which therefore deteriorate into illusion.[21] The unintelligibility of the first principle of the culminating (pre-Hegelian) system of modern philosophy leads to the unintelligibility or *negation* of the system as a whole. The entire course of Western thought, in its religious as well as its philosophical forms, terminates in nihilism. We can therefore characterize the decisive Hegelian step in his own words as the negation of the negation. Hegel assimilates the "nothingness" of his predecessors' systems at a higher and more comprehensive level. At the new level, the systems acquire a sense or positive content as moments within the Whole. But the new level is not just positivity, since that would amount to the exclusion of negativity. Hegel's system, as the negation of the negation, preserves the negativity of each finite or partial system, that is, its identity, even as he unites them in the comprehensive system of his science of wisdom, which is the identity of identity and non-identity.

In the Schellingian system, this comprehensive identity is a point of indifference between (comprehended) identity and non-identity. Whereas Schelling intended by this to convey the preservation in balance or equilibrium of subject (ego, identity) and object (non-ego, non-identity), he may be said to have forgotten that equilibrium is incompatible with spiritual activity or *excitation*. Schelling's Absolute is Nothing. Nevertheless, Schelling is right to say that subject and object must be

21. This will be analyzed more carefully in chap. 5.

each subject-object.[22] Fichte was unable to explain how his Absolute "works" or takes on determined, limited, and separate forms. Fichte could not account for the existence of the world, let alone render it intelligible. The Schellingian principle, however, provides at least the basis for such an explanation, because in it, determination is already a part of indeterminateness. This has to be explained more carefully. The subject, as the principle for identifying the variety of objects, is identical with itself, but as such (as part of the structure of that identity), it is nonidentical with its objects. The identity of the subject is defined by the non-identity of its objects. We cannot grasp the subject in its identity except by making a formal opposition between subject and objects per se. At the same time, the objects are identified as other than the subject by the process of thinking, which in fact identifies subject and object. Subject is identical with itself, but since it identifies itself by opposing itself to objects, this non-identity of subject and object is itself a moment of the identity of the subject, which is therefore identical to itself precisely as nonidentical to itself. This is the prototype for Hegel's analysis of self-consciousness as the identity of identity (consciousness) and non-identity (separation from consciousness of itself, in order to be aware of itself). And the same analysis may be made of the object, which is identical to itself as nonidentical to the subject, its principle of identification. The object is therefore, qua identical, nonidentical.

This "identity of identity and non-identity" cannot be understood as a "point of indifference" between subject and object but only as an activity or process of excitation which manifests its own essential characteristics in the production of subjects and objects, each of which is a subject-object. In terms of the previous paragraph, the subject, as principle of all objects, is indeterminate. But the production of a subject, or the

22. We see here the influence of Leibniz's doctrine of monads: material substance is "analyzable" into a cluster of spiritual substances—hence the identity of mind and matter, or of Thinking and Being, but in a way which is for Hegel Idealism, and so merely the mirror image of Materialism rather than a genuine account of the Whole.

existence of a subject at any moment, is conditioned by objectivity or determinateness: *this* subject opposed to *this* object. We see here the preservation of the Kantian thesis that the transcendental ego is actualized as the finite ego in the act of conceiving a finite object. But in Hegel's revision of Schelling, the "transcendental ego" is the Absolute Spirit whose way of acting, and so whose nature or truth, is totally intelligible within the consequences of its activity. There is no further separation between transcendental and finite egos; the former is no longer a set of static logical conditions for the possibility of rational experience, but the *life* of rational experience. It is God or the Absolute. And now that God actualizes within the thinking of man, there can no longer be a separation between phenomena and noumena. In Schellingian language, since determination is necessarily a structural moment of indetermination, the manifestation of indeterminateness is thus necessarily in the form of determinations, albeit determinations containing indeterminateness.

The Absolute manifests itself in individual form: this is one of the crucial points in Hegel's logic. The Absolute is the process of individuation. Consequently, the Absolute is not separate from but identical with itself as the differentiated individuals. If we think of the Absolute as the substantial essence and the world of individuals as its appearances, then there is an identity-within-difference of essence and appearance. It might, however, be claimed that essence, although identical with its appearances, makes many appearances, perhaps an infinite number, and so that knowledge of a finite number of appearances does not provide mortal man with absolute knowledge of the essence. But this is not Hegel's contention. On the contrary, Hegel argues that an exhaustive analysis of any appearance yields knowledge of the essence or, in the expression of an earlier chapter, that to know anything is to know everything. Since the Absolute is the formation process of anything whatsoever, it is essentially the same in everything. Differently stated, everything is essentially interrelated. Spinoza's doctrine concerning the sameness of the order and connection in the two realms of thought and extension has now been transformed from a mathematical or objective interpretation of substantial structure, into an account of the spiritual activity, source of the subject-object distinction, which acts by producing structure, and through the medium of individual egos whose cognitive processes are the same as absolute activity. Whereas in Spinoza, wisdom is a passive acceptance of man's finite status, or bondage within the order and connection of nature, which he can never completely understand, the situation is totally different in Hegel. Man is now the instrument of the Absolute: his spiritual labor may therefore be said to produce the intelligible world, albeit in accordance with a divine or necessary plan.[23]

Spinoza's sage, despite his acceptance of modern science and Cartesian reason, is still closely related to the Stoic sage of late antiquity, whose wisdom is practical rather than theoretical, in that it culminates in a condition of acceptance or resignation. Man achieves divine independence or indifference to contingency by suppressing his passions, restricting his desires, finding satisfaction in knowledge of his limitations, both theoretical and practical. The Hegelian sage, however, satisfies his desires to the fullest extent by grasping conceptually the world as the product of human labor, albeit a labor directed by "the hand of God."

23. We note in passing that Hegel's doctrine of necessity includes *contingency*. Cf. D. Henrich, *Hegel im Kontext* (Frankfurt, Suhrkamp Verlag, 1971), pp. 157 ff.

4 Contradiction in Plato and Aristotle

Contradiction and Reflection

In the course of the last two chapters, we have been gradually accustoming ourselves to the central regions of Hegel's logic. The center of the center is undoubtedly Hegel's doctrine of reflection (which includes his formal account of contradiction). The history of modern philosophy, which begins in the Cartesian distinction between immediate self-certitude and *ratio* or analytical thinking, is no more able in its concluding representatives to effect a reunion between these two intellectual powers than was Descartes. Kant requires mankind to surrender intellectual intuition in favor of the discursive understanding, yet he is unable to give a comprehensive analysis of the understanding without recourse to notions like the regulative Ideas and purposiveness, or a sense of dignity and obligation to the categorical imperative. Since these notions are grounded in reason rather than in the understanding, and are therefore empty of cognitive content, the Kantian teaching vacillates between empiricism and a philosophy of "feeling" or intuition. And despite the differences between them, when we consider Fichte and Schelling, we see in them a failure to overcome modern dualism which is, if anything, more extreme than in the case of Kant.

It is true that Kant fails to deduce the categories of discursive thinking from the "I think" of the synthetic unity of apperception, so that the object remains separate from a subject which is in turn lacking in self-consciousness, to say nothing of self-knowledge. But the "deduction" presented by Fichte in 1794 and 1797 (and followed to a considerable extent by Schelling in 1800) amounts to a systematic demonstration of the impossibility of such a deduction. To "deduce" is to analyze a general principle in the sense of dividing and collecting: a subject is identified (or classified with others of its kind) by means of predicative judgments, or the assertion that "this" is "that." *S* is *P;* however, as *S,* it is also non-*P.* The structure intrinsic to judgment is contradictory, aand this contradiction can never be overcome by another judgment, since each has the same structure. In other words, the "is" of discursive thinking is self-contradictory, and this contradiction can be resolved only by intellectual intuition. The self-contradictory character of discursively accessible Being is rooted in the manifestation of the Absolute as the reciprocal limitation of ego (subject) and non-ego (object). Since the Fichtean Absolute (as Hegel interprets it) is pure subjectivity, there is an alienation of the ego from itself (or of the finite from the infinite ego), combined with a solipsistic subjectivizing of the objective world.[1]

To put the same conclusion in another way, analytic or scientific thinking is *regulated* by the principle of contradiction. There is then no analytical reflection upon the principle itself which does not already assume the principle. Fichte's dialectic amounts to an effort to deduce all the logical (and ontological) consequences of the principle of contradiction, or the rule that *S* cannot simultaneously be *P* and non-*P*. When *S* is the subject or *ego cogitans,* then it becomes both *P* and non-*P,* or violates the principle of contradiction *by the activity of asserting it.* But given the aforementioned structure of judgment, no discursive explanation of the violation-by-assertion of the principle is possible. We may, for example, attempt to account for the violation-by-assertion by insisting that the mind is not *P* and non-*P* "in the same way," but this serves only to transform the mind into a phantom continuum, or to deprive the negative union of *P* and non-*P* of its simultaneity. In other words, it amounts to a denial of a discursive connection between the law of identity and the law of excluded middle, and so to a dissolution of the principle of contradiction itself—or else to an invocation of intellectual intuition.

Judgment is reflection, or the separation-within-connection of *S* and *P.* Every judgment may be analyzed into two conjoint forms: *"S* is *P"* and *"S* (as itself) is non-*P."* This analysis, however, which is sometimes phrased as the distinction be-

1. For Fichte's critique of the Kantian failure to provide a deduction of the categories, see the excellent analysis in Janke, *Fichte,* pp. 114 ff.

tween identity and predication, is based upon two contradictory steps. First, it affirms the principle of contradiction as a unique or self-identical law of thinking. But second, it dissolves the principle of contradiction into the laws of identity and excluded middle. We are therefore left with no way to reunite these two laws into the principle of contradiction. No explanation is given of the mental or dialectical motion from one principle or law to another. We cannot think the unity of our logical rules. In Hegelian language, an *absolute reflection* is impossible for traditional logic (including its Fichtean variant). The non-Hegelian logician must therefore rise above reflection and take refuge, whether explicitly or implicitly, in intellectual intuition. For Hegel, however, what we require is an absolute reflection or conceptual analysis of the dialectical relation between *S, P,* and non-*P*. This does not mean that we cease to be regulated by the principle of contradiction within its appropriate sphere. Instead, it means that we explain the principle reflexively.

A reflexive explanation of the principle of contradiction turns upon the previously established "sameness" of Being and Thinking, or upon the grasp of subject and object as consequences of the pure negative activity of Absolute Spirit. The activity of the Absolute is the root instance of the violation-by-assertion of the principle of contradiction. The Absolute "is and is not" the subject and the object. By the same token, the subject "is and is not" the object, and vice versa. In terms of the traditional formula, *S* "is and is not" *P*. What we require is a cognitive analysis of "is and is not" as a process, an analysis which does not vitiate itself by assuming the separation of *S* and *P,* or the impossibility of a coherent explanation of *S* as both *P* and non-*P*. We are initially justified in denying that impossibility by a "reflection upon reflection," or the previously mentioned awareness that one violates the principle of contradiction in asserting it.

This awareness smacks of paradox, and in fact it becomes unintelligible as soon as we try to grasp it from *within* the regulatory ambience of the principle itself. The paradox is obviously another version of the contradictions ensuing from the concept of "the class of all classes." To say that "the class of all classes" is self-contradictory, however, is to understand a class as a finite, stable, detached, and self-identical form. The paradox disappears only when we understand that this conception of form *is itself self-contradictory*. But it may well seem that we overcome this paradox by surrender to a still greater enigma. If to pose the principle of contradiction is to negate it (if "to be" is to be self-contradictory), have we not annihilated *S, P,* and non-*P*? Is it not now the case that we can say neither "*S* is not both *P* and non-*P*" nor "*S* is both *P* and non-*P*"? Hegel's solution to this enigma lies in his conception of negation of the negation. The negation of the principle of contradiction is at the same time a preservation of it. For example, if we can *say* the impossibility of saying (S & P & −P) or − (S & P & −P), the negation of the first is merely the affirmation of the second, and vice versa. Logical negation is not annihilation; to negate *P* is to obtain −*P*. The joint assertion and negation of *P* produces a contradiction, but the point is that we think this contradiction and understand it. A problem exists only if we cannot speak at all. To say what we cannot say is to say it.

Hegel proposes to say what is "unsayable" in the traditional logic. He claims thereby to complete or explain, and not to annihilate, traditional logic. Since his own doctrine is a completion of the tradition, we cannot understand Hegel without a grasp of the essential elements of the traditional teaching. In the balance of this chapter, I propose to indicate what these points are, and more specifically to show how the very assertion of the traditional teaching leads to what are for it *aporiai* or impassable dilemmas, but what are for Hegel themselves an anticipation of his own logic. I must, of course, restrict myself to an introductory sketch of an exceedingly complex situation. The student should bear in mind that this sketch is not a detour but a constituent element in our analysis of Hegel's doctrine of contradiction (or more generally, of reflection). The *aporiai* of Greek philosophy are for Hegel collectively the negation of the initial positioning of human thought. Hegel intends his science of logic as the negation of that negation.

Plato's Sophist: Thinking and Counting

Although the last word has not yet been said on the subject, Hegel's intensive study and assimilation of Platonic doctrines is well known and frequently mentioned in the secondary literature.[2] Nevertheless, the usual procedure is perhaps to associate Hegel with Aristotle.[3] While there is good reason for this association, which is clearly made by Hegel himself, a moment's reflection is enough to convince us that the link with Plato is of equal importance. Aristotle's writings may be taken as a continuous criticism of his great teacher; in addition, the connnection between Hegel and Neo-Platonism is scarcely intelligible without reference to Plato himself. But the decisive point is that, in Plato, we find the original principles and arguments which have sustained the entire tradition of Western rationalism, as well as anticipations of Hegel's dialectic and speculative logic. It is almost as though the Platonic dialogues are fragments of a broken mirror, hinting at some comprehensive system which is analogous to Hegel's own science of wisdom. Unfortunately, we must here restrict ourselves to some of the fragments and leave to others speculation on the possible existence of the mirror as a unity. I shall begin with a brief reference to the Aristotelian doctrine of thinking, which we have already seen to be decisive for Hegel's evolution, and in this way establish internally the connection with Plato.

2. Cf. K. Rosenkranz, *Georg Wilhelm Friedrich Hegels Leben* (Darmstadt, Wissenschaftliche Buchgesellschaft, 1963; 1st ed. 1844); W. Purpus, *Zur Dialektik des Bewusstseins nach Hegel* (Berlin, Trowitzsch & Sohn, 1908); F. Chiereghin, *Hegel e la metafisica classica;* F. Kümmel, *Platon und Hegel* (Tübingen, Max Niemeyer Verlag, 1968); H. G. Gadamer, *Hegels Dialektik* (Tübingen, Mohr-Siebeck, 1971). See also R. Wiehl, "Platos Ontologie in Hegels Logik des Seins" *Hegel Studien* 3 (1965) : 157–80; M. B. Foster, *The Political Philosophies of Plato and Hegel,* 2d ed. (Oxford, Clarendon Press, 1968); A. Kojève, *Essai d'une histoire raisonnée de la philosophie païenne* (Paris, Gallimard, 1968–73); S. Rosen, "*Sōphrosynē* and *Selbstbewusstsein,*" *Review of Metaphysics* (June 1973) : 617–42, and idem, "Self-Consciousness and Self-Knowledge: The Relation between Plato and Hegel" *Hegel Studien* 9 (1974).

3. See for example G. R. G. Mure, *An Introduction to Hegel* (London and New York, Oxford University Press, 1959). Cf. J. Ritter, *Metaphysik und Politik* (Frankfurt, Suhrkamp Verlag, 1969).

According to Aristotle, the mind, whether in its actual or potential capacity, is passive or purely receptive with respect to the forms it thinks.[4] As one scholar incisively puts it, Aristotle's mind is like the "receptacle" discussed by Plato in the *Timaeus*. Mind, "if it is to receive all forms, must itself be destitute of form."[5] In other words, mind adds nothing to the nature of the forms, even in the act of actualizing them. This "act" is, for Hegel at least, the decisive instance of pure negativity. The difficulty faced by Aristotle is how to account for an activity which is not itself an actuality or form. If the actuality of the thinking mind is in fact that of the form, then either there is no difference between the mind and the form, or else the mind is both invisible and unintelligible in itself. Aristotle certainly rejects the first alternative; to some extent, he rejects the second as well.[6] However, it is one thing to say that mind thinks itself, and another to explain the meaning of that assertion in accordance with the Platonic-Aristotelian doctrine of form. The Aristotelian teaching may be rephrased for our purposes as follows. If there is any instability or excitation associated with the forms, this cannot come from mind or the activity of thinking. This is because the actualization of mind *is* the actualization of form, and the forms must be preserved from instability. What looks like instability must therefore be explained in one of two ways. It is either the motion of genesis or the illusion of motion which ensues from our thinking now one form and now another. In sum: the forms do not undergo internal change, nor does the mind in the act of thinking; yet we think by "changing our minds" in some inexplicable way which is neither motion nor change but a sequence of instantaneous actualizations.

It would be possible to argue with great plausibility that Aristotle acquires stability of mind and form at the price of an unintelligible doctrine of genesis as the locus of motion and

4. *De Anima* Γ 429a13 ff. and the note *ad loc.* in G. Rodier, *Aristote, Traité de l'Ame* (Paris, Ernest Leroux, 1900), Vol. 2; Γ 430a17 f.

5. Cf. R. D. Hicks, *Aristotle, De Anima* (Amsterdam, Adolf M. Hakkert, 1965; 1st ed. 1907), note to Γ 429a13.

6. Γ 429b21 f.; 429b7 and Hicks's note (*nous* is knowable *kat' allo ti*); 430a19 f. (= *Metaphysics* Λ 1074b33).

change. All we need say here is that there is a discontinuity between mind and form on the one hand and genesis on the other. More interesting for us is the "identity-within-difference" of mind and form. Since the changes of genesis are not intrinsic to mind or form, and since mind itself is formless, everything depends upon whether or not form is stable. Differently stated, everything depends upon whether or not Aristotle is justified in referring to the principle of contradiction as "the most stable opinion" upon which all reasoning is grounded." [7] But this amounts to the question whether the principle of contradiction suffices to hold together the discontinuous dimensions of Aristotle's Whole.

For Aristotle, there is no *summum genus* and consequently (since sciences are defined with respect to a genus) no science of the Whole, but only discrete intuitions of the principles of the separate sciences, together with the obedience of discursive thinking to the principle of contradiction. Aristotle's intuition differs from that of the German Idealists by providing analytical thinking with its starting points; in that sense, it participates in the work of *Verstand.* The fact remains, however, that there is no deduction of the principles of the sciences from a "highest" principle, and that the separation of the principles of the sciences from the principle of contradiction is parallel to the separation of intuition from discursive thinking. The most stable opinion functions as a "regulative" Idea which serves in place of an unavailable cognitive conception of the wholeness or unity of beings. One could say that Aristotle's use of the principle of contradiction points backward toward Plato and forward toward Hegel. Whereas Plato attempts to complete the intrinsic limitations of discursive thinking, or to bespeak the Whole, by means of myth, Aristotle accepts the Platonic demonstrations of the cognitive inaccessibility of the Whole, but rejects all recourse to mythical surrogates for a cognitive account. Hegel agrees with Aristotle in rejecting myth on behalf of the principle of contradiction. Yet there is something unmistakably Platonic in his effort to provide an

7. *Metaphysics* Γ 1011b13 ff.

account of the principle itself, or to perform the absolute reflection of systematic wisdom. It is perhaps a bit too misleading to stand without qualification, yet one could do worse than to say that Hegel attempts to render the Platonic myths articulate. If I may remind the reader of a reference in an earlier chapter, Hegel tries to render Eros self-conscious as a self-differentiating unity which is both subject and object, yet neither the one nor the other. We could also say that Hegel accepts the Platonic challenge to provide a science of dialectic in accordance with an interpretation of "the Good" as both Thinking and Being. But this requires a transformation of the Platonic account of Thinking and Being. It will be convenient to illustrate the transformation in both cases by studying a brief section of the Platonic dialogue the *Sophist*.

One of the great difficulties in the interpretation of Plato is that of establishing paradigmatic passages for any specific point. The multiplicity of the dialogues, their dramatic structure, the absence of the author, and the presence of several apparent "heroes" or official interlocutors make it risky to offer pronouncements about "the philosophy of Plato" which are not subject to careful qualification. Fortunately for us, we are not concerned here to establish Plato's "private" opinions or doctrines, assuming that he had any which are not visible from a comparison of his dialogues. Our task is to show the connection between those doctrines of Plato which pervade his dialogues and have been given canonical status by Aristotle, and the teaching of Hegel. With respect to the issues under present consideration, the Plato we need to know is, so to speak, in the public domain. I think it is fair to say that the puzzles which I shall illustrate from the *Sophist* determine the contours of the fundamental modes of analysis throughout the Platonic corpus. I have chosen the *Sophist* rather than, say, the *Parmenides* (which Hegel admired very highly) because in the former the *aporiai* are much more clearly visible in their application to mind as well as form. I might add that in books on Hegel, references to the *Parmenides* tend to go too far in establishing agreement between Plato and Hegel. My own view is that the differences (as well as the agreements) are more easily extricated from the *Sophist*. But I do not deny that another text might have been used.

There are two different senses in which we may interpret the pivotal notion of wholeness, and so of unity. The first sense is that of the strict Parmenidean teaching, as that which has no parts, or "the One itself." [8] The second sense is that which, according to the Eleatic Stranger, follows from Parmenides' complete poem, and which he calls "the All," or a sum of parts. Since evidently nothing can be said of the first sense, Plato seems in the dialogues (and not just in the *Sophist*) to give the palm to the second sense, or "the All." [9] In this case, however, the wholeness and so the unity of every formal structure, or what we may call, following Socrates' terminology in the *Philebus*, its *eidetic number*,[10] is equal to, that is, the same as, the number of elements in that form. The order of the elements is not itself an additional element. But since a number is a "many," we have defined the unity of each form as a multiplicity. In addition, each unit within the multiplicity seems to depend upon "the One itself" or upon wholeness in the sense of "the Whole" for its very unicity. If each unit is an All, then we have to account for the units constituting that All, and the result is an infinite regress or a dissolution of formal structure. It should be obvious that the same difficulty follows if we replace the terms "One" or "Whole" by the term "Being." Either a Being is a specific individual thing, or it is that which is common to all things: "being qua being" in the Aristotelian expression. If "Being" designates "being qua being," then it is either a unity in the strict Parmenidean sense, or a sum of parts, with results which we have just noticed. If "Being" designates "specific indivdual thing," then again we have to account for the identity or unity or wholeness of the individual.

This general formulation (for which we have already had

8. *Sophist* 245a5 ff.

9. E.g. *Theaetetus* 204a1–205a10; cf. *Parmenides* 142b1 ff. The distinction between unity and being leads to a Whole which consists of a multiplicity of parts (Philebus 16c10 ff.).

10. *Philebus* 16c10 ff.

some preparation) is sufficient, I believe, to show that the dilemma set by the Eleatic Stranger for the students of Parmenides also applies to the doctrines of Plato. If Parmenides accepts the identification of the Whole as the All, then he must accept non-being (which I do not capitalize because it is not "opposite" to or coordinate with Being, as will shortly become clear): each part is "other than" every other part, or in the Spinozist phrase, every determination is a negation.[11] If he insists upon preserving the Whole in the strict sense (= the One itself) as therefore separate from the unity of a sum of parts or the All, then the One is invisible and unintelligible, whereas the units within the sum of the All themselves dissolve. In this case, a comprehensive Non-Being is evidently established, which one might perhaps call *Nichts* to distinguish it from the non-being or otherness of the negative determination. Whatever may be the true interpretation of Parmenides, the decision of the Platonist is evident enough. He must accept the sense of wholeness designated by the All. This has the following consequences. First, whereas the Platonist does not reject wholeness in the strict Parmenidean sense of "the One itself" but seems to have preserved it as a principle together with "the indeterminate dyad" or (pure) manyness, it is apparently not a principle which shares in, or is itself accessible to, discursive analysis. It is present in each unit of analysis, but *silently*. So far as *logos* goes, the One is indistinguishable from *Nichts*. Hence the Platonic doctrine of intellectual intuition, so closely connected to the mythical doctrine of recollection. The Platonist claims to apprehend, in some discursively inexplicable manner, the formal monad, whether with respect to an element (like a letter) within a larger structure (like a syllable), or with respect to the wholeness, unity, and Being of that larger structure itself. Second, the unity of the multiplicity, that is, of the form conceived as sum or All, must be explained in some way which both shares in the One itself (otherwise it would dissolve) and yet which does not share in the One itself (otherwise the All would in fact be the Whole,

11. Spinoza, *Epistolae*, no. 50, in *Opera*, ed. Van Vloten/Land (The Hague, M. Nijhoff, 1914), 3 : 173.

in which case we could not discern any parts). Third, Being is either form or it is not. If it is not, nothing "logical" can be said of it. If it is, then the "otherness" of one formal monad from another, that is, non-being, must be explained not as the absence of form but as the presence of form *in some other way*. Following the language of the Eleatic Stranger, non-being is, no less than the other things, within Being (*ousia*). Still more forcefully, it is to be "numbered as one form among the many forms of beings." [12]

The use of the word "numbered" is extremely important, because it underlines the connection in Plato between being and enumerability. To be is to be something, that is, a unit, or something countable. According to the classic analysis in the *Sophist,* the same holds true for non-being. Unfortunately, our study of the Whole has in effect shown us that no being can be counted. If the Whole is the One itself, then it cannot be counted because, in the Platonic formulation, a number is a multiplicity of units. If the Whole is the All, then in order to avoid dissolving it by our conceptual analysis, we must say that every form *qua* All has an eidetic (= formal) number which is one more than the sum of its parts. And that "one more" is the One itself, which cannot be counted or rendered amenable to rational discourse.

Let us first illustrate this "counting paradox" [13] with respect to the soul or mind. In the passage of the *Sophist* concerned with the critical interrogation of the "friends of the forms," [14] this paradox may be seen to apply both to the "friends" and to the Eleatic Stranger. The friends (and their historical identity is a matter of dispute) separate Being (*ousia*) from genesis. Whereas Being is always the same as itself, unchanging or impassive, genesis is always changing. The separation of Being from genesis is overcome by the soul, or rather by way of the soul's two capacities of calculative thinking and sense percep-

12. *Sophist* 258b8–c3.

13. Cf. J. Klein, *Greek Mathematical Thought and the Origin of Algebra,* p. 94.

14. *Sophist* 248a4 ff. Numbers in parentheses in the text will identify lines from the Stephanus edition.

tion. In this context, the soul constitutes an All in the sense of a *community* with Being and genesis; the term "community" (*koinōnia*) is used subsequently to refer to the weaving-together of the forms which constitutes the intelligible world and makes rational discourse possible. In the case of the community of forms, Being, change, and rest, each an independent or self-identical form, are able to connect or combine in such a way as to account for the fact that some beings change while others are at rest. In the case of soul, however, there is a difficulty. Soul is the community of Being and genesis by virtue of intrinsic capacities, calculative thinking and sense perception, and not by virtue of a community between soul (as an independent element) and these capacities. In other words, the soul, qua soul, both changes and rests. The soul, as it is ostensibly explained by the friends of the forms, is already a "community" or combination of opposing elements. If the principle of community is itself a community, then we require still another principle to explain the original principle.

This difficulty is indicated in the next series of remarks (248b2 ff.). The Stranger, who is conducting this imaginary dialogue with the friends of the forms, asks them for a definition not of soul but of community. He himself offers a definition on their behalf, which interestingly enough is the same as the definition of Being which he offered in an earlier passage to the Materialists (247d8 ff.). According to this suggestion, community is "a suffering or making, coming to be out of some power which is itself a combination of elements." The Stranger implicitly suggests that, for Materialists and Idealists alike, the principle of unity or wholeness is internally unstable. Its structure, however, is ambiguous; we cannot decide immediately whether the principle is an unstable combination of two elements or a combination of two elements in some invisible *third*. Is the soul a formal structure which arises from the combination of calculative thinking and sense perception, or are the latter two attributes of an invisible "substance?" In either case, we cannot define the soul unless we define the unity of the combination. But this is evidently impossible, for reasons which have already been suggested. A definition is itself a community of "nouns and verbs," or in the language of reflection, of subjects and predicates. The effort to define unity succeeds only in separating it; the predicates "objectify" the subject but are unable to grasp its subjectivity.

The friends of the forms, however, reject the Stranger's definition of community. The reason for this rejection is their insistence that Being is neither active nor passive: it neither does nor suffers. In other words, the friends take "suffering" to refer here to sense perception, and "doing" or "acting" to refer to calculative thinking. Since the latter "communes" with Being, it would presumably share its activity with Being as well. This passage is of special interest because we can also understand it as a Platonic criticism of Aristotle. If thinking shares its activity with Being (that is, with forms), then Being is itself either active (the same as thinking) or passive (because "to be known" is to receive or suffer a determination). The Stranger is here ruling out any sense of "activity" which is not a change (*kinēsis*). And on this point the friends agree with him. Their own position is curiously reminiscent of the Fichtean doctrine of the Absolute. The community of thinking and Being is logically prior to the distinction between activity and passivity. Unfortunately, this renders the community unknowable. In Hegelian language, it establishes an "alienation" of essence from its appearances, or of substance from its attributes.

In developing his refutation of the friends of the forms, the Stranger begins from a grammatical distinction. "To know" is in the active voice, whereas "to be known" is passive, and hence indicates that a change has taken place. In addition to this, however, the Stranger asks, with a rare (for him) oath ("By Zeus") to emphasize his question: "Shall we be easily persuaded that change and life and soul and intelligence are not present to the complete Being, that it does not live or think, but awful and holy, lacking mind, is unchanging and fixed?" (248e6 ff.). The Stranger's language does not quite make it clear whether "the complete Being" is itself the All, or whether the All is the co-presence or community of the aforementioned elements. In either case, the Stranger argues that, without change, there can be no soul, and without soul, mind is impossible. Therefore, the presence of mind requires the presence of change. On the other hand, if everything is changing, then mind is equally impossible, since sameness is impossible without rest. Unless there is a sameness of nature and of the relations of natures, mind can neither be nor come to be (249a4 ff.). Again the Stranger's language is ambiguous. It is not quite clear whether mind is itself at rest, or whether the forms are at rest, whereas mind, since it is both an activity (knowing) and a community with what does not change, is both changing and at rest. Since the Stranger has already criticized the first alternative, we must assume that he subscribes to the second. However, this gives rise to a dilemma which is *not* mentioned by the Stranger. Let us assume that mind both changes and rests. Since to know is to change, whereas to commune with sameness is to rest, and since to know is to commune with sameness, the mind is evidently passive as active and active as passive. The mind contradicts itself, or, as a unique element (whether "being" or "form" is the appropriate term here), is *already* a community of change and rest. The unity of this community is as unintelligible or as inaccessible to rational discourse as was the position attributed to the friends of the forms.

We have to continue with our examination of the *Sophist* for a little while in order to see the full force of the dilemma. Immediately after concluding his refutation of the friends of the forms, the Stranger shows how he and Theaetetus are also in logical difficulties with respect to Being. He begins with a suggested definition of Being as "change and rest" (249d6 ff.). In other words, everything which is, is either at rest or changing: both "are" equally. Since change and rest are opposites or contraries, it would seem already that Being can be described only in a self-contradictory manner. As we saw previously in another context, the contemporary reader is tempted to resolve problems of this sort by making a distinction between identity and predication. I shall discuss later the charge that Hegel himself fails to distinguish between these two. I think it can be shown that, on the contrary, the distinction serves to exacerbate an already bad situation in non-Hegelian logic.

The Stranger does indeed deny that Being can be spoken of only in a self-contradictory way. Since change and rest are neither both changing nor both at rest but both "are," "Being must be some third thing in the soul" (250b7 ff.). The Stranger gives no explanation as to why he refers to the soul at this point. If we recall the previously analyzed refutation of the friends of the forms, however, the reason becomes apparent. The soul is that "being" which *counts the beings.* It establishes a community or All by giving an account (*logos*) of beings. However, this community is rendered unstable, if it does not simply disappear, by the fact that the soul can give no account of itself. The crucial difficulty here is that of counting. The *unifying* units cannot be seen. This is why I put the "being" of the soul in quotation-marks. The soul both changes and rests qua soul; its peculiar self-identity is not intelligible as the sum of Being, change, and rest.

The same situation obtains with respect to Being. Being has a nature of its own (according to the subsequent argument), independently of change and rest. *But nothing can be said of this nature.* Strictly speaking, nothing can be said of any of the formal elements as they are in themselves, but only by connecting them to other elements through the medium of predicative discourse. Since, however, discursive knowledge is predicative by its nature, it is obvious that we can know nothing of any of the forms as they are in themselves. To know is to connect the unknowable. And as it seems, the situation is especially bad in the case of Being. Anything is said "to be" if its form combines with the form of Being. "Anything" in this context can be a form (like change) or it can be an instance of a form (like a changing object). However, it is impossible to connect Being with itself. Since Being cannot be predicated of (the form) Being, it makes no sense to say "Being is." The difficulties to which this gives rise are essentially the same as those which follow from accepting the Whole as the One itself. If it is claimed that we need not predicate Being of itself but must merely assert its identity, this overlooks the fact that the assertion of the identity "Being itself" already predicates "sameness" of Being, as is clear from the Greek (*to on auto*).

The intelligibility of Being as self-identical, ostensibly separate from predication, depends upon or includes predication. "Being itself," as follows from the analysis, characteristic of the Platonic dialogues, in the *Sophist,* is unintelligible to a discursive thinking which obeys the principle of contradiction. It "is and is not."

I trust it is now evident why I have followed this Platonic investigation in the present discussion. As soon as we analyze the Platonic conception of Being, it transforms itself into the Hegelian conception. The Platonic conception of Being (or of form generally) is intrinsically unstable. Plato makes non-being a species of Being, but the result in his case is to make Being indistinguishable from *Nichts.* Let me restate this conclusion. The Platonic analysis of Parmenides shows the need to differentiate, and therefore to multiply, the Eleatic One or Being. It would seem that this differentiation entails the famous "parricide" (241d1 ff.), or denial of Parmenides' injunction against thinking and speaking (what I have called) *Nichts.* In fact, there is a modification rather than a total rejection of the Parmenidean position. The Eleatic Stranger, as I mentioned above, introduces the doctrine of non-being as a form or class within Being, that is, as itself *being.* The result is the coordination of being and non-being within Being, and the rejection of any discursive utilization of *Nichts.* As we have seen, *Nichts* continues to be present because indistinguishable from unity or Being. But the impossibility of a rational reference to *Nichts* means that, strictly speaking, we lack an analysis of non-being itself. Instead, we have given an analysis of the "otherness" of being. Simply stated, the Stranger explains how *X* is *Y* by the doctrine of predication or the community of forms. But he does not explain how *X* is non-*Y,* since his explanation amounts to the assertion that *X* is *Z,* whereas *Z* is not the same as non-*Y.* To explain the "otherness" of *Z* from non-*Y* as in fact *A,* is simply to generate an infinite regress of analyses, each of which avoids the notion to be analyzed.

I mentioned above that *Nichts* is present in every being as the invisibility of the One itself. This is why it proved impossible to "count" or analyze exhaustively *any* being or formal structure. Unity qua Whole is, in Hegelian language, an identity-within-difference with unity qua All. It is therefore impossible to count off or separate, in any but an arbitrary or contingent manner, one formal unit from another: *each is both the same as and other than the others.* Stability, in the Platonic sense of self-identity, independence, etc., disappears. What the Stranger calls in the *Sophist* the "community of forms" loses its character as a quasi-geometrical relation and becomes a "One differentiating itself" in an almost Heraclitean sense. The Platonic doctrine, when analyzed in its own terms, shows itself as an apparently unsuspected anticipation of the Absolute Spirit, with the notable exception of any element resembling the characteristic of self-consciousness. In Hegel, Being and *Nichts* are coordinate within Becoming, as a One differentiating itself. Hegel's One, however, is self-conscious Absolute Spirit, or the Parmenidean One brought to life.

The Aristotelian Heritage

We are now ready to return to Aristotle and the principle of contradiction. As I indicated previously, Aristotle accepts the Platonic demonstration that the Whole cannot be logically thought or analyzed. Instead, he elevates the principle of contradiction (already present in Plato)[15] to a comprehensive status, which amounts to the repudiation of mythical or poetic thinking as practiced by his master. The "wholeness" of the discontinuous sciences comes from the coherence or internal consistency of scientific thinking itself. One could perhaps say that the principle of contradiction is a humanly accessible image of the coherence of the cosmos taken as actualized within the divine activity of thought thinking itself. From a Hegelian viewpoint, the Aristotelian modification of Platonism has certain advantages. For example, it gives implicitly a new and comprehensive status to thinking as formation-process. On the other hand, although the Platonic forms are brought within the grasp of thinking, they remain Platonic in

15. *Republic* 4. 436b5 ff., 439d1 ff.; *Sophist* 230b7–8.

their ontological characteristics. This is the effective reason why Aristotle is unable to achieve self-reflection in his conception of mind as pure negative activity. Aristotle does not seem to see that, in thinking the principle of contradiction, the mind contradicts itself by predicating simultaneously of itself the contraries *P* and non-*P*.

Let us move a bit more slowly here. Two preliminary remarks are in order concerning terminology. First, we normally speak today of the "law" of contradiction. But a "law" is something formulated by an intelligence, which (normally) expresses the will of the legislator, and so can presumably be changed. But Aristotle means by the principle of contradiction something which is intrinsic to rational discourse. Second, a "contradiction" refers exclusively to a discourse, let us say to two propositions which we may represent as "*S* is *P* and *S* is non-*P*." But Aristotle's principle is meant to express the nature of beings or forms, and only derivatively of discourse. Contradictory propositions cannot be simultaneously true because they do not describe a possibly existing condition or manner of being. Their conjunction is false because no being can admit contrary properties simultaneously. If we restate this by saying that "no subject can admit contrary predicates," we should not forget that "subject" and "predicate" are place-names (variables) for beings and their properties. There is no trace of nominalism in Aristotle. The mind conforms to the forms, even in being regulated by the principle of contradiction.

The previous observations should clarify what Aristotle means by referring to what we call a "law" or "principle" as "a most stable opinion." As the foundation of all deductive knowledge, it cannot be known by deduction from a still higher principle. It is "most stable" because, as Aristotle believes, it expresses our comprehensive confidence in the stability or determinateness of contraries, and so of logical discourse. Let us also be careful to notice that whereas the principle expresses how we intuit forms, namely, as *this* or *that*, it cannot be deduced from, or is not "given" by, intuition. The intuition of the form is an instance of the stability or reliability of the principle. In other words, the principle tells us what it means *to be,* whereas intuition furnishes us with an instance of being. We should also observe that since a principle is itself of formal structure, or intelligible by way of that structure, it must itself be *this* principle rather than *that,* or more generally, it must be a principle of this or of that. It is true that the most stable principle is comprehensive in the sense that it defines every *this* as *not that.* On the other hand, it is not a "first principle" in the sense of defining a universal science or account of the *summum genus* or All.[16] We have already seen that the principle of each science is generic: it defines the genus (accessible by intuition) of which a specific science gives an account. There can be no principle of principles which is comprehensive or defines the genus of all genera and to which corresponds a science of sciences or logical account of the All.[17]

Since a science follows from previous knowledge, and in this context from its principle, a science of science would necessarily follow from *its* principle, which would in turn be rendered secure by something else, whether an opinion or some higher science. We must then either ground the science of sciences in opinion or non-science, or else generate an infinite regress of "comprehensive" sciences. The latter procedure is similar to Hegel's interpretation of the history of philosophy prior to himself: a series of world-views which express or establish a "bad infinity" of mutually cancelling descriptions of the All. Hegel avoids this alternative by transforming the first alternative, or Aristotle's actual procedure, into *dialectic.*[18] What is for Aristotle unscientific discussion or opinion about the All, is for Hegel a science about the Whole. It is the science of sciences which renders the finite sciences rational by integrating them into the logical account of the identity-within-difference of the All and the Whole.

The "cosmos" in its comprehensive sense, for both Plato

16. *Physics* A 185a3–5; *Metaphysics* A 992b25–33, Λ 1070a31 ff.

17. Cf. *Metaphysics* K 1062a2 ff.

18. Some would say that Aristotle's procedure is itself "dialectical," albeit not in the Hegelian sense. This is a much-disputed point among Aristotle scholars.

and Aristotle, is a Whole in the sense of a necessary presupposition for the scientific study of "parts." At the same time, given the inaccessibility of the Whole to intelligence, it is also an All. Science in the Platonic-Aristotelian tradition proceeds upon the assumption that the Whole is logically equivalent to the All; but this is an illegitimate assumption, as I have tried to show in detail. In the absence of a science of the Whole, we are in no position to refer to scientific knowledge of the "parts." The very notion of "part" makes sense only in terms of a notion of Whole. Aristotle, to be sure, replaces the notion of Whole with allegiance to the principle of contradiction, but the resultant stability would seem to be a project of human will rather than a consequence of the natural order. What we require is a certification of the principle of contradiction which is not a deduction from some higher principle. We need a certification which proceeds by the complete development, and in that way "exhibition" or clarification, of the internal oscillations of the most stable principle itself. We need a demonstration of the self-contradictory nature of the fundamental opinion about contradiction.

If the effort to deduce the principle of contradiction from a higher principle is impossible, then our only recourse is to a demonstration of the principle *from itself*. Aristotle attempts something of this sort. He argues that those who deny the principle necessarily contradict themselves: they say either everything or nothing. This defense is clearly circular, since it is based upon the assumption that contradictory assumptions are meaningless, or do not and cannot correspond to what is the case. The Fichtean demonstration of the principle of contradiction amounts to an effort to show that the Aristotelian assumption is itself intelligible only as a result of being posed by the Absolute Ego: a spiritualized version of Kant's transcendental ego. The opposition of *P* and non-*P*, which defines the structure of the world of understanding, itself depends for its coherence upon a prior *synthesis* which, as we have already seen, is not accessible to the discursive intelligence. A Hegelian could argue that, on this issue, there is no significant difference between Aristotle and Fichte. Opposition is determinate difference, and so negation. The positivity of *P* and the negativity of non-*P* are therefore both already contained in the moment of opposition. In other words, *P* and non-*P* are contained or "reflected" within each other in the relation of opposition, which is in fact identity-within-difference.

"To be," whether as *P* or non-*P,* is always an instance of the "is and is not" structure of Being. The crux of the matter is thus the interpretation given to "negation." Plato puts us squarely in the presence of the correct solution by defining non-being as "otherness." Since every being is other than every other being, every being *is and is not.* But Plato obscures the correct solution by attempting to define being and non-being as separate species within the genus of Being. Since he cannot define or discursively think Being, it is itself indistinguishable from the Parmenidean *Nichts.* The *Nichts* cannot serve either to unite or to separate being from non-being. On the one hand, being and non-being are separated as formal elements, which is to say that the "is and is not" character of each being is dissolved in accordance with a tacit reliance upon the principle of contradiction. On the other hand, since any instance of non-being derives its reality or thinghood, and so its intelligibility, from its being (or formal structure taken in a positive sense), non-being loses any formal independence and comes to be assimilated into syntax, or how we speak about things. The things themselves now stand apart from each other, separated (and so defined) by *Nichts.* Since "to be" and "to be intelligible" is to be a form, or since the visibility of a form is explained by its positivity, whereas the negativity of a form is due to the absence of other forms, and not to an intrinsic formal element (despite the definition of non-being as a species), the negative element of negation, as external to its positive or ontic element, must be due to the relations we impose upon beings in discourse.

This helps to explain why the Platonist cannot identify a relation of formal elements as itself an element distinct from its relata. It also helps to pin-point the connection between Platonism and twentieth-century "analytic" philosophy. The unspeakability of the Parmenidean *Nichts* is present today in the nominalistic versions of Kantianism which predominate among analytic philosophers: that is to say, they reject, or have forgotten, *synthesis as unspeakable*. Doctrines like those of the unspeakability of logical form, the theory of types, the interpretation of forms as relations, and the relativity of linguistic horizons, are internally related by a Platonic incapacity to take seriously the Platonic definition of non-being.

Let us close this chapter with two illustrations of the consequences of this incapacity, the first from Aristotle and the second from Wittgenstein. There are for Aristotle as many senses of non-being as there are of being.[19] This means that the senses of non-being correspond to the categories, or how we speak of something *as* something. The "something" cannot be described as it is "in itself" or as an *ousia,* but only by virtue of its properties or predicates. This corresponds to the situation in Plato, where nothing can be said of formal elements in themselves, but only with respect to their combinations. In Aristotle's language, non-being is "potentially" being, or explained as a privation or absence of a given formal element within an actual formal structure. The doctrine of privation is thus Aristotle's revision of the Platonic doctrine of "otherness." But a privation is defined with respect to a specific, actual form. This leads to a crucial difficulty concerning the "otherness" of one generic form from another. According to Aristotle, contrariety is the "greatest difference"; each generic form is what it is by virtue of its defining differences or contrarieties.[20] We may say that two things are "other" than each other when there is no covering genus with respect to which the things differ.[21] This amounts to the assertion that one genus may be other than another. However, the two cannot be contraries, because each genus is an *ousia,* and there is no contrary to *ousia.*[22] The generically different "have

19. *Metaphysics* N 1089a16 ff.; cf. Θ 1051a34 ff.

20. *Metaphysics* H 1043a2 ff.; I 1055a3 ff. Contrariety is also said to be one of four kinds of opposition (including contradiction, correlativity, and privation): Δ 1018a20 ff.; I 1054a20 ff. and 1055a3 ff.

21. Ibid., Γ 1004a21; I 1054b23 ff.

22. Ibid., Δ 1018a9 ff.; N 1087b2.

no road into each other." [23] The "otherness" of two genera is such that no account can be given of their separateness; discussion begins with the assertion that "*X* is *X*" and "*Y* is *Y*." There is no generic form common to distinct genera; in other words, there is finally no *summum genus* or discursively accessible Whole. Consequently, there can be no "difference" or "privation" external to the genus, which defines or conditions it as the *ousia* it is.[24] But this amounts to the assertion that there is no "other" to being, because non-being is not a form which is separate from the being in question.[25] Non-being is not the genus of becoming; there is no unitary non-being which causes the categorially distinct kinds of being.[26] We cannot, then, give a logical or coherent account of non-being, any more than we could give a single, coherent account of being. In each case, there are as many accounts as there are kinds of beings. And each account *begins from a kind.* The separateness of one genus from another thus falls between the kinds of being and the correlative kinds of non-being. This "betweenness" is the Parmenidean *Nichts.*

I turn now to the second example. This is of course not the place for an exhaustive discussion of contemporary philosophy. Nevertheless, I am concerned to make as strong a case as possible for Hegel's logic, and it is part of that case to show how the classical *aporiai* remain visible in post-Hegelian philosophies of logic which ignore or deny the pertinence of dialectical speculation. I have spoken in an early chapter of the antipsychologistic tendency of contemporary analytic philosophy. If we grant the irrelevance, or still worse the inaccessibility, of the analytic intelligence to the logical and ontological significance of analysis, the practical result is the same as in the case of Aristotle. "Truth" is identified as, and derived from, a discontinuous process of the presence and absence of forms: a process which takes place upon a backdrop of nothingness. The discontinuity of logical atoms is thus in no way

23. Ibid., I 1055a6 f.

24. Ibid., I 1055a25 ff. Cf. H 1043a2 ff.

25. Cf. B 1001a31 f. and I 1054b19 ff.

26. *Topics* 128b6 ff.; *Metaphysics* N 1089a12 ff.

different from, say, the discontinuity of moments of being as described by the early Sartre. Heidegger's notorious phrase, so ridiculed by contemporary logicians, "nothing itself negativizes," is in fact a good description of the "positive" world of contemporary analytic rationalism. I note in passing the subterranean connection between Platonism and contemporary "fundamental" or ostensibly anti-Platonic ontology. The Hegelian would surely deny any decisive difference between the opposing schools of contemporary philosophy, or between these schools and Platonism, so far as the main point is concerned: in all cases, a failure to master the Parmenidean *Nichts*. *Nothing* separates "this qua this" from "that qua that." But this means that there is no formal connection between this and that. If there were, "this" and "that" would not be distinct but aspects of a continuous and coherent form. Everything would be *reflected* into everything else.

The anti-Hegelian detachment of forms as finite monads, or the separation of the law of identity from the law of excluded middle, together with the definition of negation as a syntactic operation upon a specific category, leads to an impasse concerning logical necessity which is reminiscent of Hume's impasse concerning causality. To think is to actualize as a given logical form. Whereas we may, for example, actualize twice as *P* and *Q*, there is no actualization of the entailment-relation between *P* and *Q*. The truth-function connective "$\rightarrow$" derives its significance from the combination of values assigned to *P* and *Q*. It is a syntactic convention elevated to the status of a logical definition. Whoever claims to "see" the logical necessity of "$P \rightarrow Q$" claims to grasp intuitively the logical connections between *P*, *Q*, and "$\rightarrow$." More precisely, he must grasp the connection between the values of *P*, *Q*, and the definition of "$\rightarrow$" or the connection between *P* and "$\rightarrow$" as well as between "$\rightarrow$" and *Q*. These connections are necessary ingredients of the ostensible entailment-relation "$P \rightarrow Q$." And yet, no forms correspond to them.

In the language of the early Wittgenstein, the form of "$P \rightarrow Q$" *shines forth*, but cannot be discursively or symbolically represented. Every such representation clearly makes use of the so-called form as already in operation, by way of the separation of reflective understanding. We see here the Kantian heritage of Wittgenstein's early doctrine. To grasp a logical structure is possible because of an unspoken, and unspeakable, prior synthesis. This synthesis is the modern version of the invisible Platonic "One itself," which in turn derives from Parmenides. Without recourse to this synthesis, Wittgenstein is a logical empiricist in the precise sense of advocating a logical version of Hume's skepticism.[27] But recourse to synthesis leads directly to silence, or the Parmenidean *Nichts*. Hence the paradoxical character of Wittgenstein's *Tractatus*.

In general, modern logic avoids one version of the dilemma of Platonism by dealing with relations rather than with specific or generic forms. But the relation is itself intelligible only as an intuitive synthesis of formal elements, and there is no form which corresponds to the synthetic act itself. The activity of synthesis produces "$P \rightarrow Q$" but is not represented thereby. This means that logical necessity is as invisible as causal connection, so long as we define "visibility" in terms of static formal structures. Nondialectical or analytic logic is thus essentially a continuation of the Platonic-Aristotelian ontology, if not of their specific logical "techniques." In Hegel's language, it is "external reflection" because it conceals intellectual activity and so the Absolute. We are now ready to study Hegel's treatment of reflection.

27. Cf. Wittgenstein, *Tractatus logico-philosophicus,* in *Schriften* 1 (Frankfurt, Suhrkamp Verlag, 1969), 5.134 ff. and the discussion in E. Stenius, *Wittgenstein's Tractatus* (Oxford, Basil Blackwell, 1960), pp. 58 ff. Stenius does not observe the problematic status of logical necessity. Cf. also D. Favrholdt, *An Interpretation and Critique of Wittgenstein's Tractatus* (Copenhagen, Munksgaard, 1967), p. 125.

5 Reflection

The Self-Contradictory Nature of Analytic Thinking

The Western tradition of analytic thinking, which receives its decisive orientation in the doctrines of Plato and Aristotle, may be summarized by three principles or laws: identity, difference (or excluded middle), and contradiction. It is easy to see that the principle of contradiction is the comprehensive form of the other two. *S* cannot simultaneously be *P* and non-*P* because the unit of intelligibility, and thus the subject of predication, is a finite, separate, and self-identical formal monad: hence the principle of identity, or S = S. But identity depends upon stability of identification; that is, we identify *S* through its properties ($P_1, P_2, \ldots, P_n$) by which *S* is identified as *S*. In order for *S* to remain what it is, its properties must remain the same. Let *P* equal the set of properties ($P_1, P_2, \ldots, P_n$) by which *S* is identified as *S*. To say that *S* is both *P* and non-*P* is to say that *S* is also non-*S*. The identity of *S* therefore depends upon the necessity that *P*, as inherent in *S*, excludes non-*P*, and also that *S* is either *P* or non-*P*. If it were neither, it would have no properties, and so it would be invisible, or indistinguishable from non-*S*. If it were both, it would be, so to speak, both visible and invisible, or at once *S* and non-*S*, which is again to say that the two would be indistinguishable, or that there would be no identifiable subjects or formal monads. In short, the identity of *S* depends upon the difference between *P* and non-*P*.

It should be obvious from our résumé that all three principles rest upon the finitude and stability of what I have called the formal monad. In the previous chapter, we saw that the finitude and stability of the formal monad themselves depend upon the illicit assumption that the Whole is logically equivalent to the All. I refer to the assumption that the unity of a form is the same as the "sum" (derived by analysis) of its formal elements. As it turns out, however, the One is both the same as *and* other than the many. Differently stated, a unit is a

Whole in a sense other than it is an All, yet nevertheless, the All is not some sum other than the sum of the Whole. In terms of the analytic tradition, this situation is self-contradictory or unintelligible. For either the Whole and the All are the same form, or they are two distinguishable forms. If they are the same, then the One *is* the many. In this case, the usual procedure is to ignore the One, with the subsequent dissolution of the many qua All. Or the Whole and All are not the same, but distinct forms, in which case the unit is at once transformed into an unstable dyad. In order to preserve the "sum" of Whole and All, a third kind of formal unity is required, and one which both "is and is not" Whole and All. The dilemma is merely transferred to this third kind, assuming any candidates are available, and we deteriorate into an infinite regress of unities.

Whichever side of the case we inspect, the result is apparently the same. Analysis is self-destructive. If we wish to avoid the dissolution of form, then we must ground discursive analysis in silent intuition. The difficulty with recourse to silence, however, is that it seems to be too arbitrary to repair the self-destructive tendency of analysis or discourse. How could we *identify* the content of a silent intuition except by submitting it to analysis? Apparently the decision to ground discourse in silence leads directly to the decision to ground silence in discourse. We may, perhaps, decide to do without a ground, or simply to immerse ourselves in analysis. But this decision does not free us from the need to distinguish between successful and unsuccessful analyses, at which point the need again arises to choose between discourse and silence, or as one could also phrase this, between theory and practice: or still more appropriately, between theory and production (since the modern philosopher tends to interpret "doing" as "making"). For example, we might in effect reduce theory itself to production, and define a form as the product of a human *construction*. But construction proceeds in accordance with tools and principles; if these are also constructed, then inevitably the "essence" or significance of these tools and principles will depend upon the intentions of the constructor. It is not very illuminating to be told that the intentions are defined or justified by the products of construction. This amounts to the assertion that truth is defined by power, or that whatever we can do, is true. We return to a kind of historical positivism, or celebration of *what happens* (albeit through our own constructive labor).

Let us summarize this summary. The finite and stable form, taken as the grounding principle of truth in the ontological and logical senses of the term, can be neither discovered nor constructed. Such a principle is self-contradictory. But this means that the principle of contradiction, as the comprehensive version of the Western rationalist tradition, is itself self-contradictory. The principle of contradiction unites the principles of identity and difference. According to the traditional interpretation, however, identity and difference contradict each other. The validity of the principle of contradiction thus depends upon the compatibility of contradictory properties. As we have already seen, the paradigm for the interpretation of this initially puzzling result is the activity of thinking itself. When I think the principle of contradiction, I am the ground of the synthesis by which *S* is united to *P* and non-*P* in a relation of identity (with *P*) and difference (with non-*P*). This means that *P* and non-*P* are simultaneously predicated of *S*, the first positively and the second negatively, because *P* and non-*P*, or identity and difference, are both predicated simultaneously of me, the thinking ego or subject. It is intelligible that *S* cannot be both *P* and non-*P* if and only if the ego is *both P* and non-*P*. There is an *S*, such that it simultaneously "is and is not" *P*. And this is visible with respect to *any* instance of thinking the principle of contradiction. The intelligibility of *S* not being both *P* and non-*P* depends upon *S* being both *P* and non-*P*. The antithesis of SP and $S\bar{P}$ is intelligible only within the synthesis of *S*, *P*, and $\bar{P}$. Therefore the ego is present as *S* within any instance of the principle as the synthesis of the identity and difference of its constituent terms. Since there are many finite egos, each capable of thinking the principle of contradiction, the common presence of the "synthetic unity of apperception" in each instance of such an act of thinking is the mark of the presence of the Absolute Ego in and through its manifestation as the *activity of thinking* of the finite ego.

FICHTE'S *Wissenschaftslehre* OF 1794

In the previous section, we moved from the classical to the Fichtean formulation of analytic thinking or reflection. The transition is set in motion by the separation within the classical teaching of the essence, substance, or *ousia* (Whole) from its appearances, attributes or "doings and sufferings" (All). I want now to discuss briefly the origin of the term "reflection" in modern philosophy. Since the pertinent figure in this case is Locke, we shall be able to inspect the empiricist version of the modern consequences of the Platonic-Aristotelian beginnings. This will also aid us in understanding the force of Hegel's charge against Kant (and so Fichte) that he did not escape the deficiencies of empiricism. It should also serve to reinforce my initial claim that Hegel attempts to reunite the ancients and the moderns, or in effect to preserve every major philosophical position within his comprehensive science of wisdom.

Socrates begins analytic philosophy with the question: "*What* is it?" The failure of Socrates and his students to answer this question leads directly to the modern doctrine of the substance which is unknowable in itself. To say that substance is intelligible only through its attributes is to say in effect that we know it only by what it does.[1] Hence the close connection in modern philosophy between substance as the "something, I know not what," and power as well as will.[2] According to Locke, "man's power, and its ways of operation" are "much the same in the material and the intellectual world." [3] Man makes complex from simple ideas; hence he makes species and genera. The real essences of simple ideas cannot be defined.[4]

1. *Sophist* 247d8–e4, 218c1 ff.; *Republic* 5.477d7 ff.; *Phaedo* 99d4 ff.; *Phaedrus* 270d1 ff.

2. J. Locke, *An Essay Concerning Human Understanding*, ed. A. C. Fraser (New York, Dover Publications, 1959), 1 : 230.

3. Ibid., 1 : 390 ff., 397, 400.

4. Ibid., 1 : 214; cf. 1 : 44, 145.

Therefore thinking, or the constituting of the intelligible world, arises from an uneasiness or a desire for an absent pleasure, which in turn leads us to will to consider some idea or chain of ideas.[5] The intelligible world is a product of willing or the exercise of power. The "substance" of the intelligible world is the will to power in the sense of the desire for satisfaction. But this in turn depends upon the unintelligibility of substance, except in the mediate form of human work.[6]

For Locke, man is free in the precise sense of having the power to act upon his preference or volitions.[7] If we define "Being" as the intelligible world, then it is easy to see in Locke an ancestor of the idealist doctrine that freedom is prior to Being. In the Fichtean formulation, there is for Idealism no "Being in itself" but only activity (*Handlung*). Being, as we recall, is the negation of the freedom of the ego, or a derivative concept to be understood in opposition to freedom.[8] Being, or the intelligible world of reflection, even though it is a necessary consequence of the activity of the Absolute Ego, must itself be negated or transcended in order for man to return to the original freedom of absolute spontaneity. Reflection, or the attempt to understand oneself in the work of objectivity, is therefore alienation. Satisfaction will therefore depend not upon the the avoiding of alienation or work, but upon our capacity to reconcile work and the principle of human activity. In other words, reflection is not simply an obstacle over which we must "leap" as quickly as possible; it is also the means to success.

Locke refers to sensation and reflection as the two sources of ideas. This is the modern empiricist version of the classical distinction between intellectual intuition and discursive thought. The replacement of the former by sensation means in

5. Ibid., 2 : 6, 16 ff., 23 ff., 32.

6. Ibid., 1 : 316, 327, 331, 345.

7. There is an extremely important consequence for modern logic that follows from this kind of teaching. Locke observes that the ideas of relations can be more perfect and distinct than those of substances (the relata): 1 : 430. Relations are consequences of human desire, i.e. man-made, subject to the will or to the technical power as directed by the will.

8. J. G. Fichte, "Zweite Einleitung," p. 85; *Science of Knowledge*, p. 68.

effect (as will become explicit in Kant) that the mind constructs its forms or scientific truths. Reflection is "that notice which the mind takes of its own operations, and the manner of them, by reason whereof there come to be ideas of these operations in the understanding." [9] Subjectivity, or consciousness of the self, arises from reflection: it is impossible to perceive or think without perceiving that we do so.[10] The turn inward to the self is then not so much the separation of the subject from the object as the recognition that the complex subject and object are *products* of the power of the self. On this score, Locke is somehow closer to Hegel than to Fichte, except that he cannot perform the absolute reflection required for an understanding of the "power" of the self.

For Locke, the complex subject and object are both constructed from simple ideas, the empiricist version of the Greek intuition of formal monads. The self knows itself by its operations or work, but neither as substance nor as subject. The self, and therefore its works, are visible only in the vague sense of the power of an invisible substance. This amounts to the assertion that the self, by turning inward or toward itself, inevitably turns away from its essential self. No wonder that human life is for Locke perpetual dissatisfaction.[11] It is the eternal striving for pleasure, or the alienation of man from himself, thanks to the very appetites which drive him to work, or to construct the intelligible world. In the language of Idealism, man is doomed to dissatisfaction, or to the infinite longing for perfection, which results only in infinite work, in Being rather than in freedom.

The Absolute Idealist transforms the labors of reflection into obedience to the categorical imperative, or the command that "one ought" to strive for the infinite. In the Fichtean doctrine, Locke's "dissatisfaction" is overcome in the comprehension of human life as an expression of the absolute spontaneity of the activity which actualizes in the opposition of subject and object.[12] The activity of the human ego exemplifies

9. *Essay,* 1 : 124.
10. *Essay,* 1 : 316, 327, 331, 345.
11. *Essay,* 1 : 448 ff.
12. Ibid., 1 : 162, 304.

the spontaneous activity of the Absolute or Divine Ego. Just as in Locke, however, this exemplification is not accessible to conceptual intelligence. On the other hand, Fichte's revision of the position in Locke is the immediate precondition for Hegel's own analysis of reflection. It will therefore be worth our while to make a brief inspection of the first three sections of Fichte's *Foundations of the Whole Doctrine of Knowledge* of 1794.[13] In these sections, Fichte presents his own interpretation of the three principles of reflection which we discussed in the first section of this chapter. Fichte begins his search for the "first, strictly unconditioned principle" with a distinction between thinking as activity and the principle as an expression of that activity (1.11; 93). This is, of course, a Kantian distinction, based upon the premise that thinking synthesizes its objects, or is present within every principle of thought as the synthesis of the antithetical subject and predicate. In his analysis of the synthetic unity of apperception, Kant insisted that the activity of thinking is accessible only as what we may call the antithetical articulation of a synthesis. Whereas Fichte accepts this restriction with respect to analytical thinking, his purpose is to lead us beyond the antithetical structure to an intuition of synthetic or "productive" activity itself.

Every principle of reflective thinking is already an instance of the subject-object antithesis. This is evident in the simplest case, the principle of identity, or $A = A$. The certitude of this principle is formal or hypothetical rather than existential. It does not depend upon the "being" of A, but asserts rather that, *if A, then A:* whatever we pose, regardless of its ontological status, is intelligible or posable only as identical to itself. We see here the Platonic distinction between "being" and "sameness' or "identity," a distinction which Plato does not himself always honor. This is because "being" is for Plato invisible and unspeakable apart from "sameness." Plato would no doubt

13. *Grundlage der gesamten Wissenschaftslehre* (Hamburg, Felix Meiner Verlag, 1961). The first set of numbers in parentheses in the text will refer to paragraphs and pages of Part One in this edition; the number following the semicolon refers to pages in the English translation cited fully in chapter one, note 34.

grant that "being" and "sameness" are joined in every case, or that whatever is, is the same as itself. But the distinction between the two formal elements makes sense only if there is a principle or form by which the distinction can be performed. There must be a third form which designates the unity in which "being" and "sameness" jointly inhere. In the absence of such a unity, "being" is indistinguishable from "sameness." Their conjoint appearance means that the two are one, whereas the unity of the two suggests that they are three. One consequence of this puzzle is that Plato cannot distinguish clearly between "being" and "image." If "being" and "sameness" are always conjoint, then whatever is the same as itself must "be," including imaginary or self-contradictory entities which, as "one," possess the unity of self-identity. As this problem arises in the *Sophist,* the "being" of the image (which stands for words and discursive thinking as well as corporeal instances of genesis) is at once the "non-being" of the original. Nevertheless, the image *is what it is,* or owes both its "being" and "sameness" to its "non-being" and "otherness" with respect to the original. But the reverse must also be true: the original "is and is not" the image. Therefore the original is an image of the image, which in turn becomes the original.

By his distinction between "being" and "sameness," Fichte is required to define the necessary connection between the hypothetical *A* and itself, in a source external to *A*. Otherwise, to say "$A = A$" or *A* is *A* would be to say "*A* is." The correct analysis of "$A = A$" is "if *A*, then *A*." There must be a necessary connection in the "if . . . then . . ." schema that validates the identification of *A* with itself. Fichte designates this necessary connection by the symbol *X*. *X*, as it were, stands for the license to say "*A* is *A*" without committing ourselves to the "being" of *A*. But this license is issued by none other than the reflecting ego: "For the ego is that which judges in the above proposition, and indeed, it judges in accordance with *X* as a law" (1.13; 95). In short, the ego issues a license *X in* and *to* itself: the spontaneous intellectual activity of the ego validates by that activity its own results. The licensing of the "if . . . then . . ." connection with respect to *A* is also a posing of *A*. *A* "is" in the ego: its "being" is derived not from "sameness" but from the activity of thinking which poses both "being" and "sameness" in and to itself. This is the crucial addition to Platonism: the spontaneous intellectual activity of the ego is the "third" or the principle of unification between "being" and "sameness" which allows them to be distinguished.

We began our reflection on the law of identity with a distinction between the form *A* and the hypothetical necessity that, if *A* "is," then it is the same as itself; hence we distinguished initially between *A* and *A* = *A*. The capacity to identify *A* with itself derives from the capacity of the ego to identify itself to itself as that which poses both *A* and the "if . . . then . . ." license, or X. The ego identifies itself as I = I, or as the necessary presupposition of stability, which grants validity to all instances of *X*, regardless of what *A* itself designates. But the identity of the ego (its "sameness") is also proof of its "being." If the ego were a mere form, or I, it could never license its own identification or the move to I = I by way of "if . . . then . . .". This move is the certification of "being" as self-consciousness, and is distinct from or in addition to the posing of a form. The ego divides "being" and "sameness" because it is both (or the synthesis in which they are posed) and neither (it is a synthetic activity, not a being or form). This is why Fichte calls the assertion of A = A a *judgment,* in German, *Urteil,* literally, "original division" (1.14–15; 96–97). In general, the logic of German post-Kantian philosophy is a logic of judgments, not of propositions. Any attempt to represent this logic in the calculus of propositional logic is therefore impossible from the outset.

Judgment originates in the spontaneous activity of the self-identification of the ego as I = I. The ego identifies itself as a being that thinks; hence Fichte modifies the Cartesian *cogito ergo sum* into *sum qua cogitans.* Fichte wishes to avoid even the appearance of a deduction from thinking to being. "Being and Thinking are the same." Since "being" is posed by thinking, I pose myself or am, in the act of thinking myself (1.16; 97–98). I am as thinking, namely, as I = I or as thinking myself:

"What is not for itself is not an ego." And therefore the ego is, only to the extent that it is self-conscious (1.17; 98). The ego does not "acquire" self-consciousness. It may initially think itself in an analytic manner, as an object, as for example in the process of reflection upon the law of identity. But the ego as object is the object of the reflection of the "absolute subject." In the previous example, the ego which licenses the move from A to $A = A$, possesses "objectivity" only to itself as the self-conscious subject of every object. Every object (including my objectified self) is *my* object: "One can never abstract from his self-consciousness" (ibid.). In short, since $A = A$ is valid for every object because the "if . . . then . . . " schema is constituted by the licensing power X of the thinking ego, every "value" of A is posed within the ego. "To be" is to satisfy $A = A$, which is in turn grounded in the spontaneous activity of the ego, or in Fichte's expression, in "I am" (1.18–19; 99–100).

Fichte turns next to the second principle of analytic thinking, difference: $-A$ is not equal to A, or as I shall express it, $-A \neq A$. As in the first case, he begins with a "fact of the empirical consciousness" and proceeds by an analysis of analysis to the original or "genetic" situation.[14] Everyone agrees that $-A \neq A$. The question concerning difference is its relation to identity. Fichte accepts the modern logician's view that no proof for the validity of $-A \neq A$ is available. If there were such a proof, it would have to be derived from $A = A$, which *is primus inter pares* among our logical principles. But this is impossible, because negation cannot be derived from affirmation alone. Negation, in contemporary terminology, is a *primitive operation,* or, as Fichte expresses it, $-A$ stands to A as opposition to position. If $-A$ could be derived from A alone, opposition, or the specific formal character of negation, would be indistinguishable from position (affirmation). This conclusion (2.21–22; 102–03) must be stressed, because the step from Fichte to Hegel turns upon its denial. I therefore anticipate a later discussion. From a Hegelian standpoint,

14. The term *genetic* is employed regularly in the *Wissenschaftslehre* of 1804 to refer to the constituting activity of the Absolute Ego.

Fichte's logic is not genuinely dialectical because, despite its reliance upon the activity of an Absolute Ego, there is no continuity of development. The "spontaneity" of the Fichtean Ego is discontinuous, as is evident in the separation between identity and difference. One could say that Fichte has two different senses of negativity, of which the first is conventional or static and the second is unnoticed. This duality goes back to the Platonic-Aristotelian heritage, where negation qua "otherness" or "privation" cannot be invoked to explain the difference between two generic forms. Or again, Fichte fails to make a dialectical interpretation of the Platonic "otherness," which contains the clue to the identity of identity and difference.

To return to Fichte's analysis, the nondeducibility of negation from affirmation means that the form of the principle of difference is independent of the form of the principle of identity. It is a possible activity of the ego, and not grounded through any higher principle (2.22; 103). On the other hand, the content of the principle of difference (*A*) is clearly dependent upon the principle of identity, and therefore upon the self-conscious structure of the ego (I = I). In order to oppose *—A* to *A*, we must first pose *A* and certify it as the self-identical object of reflection within the negative and affirmative constituents of the principle of difference. We have already seen that the posing of *A*, as well as its identification, depends upon, or takes place within, the ego. The posing ego is identical to the reflecting ego: I = I (2.23; 103 f.). However, we recall that *this* identity is not licensed by an antecedent capacity which is accessible to analytic intelligence. I = I, as Fichte will later express this, is an *image* of the unity of the Absolute Ego, the pure spontaneous activity which expresses and therefore conceals itself as the identity of positing and reflecting. The formula I = I is *already* a product of reflection: the ego cannot "identify" itself except by posing itself as subject and object. "I am originally neither the reflecting nor the reflected, and neither is defined by the other, but I am *both in their unification*, which unification I cannot indeed think, precisely because in thinking, I separate the reflected and the reflecting." [15] Whereas Fichte can distinguish between original and image, he is no more able than Plato to bring the original within the domain of theoretical science. This step is taken only by Hegel.

In any event, Fichte explains the transition from position to opposition as grounded in the identity of the ego. There is a material connection between *A* and $-A$; in both cases, the *A* is the result of the ego's activity. The unity of identity and difference is not formal but inheres in the ego as acting. The unity of activity accounts for the identity *and* difference linking *A* to $-A$. However, the discontinuity of the formal elements of position and negation underlines the inaccessibility to analysis of this unity. The closest we come to representing it is by *A*, which obviously says nothing at all. The step to Hegel requires an account of the unity of identity and difference, an account which must turn upon the dialectical connection between position and negation. Since Fichte is unaware of this dialectical connection, he cannot explain why or how the ego moves from *A* to $-A$.[16] This "transition" is in fact the Parmenidean *Nichts* of the previous chapter. And since the Absolute Ego is defined solely as pure activity, it, or Absolute Being, is in Fichte the same as *Nichts*. Again, it will remain for Hegel to explain the sameness of Being and *Nichts* as pure negative activity, or the reciprocal determination of position and negation.

In the present context, Fichte argues that, just as $A = A$ is grounded in $I = I$, so $-A \neq A$ must be grounded in $-I \neq I$, or the opposition of the ego and non-ego (2.24; 104). In other words, since the original act of self-consciousness, upon which everything else is founded, amounts to the assertion "I am," the "posing" of negation can only be understood originally as the "opposing" of the non-ego to the ego. However, since whatever is posed, is posed within the ego, the same must be the case for the non-ego. The object opposed to the subject by the activity of reflection is both the same as (= posed within)

15. "Zweite Einleitung," p. 76; *Science of Knowledge*, p. 60.

16. Cf. *Wissenschaftslehre* (1794), pp. 80 f., 97; *Science of Knowledge*, pp. 149 f., 163 f.

and other than the self-identical subject, whose identity is connected to or determined by its opposition to the object (which, in the original case, I = I, is the subject itself). In other words, *we have a discontinuous continuity of the principles of identity and difference.* On the one hand, there is the self-conscious version of the synthetic unity of apperception, which holds together identity and difference within itself as activity. On the other hand, the antithetical articulation of subject and object in the case of difference or opposition can be explained neither by way of identity nor on the basis of synthetic unity (the original instance of identity). In simple and accurate language, Fichte offers us an explanation of why reflection or analytical thinking is grounded in the identity-structure of self-consciousness. But he offers no explanation as to how the self-conscious ego is able to go outside itself or to pose (= think) the objective world as external (= opposed) to itself. This is why Hegel takes Fichte to be a *subjective* Idealist, or one for whom the object is opposed to the subject within subjectivity itself. Fichte does not seem to be able to avoid the charge of solipsism; in Hegelian language, there is no genuine externalization of Spirit as nature.

Fichte himself puts the point in this way: whereas no deduction can be given of the principle of identity with respect either to form or to content (since both originate in the spontaneous self-posing of the ego), the content of the principle of difference is shown to be equal to the non-ego. But this, we may add, is the result of two separate steps: the unity of content and the spontaneous negation of that content in the principle of difference. No deduction has taken place of the second from the first principle, whether with respect to form or to content. In any case, Fichte claims, now that we have *two* principles, the deduction of a third is possible: namely, a third which is formally conditioned by the two principles already discovered (3.26; 106). In order to explain Fichte's meaning, I shall deviate slightly from his own order of argument. Our results thus far may be summarized as follows. The original content ("I am") is differentiated by two forms, identity and negation or difference, which occur spontaneously as position and opposition. Since the content is the same in all cases, it contributes nothing to a deduction of a principle which reconciles identity (position) and negation or difference (opposition). On the other hand, since identity and negation both occur within the unity of content, this is tantamount to the assertion that the *unity* of content reconciles the two formal elements. We are very close to Schelling's doctrine of an "indifference-point" between subject and object, or in other words, to the notion of a "One differentiating itself" which we discussed previously. But this notion cannot achieve the status of a proof or deduction unless the "One" or *unity* in question is intelligible independently of identity and negation. According to Fichte, such intelligibility is out of the question, since to understand is to *divide* a unity. We can say "the One is identity and negation," but this already conceals unity by expressing it as a synthesis of position and opposition (or of thesis and antithesis).

For this reason, a "deduction" of the third or comprehensive principle is possible only in the sense that we can define the infinite task facing intellectual activity (3.26; 106). If every object is posed within a subject or ego by the ego itself, and since all objects other than the original object (in the case of self-consciousness) are, as other, equal to the non-ego, then we may formulate the third principle as follows: the ego opposes within itself a divisible non-ego to a divisible ego (3.30; 110). The pure spontaneous activity of the self-conscious synthetic unity of apperception takes the original (self-concealing) form (= image) of a reciprocally determining ego and non-ego, the borders of which vary from case to case. Thinking is thus visible as *judging:* the Absolute Ego presents itself in an infinite series of images, each of which divides the presentation into finite ego and finite non-ego. Fichte calls this the principle of the ground: opposites are unified within the Absolute Ego. This is the reinterpretation of the traditional principle of contradiction. To assert the principle is to contradict it. Unfortunately, the unintelligibility of the Absolute Ego leaves the contradiction-by-assertion of the principle of contradiction hanging in the void or *Nichts.* It possesses significance only as a *Sollen* or infinite "project" for analytic thinking. The project can be finally accomplished only by an eventual act of force of Reason, that is, a leap over the discursive understanding and its finite beings into the *Nichts* of the Absolute: into the *unity* of the "One differentiating itself." So long as we remain within analytic thinking, every "step" in our demonstration of original unity will be accomplished only by the posing of a new subject-object opposition.

According to the principles of identity and difference, the non-ego is both opposed to and posed within the ego. The assertion of the two principles is thus equivalent to their cancellation (*Aufhebung*). Our task is to find a principle which expresses the preservation of the identity of self-consciousness despite its internal contradictions. This principle is the consequence of an activity *X* which unifies the oppositions in question. The ego and non-ego are produced by *X*, which is the activity of the original or spontaneous self-posing of the ego (3.26–27; 106–07). More precisely, the Absolute Ego spontaneously poses itself by an original activity of limitation, designated as *Y*. The limit which results from this activity is *X*, or the boundary, in any manifestation of *Y*, between the reciprocally determined ego and non-ego (3.28; 107–08). The reason for the distinction between *Y* and *X* is to establish the character of reflective analysis as produced by an activity which is itself inaccessible to reflection. Reflection divides (= judges) the *Y*-activity into an ego and a non-ego, separated by a limit *X*, which is thus an image in analytic terms of *Y*. Since *X* is the act by which I pose myself as a finite, reflecting ego, and since *X* is "actualized" by the Y-activity, which acts *as X*, the act by which I pose myself is the same as the activity by which the Absolute Ego poses me (3.29–30; 109).

We see here the result of a line of development from Aristotle via Neo-Platonism to Spinoza and Kant. The principle of contradiction (as the comprehensive form of analytic thinking) and the doctrine of "thought thinking itself" combine to provide the structure of self-consciousness. The intelligibility of the principle of contradiction is the clue for its *Aufhebung* or interpretation at a higher, more comprehensive level. The principle of contradiction is not rejected but given an immanent explanation. In thinking itself, thought is both subject and object, thesis and antithesis, affirmation and negation, or identity and difference. In Fichte, however, the last step has not yet been taken. Since Fichte regards affirmation or identity and negation as detached, independent forms, he cannot provide an analytic account of his own hypothesis about their systematic or deductive relation. The thought which thinks itself is therefore concealed by itself as the consequence of that thought. This thought is the Parmenidean "One itself" or *Nichts:* it is Spinoza's "god or substance," hidden within his attributes, which are in turn visible only as modes. There is a final consequence to be drawn from this line of development. If thought "predicates" *P* and non-*P* of itself in thinking the subject-object structure of reflection, then *P* and non-*P* are *essentially the same. P* is essential to the definition of non-*P,* and vice versa. If we conceive of this "essence" as pure negative activity, then the fact that there is "nothing" between *P* and non-*P* does not mean that they are annihilated. It means rather that to pose one is to pose the other. In short, Fichte's Absolute Ego is now explained as the process of position-opposition-assimilation itself. This process cannot be separated from its products because the products are not separate (although they are distinguishable) from the process and from each other. "The true is the Whole." And the Whole is a continuum-process, or the sameness of Being and Thinking. Since Thinking is pure negative activity, the sameness of Being and Thinking is also the identity-within-difference of Being and Nothing. Hegel thus arrives at his understanding of the Whole as the "One differentiating itself" by solving the riddle of the Parmenidean *Nichts.*

HEGEL'S ANALYSIS OF REFLECTION: THE OVERCOMING OF NIHILISM

Hegel does not claim to have "invented" a new philosophical position but rather to have accomplished the completion of the history of Western philosophy. This is why it is essential to discuss so many of Hegel's predecessors. In our study of these predecessors from Parmenides to Schelling, we have been assimilating specific elements in Hegel's own science of wisdom. This history corresponds to the logical development of the concept of the Absolute Idea.[17] We are now prepared to analyze the main points of Hegel's treatment of reflection. Fichte's interpretation of the three fundamental principles of discursive thought shows both the necessity to unite identity and difference in a comprehensive ground and the impossibility of doing so in the terms of traditional logic. The core of the problem lies in Fichte's "classical" attitude toward negativity, or in his acceptance of the finite, separate, self-identical, and stable formal monad. In Hegel's language, Fichte remains faithful to the logic of understanding; he does not move significantly beyond Kant, for whom a "logic" of reason is "dialectical" in the pejorative sense of the term. Reason is indeed dialectical and negative because it dissolves the fixed definitions of the logic of understanding. But it is speculative and positive because it creates the universal from the elements of dissolution. The concept is constructed as a continuous totality by the pure negative activity of Absolute Spirit; and this is the "absolute method" of knowledge.[18] A genuinely philosophical method requires knowledge of the inner self-excitation of the content of form. And this depends upon knowledge that the negative is also positive, or that contradiction does not annihilate its terms but only their particularity (1 : 35–36; 54). The task of speculation is to see the unity of opposites (1 : 38; 56).

It should go without saying that for Hegel, "method" is equivalent to the science of logic as a whole. Nevertheless, the crux of the logic is the doctrine of pure negative activity, and Hegel analyzes this in the central section of the *Science of Logic*. The *Logic* is divided into three books: *Being, Essence,*

17. *Einleitung in die Geschichte der Philosophie* (Hamburg, Felix Meiner Verlag, 1959), p. 34.

18. *Logik,* 1 : 6–7; *Logic,* p. 28. The first set of numbers in parentheses in the text refers to volume and page of the German edition of this work. The second number refers to the English translation, fully cited in chap. 1 n. 23.

and *Concept*. Despite Hegel's regular insistence upon the identification between the history of philosophy and the stages of conceptual development, it would be dangerous to take him too literally on this score. Hegel understands the history of philosophy in a cyclic as well as a linear or chronological sense. Whereas his own logic is intended as a comprehensive conceptual analysis of the history of philosophy, his standpoint is not chronological but that of God "as he is in his eternal essence before the creation of nature and of finite spirit (1 : 31; 50). Since the eternal is complete and present implicitly in each moment of temporality, one or another of its aspects may become visible to mortal thinkers at various times. I do not deny, of course, that Hegel claims a kind of regular development in the history of philosophy; I rather add the qualification that there are cycles of repetition within this development. With this proviso, it can be said that, very generally, Book One of the *Logic,* or *Being,* corresponds to the period of philosophy stretching from the Greek origins to the emergence of modern science in Newtonian calculus and mechanics. Book Two, or *Essence,* corresponds approximately to the period from Spinoza to Schelling. Book Three, or *Concept,* is more difficult to characterize in these terms. The analysis of essence is intended to show the process by which classical dualism leads to the development of subjectivity, which is completed in Hegel's logic. The completion amounts to the overcoming of *subjectivism* by a genuine reconciliation of subject and object in the concept, which is thus total self-consciousness or self-knowledge: Spirit "grasping" (a sense contained in the German word for conceiving, *begreifen*) itself in the Absolute Idea. In a real sense, then, Book Three, which has as its full title *Science of Subjective Logic or the Doctrine of the Concept,"* recapitulates all of Books One and Two (which make up the "objective" logic) from a higher standpoint. Nevertheless, this standpoint is obviously that of Hegel himself, or the final stage of the history of philosophy.

Our general concern is with the logic of essence. Essence is "the truth of Being." The German word for "essence," *Wesen,* is derived from the past participle of the verb "to be" (*Sein*).

As Hegel says, however, essence is the "accomplished" (literally, "past": *vergangene*), "but atemporally accomplished Being" (2 : 3; 389). This is because the historical achievement is itself an exhibition of the process of the Absolute. There is a serious difficulty here, to which we shall return at a later stage of our analysis. For the moment, suffice it to say that, in the development of Being, the mainspring of the dialectic has been the excitation of unity and multiplicity, or of identity and difference. This excitation is one of separation (the classical ontology of form), albeit of separation attempting to achieve unification (the classical doctrine of thinking). In Hegel's language, the stage of Being is characterized by a separation between the "in-itself" and the "for-itself." These terms correspond approximately to "identity" and "difference." Being-in-itself is a unity; yet every attempt to think or describe that unity leads to the dualisms of reflection. By seeking itself reflectively (as it is for-itself), Being (in the form of the thinker) separates itself from what it is in-itself. In order to bring together the in-itself and the for-itself, we require a reconciliation of identity and difference within the ground, or correctly understood principle of contradiction, which is, needless to say, Absolute Spirit. When this is achieved, Being may be said to have recollected itself, or accomplished its truth. This accomplishment may also be described as the reconciliation of essence with its appearances, or the transition from Being to existence, and thus to actuality. Only then, when Being is understood as a totality, can the final stage of conceptual self-knowledge occur. Only then is the truth of Being rendered wholly accessible to Thinking. Thus the final reconciliation of subject and object depends upon the identity of identity and difference (2 : 5–6; 390–91).

The book on essence is subdivided into three major parts: "Essence as Reflection into Itself," "Appearance," and "Actuality." We shall be concerned here with the first part only. In this part, there is again a tripartite division, with chapters entitled "Illusion," "The Essentialities or Determinations of Reflection," and "The Ground." The reflection of essence into itself is the process by which the fundamental dualism of

Being leads to the negation of the significance of both elements in the dyad. The "substance" of modern philosophy "underlies" appearances as their ground or essence. However, substance in itself is unknowable and invisible. It is nothing, or the Parmenidean *Nichts*. But if the essence of appearance is nothing, then appearance is itself emptied of significance. Hegel calls this "illusion," which in German (*Schein*) also carries the meaning of "shine": in this case, almost like the colloquial English "moonshine," or in a more somber vein, the "shining" blackness of *Nichts*. In historical terms, the unknown substance of Locke becomes the unknowable thing-in-itself of Kant. "Being" is then understood as the presence of absence. Kant's "intelligible world," or the Fichtean domain of reflection, is an illusory manifestation of what is in itself the self-negation of consciousness. As Hegel puts it, "The shining of essence in itself is reflection" (2 : 7; 394). In other words, since the subject of modern philosophy sees himself only as conditioned by an object, and since that object is at once "subjective" (an aspect of the self-limitation of the subject) and "objectifying" (because it conceals the essential subject behind the finite properties or predicates of analysis), the subject sees a reflection of himself which is also an illusion. Hegel calls this illusion "reflected immediacy," and adds that it is "the phenomenon of Skepticism, or also the appearance of Idealism" (2 : 9; 396).

Hegel's deprecatory terminology should not disguise the crucial importance of this step in his analysis. I remind the reader of the general context: modern philosophy terminates in nihilism, or the reciprocal negation of essence and appearance (identity and difference). Since the "essence" of an illusion is itself illusory, there is no difference between the two. The "given" is not merely grounded in but is itself nothing. The identity and difference of the modern subject-object relation are grounded in a reciprocally annihilating contradiction. In Hegelian language, illusion (whose essence is negative) is *the negation of negation*. Becoming (the Whole of illusion) is a process in which each moment emerges *from* nothing, negates its predecessor by showing itself *as* nothing, and in the very act of appearing, disappears or returns *into* nothing (2 : 11–13; 387–99).

Allow me to paraphrase this initially peculiar formulation as follows. Let us assume the worst, namely, that human experience lacks all substance, or is an illusion in the sense that it implies a deeper meaning where none exists. When we discover this fact, our initial inclination is to despair, or to lapse into one species or another of nihilism. However, it is possible to understand the absence of a "deeper" meaning in a positive sense. Were there such a meaning, it would necessarily be separate from experience, whether in the sense of "beyond," "beneath," or "behind" its appearances. But then the existence of a "deep" meaning *would itself produce nihilism.* (This is of course the view subsequently advocated by Nietzsche.) Since man can only experience what he experiences, the "deeper" meaning would be forever beyond his reach: it would amount to a *Nichts* which, since it is defined as the absent essence of experience, transforms experience, as the "appearance" of the "deeper" meaning, into illusion. Once we recognize that there is *no* deeper meaning, we are not condemned to regard our lot as an illusion, but are now freed *from* illusion, or enabled to regard our experience as the totality of significance. The rejection of the "deeper" meaning is thus the negation of negation, which does not annihilate but preserves both experience *and* meaning.

In my paraphrase, oversimplified as it is, I have gone beyond the passage in the text in order to emphasize its importance. The overcoming of nihilism depends upon the capacity of the negation of negation to preserve content, or to yield a genuine Whole, and not simply to establish an analytic sense of structure for the Whole qua *Nichts.* Whether the former is possible can scarcely be decided without a closer study of the latter. Let us be clear, however, that the structure Hegel has in mind is not quite so obscure as it may initially seem. I shall try to illustrate this with a pair of closely related examples that may already have occurred to the reader. The Whole or Absolute, which I previously defined as the activity represented in the principle of contradiction, shows itself fully, *as* activity, in

each moment it produces. Each moment is the grounded reconciliation of identity and difference. In slightly different terms, it is the simultaneous or antithetic relation of position and negation, which antithetic relation is the synthesis or negation of negation. Since the Absolute exhibits itself in each moment, or is itself the principle of individuation, it must itself possess the same structure as its moments. The Absolute acts by posing a moment (of whatever content) which, as posed (hence positive or determinate or identical to itself) thereby separates itself from the Absolute and from every other moment, or poses itself by negating itself. As in the case of the Spinozist maxim, "Every determination is a negation." To pose is to negate in the sense of separation from every other moment, and, as an affirmation of position, from the Absolute as that which affirms. However, in the determinate negation of the posed moment, the moment is preserved (as is *P* within non-*P*). The negative element of each moment is its union with the pure activity of the Absolute by which moments are posed. When one moment is replaced by another, it is not annihilated but returns to the Absolute which it has never totally left. There is an accumulation or enrichment of content, made possible by the continuity of negative activity. This continuity is the negation of negation.

Our first illustration of this process is the phenomenon of time. The fundamental structure of the temporal process is the emergence of a moment from an invisible or indeterminate source. The moment occurs, or poses itself; but in so doing, it is already disappearing not in the sense of annihilation, but in the sense of a negation which preserves it in the past. *The present moment of time occurs as that which is disappearing into the past, even as it is turning into the future.* In other words, the invisibility or indeterminateness of the source of time was due to our initial failure to notice that *time is its own source.* It does not emerge from a detached *Nichts* but contains Being and *Nichts* within its own activity. The flow of time is therefore both cumulative and circular. It is cumulative because there are ever more moments occurring. But it is circular because the process of accumulation or occurrence, represented by the structure "past-present-future," is always the same. Instead of time, we might also, and perhaps more adequately, turn to the second illustration: the process of genesis, or Becoming. Each moment of Becoming emerges from what is initially an invisible source, and it emerges as both decaying and giving birth to the next moment. Here we see more clearly than in the case of time that negation is not annihilation. The transformation of one moment into the next is not the annihilation of genesis up to that point but its continued presence, or continuous assimilation into the next moment. This continuous assimilation is precisely the continuity of genesis: the circularity or eternity of itself as process. The Whole is present in each moment, albeit we, whose lives are temporal, require a "stretch" of moments from which to comprehend the structure altogether. Again, what seemed to be an invisible source was in fact the result of our failure to see that genesis "produces" itself.

Becoming does not emerge from Nothing (*Nichts*) or from Being, but it contains both together as the identity of identity and difference. There is, then, never a transition "taking place" from Being to Nothing and thence to Becoming; instead, such a transition has *already* taken place relative to any moment which we choose: the transition is continuously occurring.[19] This is Hegel's solution to the dilemma of the Parmenidean *Nichts*. Hegel's doctrine is "Platonic" to the extent that Nothing is indeed the "otherness" of Being, or its *dynamis* for self-differentiation. Thus Hegel denies a creation *ex nihilo:* the world is always present to, and so inseparable from, its creator.[20] But Hegel's doctrine is "Christian" be-

19. Cf. H. G. Gadamer, *Hegels Dialektik*, p. 61.

20. This point is one of the most difficult in Hegel's entire teaching. Whereas Hegel never (to my knowledge) denies it, he does not, as I shall argue in my conclusion, defend it in a consistent manner: cf. below, p. 266. M. Theunissen, *Hegels Lehre vom absoluten Geist als theologisch-politischer Traktat* (Berlin, Walter de Gruyter, 1970), contradicts himself on this point (which is central to his overall argument). He does not seem to notice the inconsistency of attributing to Hegel a doctrine of a God who is always distant from the world (p. 119), while also accepting that there is no separation of the *ewige Insichsein* and the created world (pp.

cause the presence of the world (object) to its creator (subject) is the eternal structure of self-consciousness. In the terms of Hegel's logic, this structure is the negation of negation. The phrase itself obscures the presence of content or position from the start. Just as the science of logic begins necessarily with Being rather than with Nothing, so the first negation is a determination of initial positive content. Just as Being and Nothing determine each other eternally in Becoming, so the second negation preserves the positive and negative aspects of the first negation. The self-consciousness of Becoming, understood as the negation of negation, is thus the immanent interpretation, or *absolute reflection,* of the principle of contradiction. And Becoming is necessarily self-conscious, since otherwise the subject and object would separate; the human capacity to think beings would be inexplicable.

Hegel's procedure is similar to that of Greek dialectic in its reliance upon the *reductio ad absurdum*. His dialectic looks excessively odd to the beginner because, whereas Greek rationalism justifies the *reductio* argument by reference to the principle of contradiction, Hegel applies the *reductio* to the principle itself. Hegel insists that Being and Thinking are both internally contradictory, and that the opposition in each case is the pure negative activity of Absolute Spirit, which therefore holds each together by identifying them with respect to their *actuality*. This means that, whereas Being provides the content of each moment of Becoming, the "activity" or excitation of this content, and so its dialectical capacity to assimilate content, whether of distinct generic form or of a contrary nature, arises from "otherness" or Nothing. If such a distinction is legitimate in the present context, then Being is "passive," whereas Nothing is "active." In post-Hegelian philosophy, this distinction leads to the priority of possibility to

---

247 ff.). Theunissen sees Hegel as an orthodox Lutheran, yet often cites texts which contradict this interpretation (cf. pp. 370 ff). Theunissen argues that Hegel retains the Christian eschatology, even while citing Hegel to the effect that the future divine realm *has already begun*. For the correct interpretation of Hegel's "eschatology," see P. Cornehl, *Die Zukunft der Versöhnung* (Göttingen, Vandenhoeck und Ruprecht, 1971), pp. 141–49.

actuality. For Hegel, of course, such a priority is senseless, given the eternal actuality of the Whole as Becoming. Nevertheless, I think it is true that Nothing has a certain priority of status in Hegel's teaching. The positive aspect of determinate form is derived from Being, and, apart from Nothing, it would be inert or as stable as Greek form. The negative excitation of form is the presence within human experience of Absolute Spirit, or the pure negative activity which posits and negates but which can do this because it is itself *formless*, like Aristotle's "thought thinking itself."

Perhaps it is this priority of Nothing that has led some of the best students of Hegel to criticize him on the ground that the negation of negation erases content or is unable to accumulate it.[21] In my view, the criticism seizes upon a genuine difficulty, but from the wrong end. The negation of negation does not cancel its content but holds it together, as becomes much easier to see when we drop Hegel's terminology and consider it as the activity of a divine intelligence. The problem lies rather in the total presence of content within the divine intelligence throughout eternity. The negation of negation is the pure negative activity of the One differentiating itself into a continuum of onto-noetic "places" for content. But this activity does nothing to render intelligible what Hegel insists upon as *the necessary order of development* of this content. Since I shall have to return to this criticism on more than one occasion, I state it here in an introductory manner. I suggest that Hegel cannot demonstrate, whether with respect to logic or to history, his central contention that the activity of thinking (in its theoretical or practical manifestations) proceeds necessarily from Being and Nothing through Becoming in the precise sequence of steps as articulated in the *Logic*. We have to distinguish between a logical recipe for making the world and the activity by which the world is made. Since every category of the Whole is simultaneously present in each of its moments, or since the essence of time is eternity, the logician might at any moment begin with *any*

21. E.g. D. Henrich, *Hegel im Kontext*, pp. 95 ff.; P. Rohs, *Form und Grund*, in *Hegel Studien, Beiheft* 6 (1969) : 258.

category, and so move "backward" or "forward" along the perimeter of the circle of wisdom (to use Hegel's own metaphor). Of course, after the logician has thought through the Whole, it might be possible for him to analyze the logical results in the form of a systematic deduction. But this would be to separate form from content in a way which Hegel cannot condone. The demonstration of a logical system is not the same as a demonstration of *eternal history*. How can there be an order in the process of creation if that creation is eternal, that is, simultaneous, or Whole from "moment" to "moment" of eternity? If this objection is sound, then it no longer makes sense to explain human history as developing in the same order as eternal history. Let us bear this in mind as we return to Hegel's analysis of reflection.

Identity, Difference, and Contradiction

I interrupted the order of Hegel's exposition for some general remarks which may lessen the feeling of strangeness (not to say alienation) that an initial contact with his logic is liable to produce. At least such was their intention. In my paraphrase, I covered the essential points of Hegel's explanation of Becoming (apart from all question of content) as negative process (2 : 13–23; 399–408). The positing of a moment of this process as the negation of its source presupposes and returns to it in and through its negativity. Hegel calls these three steps positing, external, and determining reflection. Determining reflection, as the unity of the first two, corresponds to the negation of negation. In this context, Hegel distinguishes between two senses of "negation": quality and reflection. Quality is "negation simply as affirmative," or the identity of a thing as different from everything else. Reflection is "positedness as negation," or the pure negative process of Becoming, independent of any specific content, which is the life-pulse of the Absolute (2 : 20–23; 405–08). This distinction corresponds to the previously mentioned distinction between non-being qua otherness, and the Parmenidean *Nichts*. In Hegel, however, they are ultimately the same: pure negative activity is visible in the world as the "affirmative negation" of qualitative determinateness.

We turn now to Hegel's interpretation of the "determinations of reflection," or identity, difference, and contradiction. Since Hegel explains contradiction as equivalent to Leibniz's law of the ground, it is obvious that, in this section, the argument amounts to a criticism of Fichte. Whereas identity and difference may be symbolized as usual by $A = A$ and $-A \neq A$, the law of contradiction or the ground requires a fuller statement: A and $-A$ constitute an opposition which must have a ground. In Fichte, the ground is invisible. A and $-A$ are separated by nothing, yet by a "nothing" so static that it is unable to relate or contrast the two terms. Hegel will try to show that the three principles of discursive thinking correspond to the three aspects of determinate reflection: origin, position, and return. Stated more fully, the dialectical motion from identity via difference to contradiction will be shown to correspond to pure essence externalizing or "appearing" as a determinate moment (position), which, as opposed to essence, is both positive (self-identical) and negative (different from essence). But, as self-identical, the positive moment is precisely a moment of negativity (its essence is pure negativity): as positive, it is negative; but as negative, or different from essence, it is the same as, and in this sense "returns to," essence. The opposition of position and negation expresses itself *as* it "returns into its ground" (2 : 23: 409).

Hegel fleshes out this rather abstract schema by operations upon identity and difference themselves. He first observes that there is something arbitrary in the designation of identity, difference, and contradiction alone as universally applicable. For example, since Aristotle's categories, still accepted by Kant and Fichte, specify properties or predicates of being, each could be taken to assert a necessary law of thought. But the main point is that no set of "laws" can be selected as independent axioms from which the rest of logic follows deductively. The contemporary logician might be inclined to agree that there is something arbitrary about our choice of axioms. Hegel goes farther: all laws or axioms are interconnected by pure negative activity in such a way as to be continuously turning into each other.

Hegel provides the following anticipatory illustration of his main argument. If $A = A$ is taken separately as a universal law of thought, that is, if everything is self-identical, that property in itself excludes difference. The result is a universe of nonarticulated monads, each indistinguishable from the others. Hence each collapses into the others, and the result is *A*, or the Parmenidean One, which cannot be distinguished from *Nichts*. On the other hand, if we assert separately $-A \neq A$, then no two things are the same, in which case there is no basis for them to be compared or related. A universe of radically disjunct monads, however, provides no basis for distinguishing one from the other. In historical terms, the doctrine of atoms in the void is indistinguishable from the Parmenidean One of which it is the intended multiplication. We cannot assert the non-identity of *A* and $-A$ except on the basis of the identity of the two *A*s. In the Fichtean analysis, the sameness of content is distinct from the difference of form. But the law $(-A \neq A)$ itself asserts that no two things or instances of content are identical. In other words, only because form and content are not detachable from each other in the Fichtean manner can the law be asserted at all. The law contradicts itself, or asserts simultaneously that $A = A$ and $-A \neq A$. In this contradiction is expressed the law of contradiction or ground: *identity and difference are identical-within-difference*. Fichte could not achieve this formulation as a unity of opposites, but it remained for him a goal infinitely distant from discursive or logical thinking. Fichte's failure, as we have seen at sufficient length, was due to his misunderstanding of negativity or reflection. For Hegel, however, wherever we begin in the assertion of a logical law, we engender a contradiction or return to the origin of the separated moments of reflection in such a way as to join them without erasing their distinct determinations. The law of contradiction is thus revealed as the grounded ground, that is, the Whole (2 : 25; 411).

This illustration makes sufficiently clear Hegel's analysis of identity. I therefore turn directly to some aspects of his analysis of difference. In order to identify anything, we must distinguish it from everything else. *A,* taken by itself, cannot be identified because it is not distinguished in any way, or is indifferent to difference. In order to identify *A* even with itself, we must distinguish it from itself as what Hegel calls the "pure other" with which we are identifying it. *A*'s indifference to difference is thus already the seed of the negation of negation: it constitutes the *instability* of the ostensibly stable formal monad. I repeat: the Fichtean *A* is distinguished with respect to form and content. The content is then joined with the (positive) form in an inexplicable manner, even though both are consequences of the activity of Absolute Spirit (in the Hegelian terminology). The Hegelian *A,* however, is already a union of form and content; since this union is itself negative activity, *A* is at once *–A*. Difference qua difference, or what Hegel calls "absolute difference," is the same negativity of reflection as identity qua identity. Hegel puts this in his usual crabbed way, but we should be able to discern his meaning: "The *other of essence* . . . is the other in and for itself, not the other as other of another existent outside itself" (2: 33; 417). I paraphrase: essence or pure negative activity externalizes or becomes other than itself in its appearances, even while remaining the same as itself. For Hegel, difference, as difference of itself from itself (that is, the self-differentiating One), is not different from identity. The two are one in the third of "the essential nature of reflection and . . . the specific, original ground of all activity and self-movement" (ibid.).

Hegel turns next to an analysis of *diversity,* or the separate moments of the continuum of identity and diversity. Diversity is the difference of external reflection. In other words, identity and difference are not yet thought as dialectically the same; this is the stage of Kantian and Fichtean rationalism. Identity and difference are externally determined; each is related to the other as distinct from it. Each is therefore both like and unlike the other. This instability takes the following shape.

In themselves, the diverse moments are indifferent to each other. Relations of identity and difference, or of like and unlike, are imposed upon them by an external observer. The instability of these external relations is equivalent to subjectivism. The observer "divides and collects in accordance with kinds," but the "kinds" are subjective constructions. The likeness of the like comes not from itself but from the observer, to whom it is itself unlike. Or, rather, it is like the observer who furnishes likeness but not like itself, since it has no self except for what it receives externally. The same analysis holds good for the unlike. Both "like" and "unlike" *are unlike themselves;* qua themselves, they are opposed to themselves (2 : 34–38; 418–21).

The moment of diversity thus moves internally from the separation of identity and difference to their connection by opposition. Each diverse moment is internally articulated by the antithetical dyad of position and negation. It is therefore a synthesis of the thesis (position) and antithesis (negation), or what Hegel called previously "determining reflection." Whereas the principle of diversity is intended to establish the stability of the finite, self-identical monad, Hegel has demonstrated its self-contradictory nature, or the intrinsic interconnectedness of the formal elements separated by Fichte. To give only the crucial instance: the affirmation of *A* is already the denial of $-A$, whereas the affirmation of $-A$ already affirms *A* in order to deny it (2 : 40–44; 424–27). Our study of difference, in short, is at the same time a study of identity and contradiction. I am well aware that to many readers this conclusion will seem like logical hair-splitting, or for that matter, sophistry. Before this opinion becomes hardened in the dubious reader's mind, I ask him to reconsider Hegel's conclusion in the light of my entire exposition, and especially as the immanent consequence of Hegel's critical interpretation of nondialectical logic and ontology.

For better or worse, Hegel is engaged in the philosophically necessary task of describing the horizon of discursive analysis in a way that begs no questions. His guiding insight is the self-contradictory nature of our experience, both in its parts and as a Whole. If I could express this in terms of a historical metaphor, the extraordinary character of the Platonic dialogues is that they give us a rationally constructed portrait of the Whole, yet no "interpretation" of a consistently discursive kind of this Whole. The attempt to submit Plato's dialogues to a rigorous interpretation leads almost immediately to contradiction, or what we may call the "thesis" and "antithesis" of the history of philosophy. I am suggesting that Plato is the "synthesis," but a *silent synthesis.* Hegel attempts to make this synthesis articulate. In slightly different terms, he tries to provide us with an absolute reflection upon the contradiction which is the underlying structure of the Platonic portrait of the Whole. In still another Platonic image, what may look to some as the "sophistical" character of Hegel's logic is due to the fact that the Whole, or Becoming, is itself a "Sophist." The Whole continuously changes its shape or pretends to be what it is not: it eludes every attempt by the nondialectical logician to "classify" it or to provide us with an analysis of its structure by the method of the division and collection in accordance with kinds. This is the comprehensive problem of Plato's *Sophist,* or rather, of his entire corpus. It is the problem which Hegel believed himself to have solved.

In Book One of the *Logic,* Hegel followed the procedures of a mathematical ontology by describing the structure of the Whole exclusively in terms of Being-Nothing-Becoming, or Quality-Quantity-Measure as the elements in the continuous process of appearance. He showed that such an account cannot "save the appearances," or explain the intrinsic nature of human experience. On the basis of this account, the following situation arises. The fundamental structure of the continuum (= the Whole) includes Being *and* Nothing, whether in the Platonic or Democritean (atoms and the void) sense of these terms. There is, then, "nothing" (*Nichts*) outside the continuum, because the "outside" is the externalization of the "inside." In the present context, this can be taken to mean that difference is necessarily contained within identity in a self-sufficient Whole: otherwise, philosophy is superseded by theology, or the Whole becomes either a part or a *deus ab-*

sconditus. On the other hand, the presence of difference within identity, as we have seen at length, cannot be explained by traditional logic. The very analysis of the continuum into "inside" and "outside" proceeds by reflection, or the abstraction of one aspect from the other. This process is absolutely necessary in order to conceptualize the details or elements of the process, but it has the undesirable consequence of "alienating" one element from the other in the consciousness of the reflecting logician. From the standpoint of God (which Hegel claims to be his own in the *Logic*), the separation of reflection is essential for the manifestation of the Absolute *as* its appearances. This manifestation is predicated upon an underlying community which we mortals must recover in order to achieve reconciliation with God. Unfortunately, by separating the "inside" from the "outside," we in effect hypostasize Nothing, which becomes *Nichts.* The process of manifestation now seems to transpire from an invisible source. We may refuse to pay any attention to the *Nichts,* ostensibly in obedience to the dictum of Parmenides; the result is both a loss of self-consciousness and a self-contradictory logic. Or we may treat the invisible source as an external ground rather than as a dimension of the process itself. Instead of grasping that "nothing outside" (*Nichts*) is the externalization of the pure negative activity (as the identity of identity and difference) of Absolute Spirit, we take it to be the external identity of an inner *Nichts.* One could perhaps call this *Seinsvergessenheit* (*the forgetting of Being*): by rendering *Nichts* substantial, we forget about the presence of essential Being within appearance itself. In this sense, Hegel attempts the "reappropriation" or "recollecting" of Being by an analysis of *Nichts,* and so its reformation as Nothing or as a dimension within the Whole. The coherence of the "inside" and the "outside" is then found within the shining of "appearance." This is how Hegel tries to save the appearances.

I summarize this reflection by returning to Hegel's treatment of contradiction. Identity and difference are inseparable but distinguishable features of opposition as the general characteristic of positing, or the manifesting of appearance, a positing which is, as such, a self-negation. Granting the thesis of radical skepticism, phenomenalism, and others that there is no substance or essence, Hegel arrives at his doctrine of contradiction as *the structure of the absence of essence.* In other words, an antimetaphysical empiricism itself furnishes us with the basis for proving the validity of Hegelian logic. On the basis of all that has gone before, we should now have no difficulty in following Hegel's discussion of contradiction. Since contradiction is the identity of identity and difference, we have in effect already mastered Hegel's doctrine of contradiction. Contradiction is the structure of positionality, since *A* can be posed only as opposed to $-A$. Which counts as positive and which as negative *depends upon one's position.* The total situation is both (and the element of totality is of course essential here to preserve Hegel from a vulgar relativism), and within both, each as itself and the other. But how each is "identified" within a given analysis depends upon the perspective of the analyzing consciousness. The Whole, as opposed to a perspective of the Whole, is self-contradiction. Like the Platonic Eros, it is that which ceases to be what it is, and is in the course of becoming what it is not (2 : 56; 438).

We can now state briefly how the study of reflection is in fact the study of pure negative activity. What is true of the Whole is true of any moment of the Whole. Each moment is posited and so other than its source; but as so posited, it returns to its source while being replaced by its successor or opposite, which is nevertheless structurally the same as it. The position of opposition is thus the destruction of opposition. The posited element returns to its ground or is *zugrunde gegangen.* The meaning of this German pun is that what looks like extinction is in fact a reunion of appearance and essence. This is the transition to the next section of the logic, which we shall not study here. Essence is the grounded ground, thanks to the accomplishment of absolute reflection. The Whole is a self-differentiating continuum of moments, each of which presents itself as what it is, but thereby as essentially related to what it is not. A moment is determinate, hence self-identical, precisely as exemplifying the excitation of the continuum or Whole which manifests that moment. The analysis of manifestation per se, or of appearance qua appearance, is also the critical assimilation of the Fichtean doctrine of reflection, and reveals the structure of identity-difference-contradiction that we have just studied.

6 From Logic to Phenomenology

The Relation between the *Phenomenology of Spirit* and the *Science of Logic*

In this chapter I propose to make a transition from the analysis of Hegel's logical doctrine to selected themes from his first major work, the *Phenomenology of Spirit*. Since the *Phenomenology* is normally regarded as the introduction to the science of wisdom, the reader may wonder why I have begun with the logic. The first task is therefore to consider the much-discussed question of the relation of the *Phenomenology* to Hegel's system. A closer acquaintance with Hegel's writings, to say nothing of the secondary literature, soon reveals that Hegel changed his mind about the function of the *Phenomenology* after its completion. This is evident from a comparison of the preface of the *Phenomenology* (written after the main text and intended as a preface to the entire forthcoming system) as first published in 1807 with a variety of later texts.[1] Hegel first speaks of the *Phenomenology* as follows: "This becoming of science in general or of knowledge, is that which this *phenomenology of Spirit* presents as the first part of the system of this science." Shortly before his death in 1831, Hegel was engaged in the preparation of a new edition of the *Phenomenology*. He then struck out the phrase "as the first part of the system of this science." At the same time, however, he left unaltered (in the course of revising for a new edition of his works) a passage in the *Science of Logic*, dating originally from 1812, in which he refers to the *Phenomenology* as "the science of appearing

1. Cf. P.-J. Labarrière, *Structures et mouvement dialectique dans la phénoménologie de l'esprit de Hegel* (Paris, Aubier-Montaigne, 1968), pp. 17 ff. For an exhaustive analysis of the problem, cf. H. F. Fulda, *Das Problem einer Einleitung in Hegels Wissenschaft der Logik* (Frankfurt, Vittorio Klostermann, 1965). See also O. Pöggeler, "Qu'est-ce que la 'Phénoménologie de l'Esprit'?" *Archives de Philosophie* (April–June 1966) : 189–236.

Spirit," the "presupposition" of the *Logic*.[2] Finally, we may refer to a passage from the *Encyclopedia*, published first in 1817 and for the last time in 1830, where Hegel says that the *Phenomenology* "was intended for this reason at its publication as the first part of the system of science," namely, to show the dialectic of Spirit "from its first, simplest appearance . . . up to the standpoint of philosophical science." But the very function of the *Phenomenology* prevents it from remaining "in the formal element of bare consciousness." The *Phenomenology* presents us with the development of the concrete forms of consciousness, for example morality, ethics, art, religion. This content is "presupposed" by the standpoint of philosophical knowledge. "The development of the *content* of the objects of the individual parts of the philosophical science falls therefore together in what seems at first the development of consciousness which is restricted to the formal. That development must proceed, so to speak, behind the back of the formal, insofar as the content relates to consciousness as the *in itself*. The exhibition becomes thereby more complex, and what pertains to the concrete parts partially coincides already with that introduction." [3] In other words, the *Phenomenology* is an introduction to the system or science of wisdom, of which logic is the first part.

In my opinion, the fair conclusion to be drawn from these passages (together with less important supportive texts) is that Hegel came to see the *Phenomenology* as a general introduction to the science of wisdom, even though not a part of the system itself. I therefore agree with scholars like Fulda and Labarrière, who insist that Hegel never "abandoned" the *Phenomenology* and continued until his death in the view that it was a work of philosophical importance. On the other hand, this does not solve the problem of whether, or to what degree, the *Phenomenology* is able to fulfill Hegel's intentions. These intentions, although clear with respect to the main point, leave room for conflicting interpretations on the exact sense of an "introduction" or "presupposition" to the science qua

2. *Logik*, 1 : 53; *Logic*, p. 68.

3. *Enzyklopädie*, p. 59 (par. 25); *Encyclopedia–Wallace*, pp. 58 f.

system. Let me illustrate this by means of another passage from the *Encyclopedia.* So far as the beginning of philosophy is concerned,

> it is the free act of thinking to place itself at the standpoint where it is for itself, and where it itself generates its object and presents it to itself. Furthermore, this standpoint, which thus seems to be immediate, must make itself into the *result,* and indeed, into the last result, of science, in which it achieves again its beginning and into which it returns. In this way, philosophy shows itself as a circle that returns into itself, which has no beginning in the sense of the other sciences; thus the beginning has reference only to the subject which will resolve itself to philosophize, and not however to science as such.[4]

As has been pointed out by H. Brockard among others, this could be understood to mean that there is no transition in the act of resolution by which we are transported to the level of the Absolute; but nothing rules out the obvious need for an introductory preparation that brings us to the point of resolution.[5] I agree with this judgment. If we take together the two passages just quoted from the *Encylopedia,* they say, although not with the clarity one might desire, that *logic* is the first part of the science of wisdom (a point that is clear from the organization of the content of the *Encyclopedia*), and that the individual cannot arrive at the standpoint of logic unless he has gone through a process which is described in the *Phenomenology.*

This is by no means the end of the matter, however. Given the "circularity" of science, or the need to reappropriate the content of the development of self-consciousness in the formal categories of the logic, it is obvious that this content is not fully intelligible in itself. As O. Pöggeler puts it:

> Phenomenology considers the spirit as consciousness. Consciousness and the being-in-itself of the ideal as it develops

4. Ibid., p. 50 (par. 17); *Encyclopedia–Wallace,* pp. 27 f.

5. H. Brockard, *Subjekt, Versuch zur Ontologie bei Hegel* (Munich and Salzburg, Verlag Anton Pustet, 1970), p. 61.

> in the system, are in reciprocal causality; the progress of the one is thus the progressive formation of the other. However, in the progressive formation of consciousness, in the phenomenology, one does not yet perceive the necessity of the progressive formation. This necessity is perceived only in the logic which arrives already from Absolute Spirit.[6]

I entirely agree with this part of Pöggeler's argument (which can be separated from his claim that Hegel changed his mind in the midst of composing the *Phenomenology* and never harmonized the two parts). There is, in other words, a difference between preparing oneself to engage in the science of wisdom, and in fact engaging in wisdom. But the crucial difficulty is now visible. Since the preparation for science is not itself scientific, or cannot be understood until we *acquire* (and not simply "begin") the science of wisdom, what is its connection with the act of resolution by which we seem to enter immediately into the circle of wisdom? Furthermore, since the immediacy of the beginning of science is only apparent, or is "in and for itself" the complete science of wisdom, and since this science is itself the reappropriation of the content of consciousness acquired during our preparation for the act of resolution, how can science itself take place? On the one hand, science has nothing to do with the prescientific. On the other hand, the prescientific is the *content* of science.

One could reply that after science "begins" the content is raised to the level of the Absolute by the development of form, so that the apparent separation of content and form is overcome. But this suggestion amounts to the assertion that the science of logic, and not the *Phenomenology,* is the ladder to the Absolute. First we accomplish the process of spiritual development as described in the *Phenomenology,* but *without understanding what we are doing.* This coincides with the interpretation of the history of philosophy, culminating in Kant, Fichte, and Schelling, as nihilism, or the negation of the initial position (the original philosophical "project" of

6. O. Pöggeler, "Qu'est-ce que la 'Phénoménologie de l'Esprit'?" p. 222.

Parmenides). The science of logic is then the negation of negation, or the assimilation upward (*Aufhebung*) of the nihilistic history of consciousness appearing to itself. It is the "positive" reinterpretation in and as the circle of wisdom of what, at the lower level, is a series of self-cancelling parts. One might argue further that the last chapter of the *Phenomenology*, "Absolute Knowledge," is the conclusion of our preparation for the journey upward, a "prophecy" of reconciliation rather than its accomplishment. I am myself very sympathetic to this suggestion. However, it still does not solve the dilemma of the connection between the *Phenomenology* and the science of wisdom, or logic, the first part of that science.

The difficulty now turns upon the distinction between phenomenological experience as the preparation for logic, and the comprehension that this experience is the preparation for logic. This difficulty has two aspects. First: once we have completed our phenomenological experience, how do we as "subjects" rise from the first to the second negation, that is, from the *Phenomenology* to the *Logic*? Obviously, we can do so only if we have properly understood our experience. There is no invisible historical necessity in Hegel, separate from the concrete thinking of individual human beings. But such an understanding is impossible without the knowledge of logic. Second, we may claim that the development recorded in the *Phenomenology* is not an "interpretation" but a scientific description of the process by which the human spirit evolves into the philosophical subject who finally raises himself up to the level of the Absolute. In this case, the structure of the *Phenomenology* must be identical with, albeit the temporal or historical manifestation of, the *Science of Logic*.[7] It therefore follows that we are within the circle of wisdom *from the outset*, but in this peculiar sense. As finite subjects, we develop from consciousness to self-consciousness, or to the recognition that the totality of human experience is self-contradictory. The completion of the historical development of self-consciousness is then nihilism, and we still require assistance external to the

7. A. Kojève, *Introduction à la lecture de Hegel* (Paris, Gallimard, 1947), p. 420.

ostensibly necessary phenomenological process in order to understand its significance, that is, to negate our negativity or rise to the Absolute. Or else our comprehension of nihilism is itself the negation of negation which raises us from phenomenology to logic. But this means that the comprehension of phenomenology is *identical* with the comprehension of logic. And this Hegel regularly denies.

The *Phenomenology* is "the science of appearing Spirit." In his *Logic,* Hegel discusses "appearance" as the stage intermediate between "the essence of reflection into itself" and "actuality." When we have completed our analysis of reflection, we see that "the essence must appear" or show itself in what was previously regarded as nonessential illusion. "Thus essence appears. Reflection is the shining of essence in itself," and again, it "is that which the thing-in-itself is, or its truth." As such, the enduring, manifest, existent "show" of essence, appearance is finally actuality.[8] The logical analysis of "appearance" must be completed in that of "actuality," in order to pass on to the final stage of logic: the development of the concept. The "science of appearing Spirit" is not yet the science of appearance. The same conclusion may be drawn from Hegel's remarks on time in the *Phenomenology:* "The whole Spirit only is in time, and the forms, which are forms of the whole Spirit as such, exhibit themselves in a succession; for only the Whole has genuine actuality, and thus the form of pure freedom as opposed to anything else, and it expresses itself as time." And again: "Time is the concept itself, which *is there*" [= exists]. . . . Therefore Spirit appears necessarily in time, and it appears for so long in time as it does not grasp its own pure concept, that is, as it does not annul time. . . . Time appears therefore as the fate and the necessity of Spirit, which is not completed in itself." [9]

The temporal appearance of Spirit is a mark of its incomplete self-comprehension. The totality of the appearance of Spirit to itself, *at any given stage of its development,* is actuality, or time as the existing concept. But the completion of the

8. *Logik,* 2 : 101 f.; *Logic,* pp. 479 f.

9. *Phänomenologie,* pp. 476, 558; *Phenomenology,* pp. 689, 800.

appearance of Spirit results in the annulling of time, or the negation of negation by which the stage of actuality is assimilated into the stage of the concept. Although the process of conceptualization undergoes a development, this "excitation" is not temporal but eternal. In other words, the process recorded in the *Phenomenology* must be recollected at the level of the *Logic.* Since the *Logic* proceeds, in Spinoza's phrase, *sub specie aeternitatis,* the transition here from appearance to the concept cannot be the same as the transition from religion to absolute knowledge within the *Phenomenology.* The science of appearance as a logical category is not the same as the science of Spirit in the temporal process of appearing to itself. The question therefore necessarily arises how Spirit knows that it has completed its temporal appearance, that is, how we can explain the transition from religion to absolute knowledge within the *Phenomenology* itself. The transition, as the culmination of experience, cannot be its own explanation; if it were, the *Logic* would be superfluous. This transition is made not by Spirit as appearing but by the Spirit which has completed its appearance, or already achieved the level of logic, in a way not explained by the phenomenological history of man. This Spirit is present in the *Phenomenology* as the reader's guide, leading him, more fully than Vergil led Dante, to a reappropriation and therefore an interpretation rather than a "scientific" description, of past human experience. The guide, of course, is Hegel himself, present somewhat ambiguously as the "we" within the narrative of the *Phenomenology* and unambiguously as the speaker of the monologue that is intended to prepare us for the science of wisdom.[10]

My conclusion, then, is that the *Phenomenology* is not genuinely intelligible without a knowledge of the *Logic.* As Hegel's Jena manuscripts make clear, he had already developed the main points of his logic by the time he composed the

10. This guide is Hegel's analogue to the unidentified guide in Plato's *Symposium* (210a4 ff.) who, according to Diotima, will lead the young man up from beautiful bodies to the beautiful itself. In each case, the guide must already have made the journey and subsequently descended to assist neophytes.

Phenomenology. In my opinion, this development was a result of Hegel's study of the history of philosophy, and especially of those figures whom we have analyzed in earlier chapters. Hegel no doubt convinced himself that what he had discovered from history was in fact the last step of a necessary historical process. He then wrote the *Phenomenology* in the quick inspiration peculiar to geniuses of the highest order, to demonstrate that human experience is the record of the progress of Spirit toward reconciliation with itself within Logos. Like other geniuses, however, in confusing himself with God he seems to have forgotten that only his individual presence, as one who has already taken the upward journey and has now descended to assist his lost fellow creatures, provides the necessary mediation between time and eternity. The ladder to the Absolute is not historical necessity, or even the negation of negation, but the spirit of the philosopher.

Time and Eternity

It is always unsatisfactory to be offered a psychological explanation for a philosophical difficulty. In order to give theoretical substance to my suggestion at the end of the previous section, I want to restate the problem which underlies the apparently biographical or philological question of the relation between the *Phenomenology* and the *Logic*. This is the problem of the relation between time and eternity in Hegel's science of wisdom. We recall the general terms of the difficulty. On the one hand, the structure of time is the same as that of eternity. On the other hand, whereas eternity is complete from the beginning, or a circular process of extra-temporal excitation, time must develop toward completion, in the sense that history is completed only by the completion of philosophy. The circularity of eternity, understood as absolute reflection, is necessarily present within each moment of time in its entirety. Since the circle of eternity is the Whole, it must encompass time as a whole. Eternity is altogether in time, and time is altogether in eternity. But time is the externalization of eternity, or the process of its appearance. The completion of eternity is therefore dependent upon the completion of *historical time*. This is clear from the fact that the actuality of Being and Thinking are the same. This actuality manifests itself to itself only in the mind or spirit of the individual who has achieved wisdom, and who therefore comprehends the truth of the identity of the actual and the rational. In short, whereas eternity is always complete with respect to time, the completion of eternity, as inclusive of history, is incomplete with respect to time, until the last epoch.

It should be mentioned that this problem is not simplified but made more pressing if we take the frequently suggested line of interpretation which denies the completion of history in wisdom. There are undoubtedly passages in Hegel which give some support to this interpretation, such as his references to the new life of Spirit following upon the accomplishment of wisdom, or his various remarks, usually in the "popular" lecture courses, on the next epoch of world-history.[11] I have already made evident my position on this issue. Whatever empirical history may bring, it will not include a new stage in the science of wisdom. To say otherwise is to deny the reconciliation between God and man upon which Hegel's entire science rests. In terms of the present section, the "openness" of the future means that the circle of eternity is broken, or transformed into a straight line, and thus a "bad infinity." In slightly more technical language, it means that absolute reflection is impossible. Each interpretation of historical time up to a given point (one's own epoch) deteriorates into a *Weltanschauung*, and Hegel's "wisdom" is transformed into the radical perspectivism of Nietzsche, for whom eternity is the temporal instant. Since Nietzsche's teaching is in Hegelian language a return to the intellectual intuition of Jacobi, Fichte, and Schelling, or an effort to transcend the divisiveness of reason in the unity of will, this strikes me as an unacceptable manner of reading Hegel.

If one is a "strict constructionist" with respect to the identity of time and eternity, Hegel's claims for his science of wisdom remain intelligible, however paradoxical. The paradox can be formulated in a way which is connected to, if not the same

11. *Phänomenologie*, pp. 476, 558; *Phenomenology*, pp. 689, 800.

as, Hegel's interpretation of the principle of contradiction. We begin again with the fact that the Absolute must be both eternal and temporal. What I have called the "formation-" or "pulsation-process" of the Absolute is always and everywhere the same. Nevertheless, this cannot be said of the consequences of that process. The circularity of the tripartite activity of position-negation-negation of negation serves, as we may put it, to preserve Becoming as a continuum of logical "places." But each of these places must be filled with logical content. Despite Hegel's regular insistence that the traditional distinction between form and content is inadequate and unstable, the fact remains, as we saw earlier in the reference to paragraph 25 of the *Encyclopedia,* that something similar obtains in his own science of wisdom. The process of filling with content the logical places on the continuum of Becoming is not simply identical with the process of keeping the continuum both "open" (to receive content) and "closed" (as circular or eternal). If these two processes were the same, there could never be any development in Hegel's Whole. Everything would be everywhere complete. Unfortunately for his interpreters, Hegel both affirms and denies the identity of these two processes. As we just saw, he insists that the Whole is everywhere complete, but that part of its completeness is to be developing toward completion within the domain of historical time.

We can put our question in two different ways. First, if divine and human "history" are the same, then must not the Whole, while it is unfolding toward its completion, be necessarily incomplete? In this case, must not each "moment" of reflection be internally dissolved, so as to produce an infinite multiplicity of discontinuous temporal instants? Second, if each negation of negation raises the antecedent position and negation to a higher or more comprehensive level, then how can the logical process be circular or history complete? Must not each successive mediation of the two preliminary stages be at a higher level than its predecessor?

There is at least a terminological distinction in Hegel which addresses itself to the second version of our two questions. One could say that the "completion" of history is not existential but logical. In the logical concept of the Whole, "incompleteness" is itself a necessary moment. However, we must distinguish within the nature of incompleteness between a *transition* (*Übergehen*) to some higher or more comprehensive stage of history, and a *development* (*Entwicklung*) of actuality within itself, as fully present or logically complete.[12] Nevertheless, granting that the actuality of eternity is a development rather than a transition, this does not explain the relationship between eternity and temporality within actuality itself. We might be tempted to suggest that eternity and temporality are the interior and exterior of a continuum which, as self-differentating Whole, is at once One and three. The crucial defect of such a suggestion, however, is that eternity is not the interior but the process as a Whole. It makes more sense to say that eternity actualizes as time or history, but again, the distinction between "transition" and "development" is left unexplained.

I think we can now see that at least part of this explanation must turn upon an *inversion relation* between eternity and time. In terms of a previous formulation, the Absolute is the "principle of individuation" which manifests itself *as* individual, and so is present in and as each individual. The temporal moment, truly or logically grasped (= conceived), *is* eternity; eternity, or the totality of the structures in the logical concept, *is* the temporal moment. Each "moment" is thus *self-contradictory*. There is in fact a certain similarity between Nietzsche and Hegel on this score. The "instant" may be understood as the gateway between eternity and temporality. However, in Hegel, we can only pass through the gateway on the basis of a total comprehension of historical experience; and once we have moved from time to eternity, we must "recollect" the thoughts of God (as recorded in the *Logic*) by thinking through the structure of eternity as the concept. It is no accident that both Hegel and Nietzsche were influenced by Heraclitus. However, Hegel's reconciliation of opposites is achieved by the hard work of conceptual thinking, whereas Nietzsche turns to a conception of cosmic play. The moment in

12. *Enzyklopädie*, pp. 140 (par. 142), 151 (par. 161); *Encyclopedia–Wallace*, pp. 257 f., 288 f.

Hegel is the exemplification of the "principle" of contradiction, and philosophy is transformed into wisdom by the process which renders this principle self-reflective. The self-contradictory nature of each moment also explains the instability of every partial resolution to the dualist problems of life, whether as theory or practice. The assertion of *P* is at once the assertion of non-*P*.

We are very far from having "solved" the problem of the relation between eternity and temporality. I shall have to return to this question in the conclusion to the present study. In this chapter, my goal is to provide an introductory analysis of the crucial element of the "inversion process," or in the language of the *Phenomenology,* of the dialectic of *the inverted world.* Such an analysis is essential for our understanding of the transition from logic to phenomenology; it helps to explain what I have been defending as the cognitive priority of logic to an understanding of the phenomenological process. The Absolute as the "gateway" or structure common to eternity and temporality is itself both eternal and temporal. Eternity is the *Aufhebung* of the eternal and the temporal, and therefore self-contradictory. But this contradiction is preservative rather than annihilating. In human terms, experience is both logical and historical. As a preparation for the analysis of the inverted world, I shall conclude this section with a summary restatement of the historical appearance of the logical excitation of reflection. This will also help us to understand the significance of the title *Phenomenology of Spirit.* To be able to give a *logos* of the *phenomena* requires the presence of logic within the phenomena; and this in itself is the minimal structure of the dialectic of the inverted world.

In human terms, wisdom "grows" with the spiritual history of the race. The growth of the Spirit, of course, is not the same as the body's growth. In an obvious sense, the human body has remained more or less the same, except for a limited increase in stature, throughout human history. But man's understanding has undergone an extraordinary transformation during that time. Consider as an example the previously mentioned thesis of the "mastery of nature." Man acquires dominance over his environment by understanding it.[13] This process of understanding is a necessary consequence of the initially hostile or intractable character of nature. Whereas the desire to exist, and hence to satisfy one's appetites, is natural, so too are the obstacles placed in the way of this satisfaction. Human (as opposed to merely animal) existence may be said to originate in the recognition of the *contradictoriness* of nature. This is the "existential" root of the logical principle of contradiction.[14] It is perhaps a trivial observation that man begins to die at the moment of his birth. The observation loses its triviality when we consider all of its implications. By a very slight exaggeration, we could say that the very circumstances upon which our existence depends are continuously striving to deprive us of our existence. Similarly, we maintain our existence only through the destruction of other living things. Whereas the process of absolute reflection is present in each instance as the individual person, the structure of "personality" is self-contradictory. This is why Hegel connects the discovery of self-consciousness with the struggle for recognition in the dialectic of master and slave.

The simple process of eating is already a paradigm of war. The "mastery of nature" is implicit in the desire to eat rather than be eaten. In order to satisfy this desire, intelligence is required. But the more we exercize our intelligence, the more sophisticated becomes our taste in food.[15] By the natural process of the satisfaction of physical appetites, which is rooted in the necessity of war or "the struggle for existence," spiritual appetites are awakened, and man turns inevitably to the pursuit of "food for thought." The significance of life shifts for

13. Cf. *Enzyklopädie,* p. 309 (par. 375); *Encyclopedia–Miller,* p. 441: natural death is overcome by Spirit in the identification of the universal and the particular in the individual; i.e. I am God. Cf. p. 313 (pars. 381–83); *Encyclopedia Wallace–Miller,* pp. 8 ff.: nature "disappears" or is assimilated, and so mastered, in the truth of Spirit. This is freedom (i.e. freedom from enslavement *to* nature).

14. *Enzyklopädie,* p. 296 (par. 359); *Encyclopedia–Miller,* pp. 384 f.; and chap. 2, n. 5, above.

15. Cf. Plato *Republic* 2.372d4 ff. Philosophy enters the just city only with meat-eating and luxury (and so with injustice).

us from a natural to a spiritual plane. Needless to say, we continue to satisfy corporeal desires, but this no longer defines the purpose of existence. Instead, it has become a means to a higher, more comprehensive end. No longer are we content with food at a level sufficient to maintain life. We seek more food than our neighbor, a supply to guard against hard times, delicacies rather than common fodder, food for our children and friends as well as for ourselves. Step by step, the desire for food transforms itself into what may be called generally *the desire to satisfy this desire.*[16] Life defines itself, in a sense emphasized by Locke, as work. And this definition in turn differentiates itself into the political, scientific, and speculative activities of the human spirit. Man discovers himself as genuinely human, or begins the genuinely human history of the development of self-consciousness, by a process which is rooted in, or the expression of, the self-contradictory nature of existence (which is fundamentally discursive or reflective: the medium of significance). Existence negates itself as it poses itself, but at the same time it preserves the positive content by a negation of negation. Natural existence is raised up into (primarily spiritual) history by the process of growth bearing the logical names of "mediation" or "assimilation" (*Aufhebung*): literally a "digestion" and so reformation at a higher level of development.[17]

Hegel accepts the Hobbesian doctrine that the natural situation is war rather than peace.[18] In Heraclitean language, "War is the father of all things." This doctrine, in its modern form, is inseparable from the emergence of the new physics. Nature is now understood not as a divinity, nor as the principle of life, but as matter in the void. This matter is characterized by

16. *Phänomenologie,* pp. 296 ff.; *Phenomenology,* pp. 433 ff.

17. *Enzyklopädie,* p. 285 (par. 338); *Encyclopedia–Miller,* p. 277: life is a self-mediating activity.

18. Hegel praises war in a way that embarrasses contemporary liberal readers: *Philosophie des Rechts,* pp. 280 f. (par. 324); *Philosophy of Right,* pp. 209 f. Cf. the justification of the behavior of world-historical individuals or heroes like Caesar: *Die Vernunft in der Geschichte,* pp. 103 ff.; *Philosophie der Weltgeschichte,* pp. 711 ff.; *Phänomenologie,* pp. 139 ff.; *Phenomenology,* pp. 225 ff.

motion which can be measured, and to that extent "tamed" by man. One could even say that the process of taming matter has a natural root, since human passions spring from the motions of our corporeal parts. Let us also notice that the taming of matter entails our turning away from an effort to grasp its "essence" or "substance," toward the study of the *relations* of material elements: in slightly paradoxical terms, we digest the "substance" of matter by ignoring it as substance. The soul, spirit, or intelligence is then regarded as the epiphenomenon or consequence of corporeal motions, or else as an independent component, granted to us by the generosity of God rather than through the indifference of nature.

Whether granted by chance or by God, the human spirit finds itself in an essentially hostile universe, and survives only by declaring war against nature.[19] (This can be justified within the religious tradition as a necessary consequence of free will.) The epitome, or rather the most powerful human weapon of this war, is science: mathematical physics. In general terms, Hegel accepts this analysis. Needless to say, he develops it in such a way as to overcome the vitiating dualism of nature and spirit, but the development is of the initial condition of war. Dualism is overcome not by mathematical physics but by a comprehension of the spiritual significance of the struggle which produces mathematical physics. As one might put it, mathematical physics, and so too the modern epoch, is necessary but not sufficient. For Hegel, peace is acquired only through the development of spirit from the initial condition of war in nature, to the completion of essential history in science or wisdom. Peace is the essential satisfaction of desire in spiritual nourishment. The highest form of this nourishment is contained in Hegel's logic. This logic combines form with the content of life; its difficulty is due to its extraordinary *concreteness*.[20] The logic recapitulates, at the level of divine thought, the totality of the significance of human experience

19. Cf. G. Sebba, "Descartes and Pascal: A Retrospect," *Modern Language Notes* 87, no. 6 (November 1972): 96–120.

20. For Hegel's use of "concrete," see *Enzyklopädie*, pp. 153 f. (par. 164); *Encyclopedia–Wallace*, pp. 294 f.

and so the process by which that experience is transformed into recognition of the structure of the "gateway" as the identity-within-difference of God and man.[21]

The circularity of eternity thus guarantees the identity of logic and history within human experience and so makes possible the acquisition of wisdom.[22] The human spirit develops toward completeness in a way which is itself both incomplete and complete. Absolute Spirit, as the principle of individuation, manifests itself in and as each individual moment. The pulse-beat of the moment is everywhere the same, but the "content" (a unity of logical form and logico-historical content) is everywhere different.[23] Within this "content" we must distinguish between the logical and the historical component. The logical component is in each a moment or category of the Whole as concept, and these moments are finite or circular. Stated with utmost simplicity, in a given number of historical stages, the totality of these logical categories is revealed. After this revelation, empirical history continues (the Absolute does not cease to individuate), but the logical categories repeat their appearances. Nothing *logically* new can occur. Up to the moment of the accomplishment of wisdom, or the complete recollection of the logical categories (to give the essential condition), the self-contradictory nature of the instant is not understood. There is no absolute reflection; therefore, each interpretation of history contradicts itself or dissolves into a series of paradoxes and antinomies. More sharply still, each interpretation of the Whole, since it sees only a part, inverts itself by its very assertion into its opposite. History is visible only because we discern it as eternity; but our perception of eternity is within a historical perspective. To see eternity is thus to see temporality; to see temporality is to see eternity. Therefore, human history, up to the moment of its (logical) completion, is

21. *Enzyklopädie*, p. 47 (par. 13); *Encyclopedia–Wallace*, pp. 22 f.

22. *Phänomenologie*, p. 559; *Phenomenology*, p. 801; *Enzyklopädie*, p. 50 (par. 17); *Encyclopedia–Wallace*, pp. 22 f.; *Logik*, 2 : 504; *Logic*, p. 842.

23. *Logik*, 2 : 503; *Logic*, p. 841: Method, although circular, cannot anticipate within temporal development "that the beginning is as such already derived."

not merely the story of man's triumphant progress toward God, but also of his alienation or loss of satisfaction in its ostensible (because momentary) acquisition. As a historical being in the ordinary sense of the term, man is *not at home*. Nevertheless, man is a historical being since history is the medium of his struggle to return to his home (which is itself the "inversion process" of eternity and history). For those who lack Hegelian wisdom or perfect satisfaction, life is essentially tragic. In a striking Hegelian phrase, history is a *slaughterbench,* both of persons and philosophical doctrines, or the tragic record of partial efforts to overcome alienation by a return to paradise.[24]

Hegel maintains in effect that all thinkers prior to himself have suffered from the tragic sense of life, even if in their various inadequate efforts to insist upon their own happiness. This unhappiness follows necessarily for the highest individuals, since their overriding desire is to achieve wisdom; instead, they imitate wisdom in resignation. As we have already noticed, the world-historical individual in the political sense can acquire a kind of satisfaction in fulfilling his role within history, but this cannot be complete satisfaction because it is not discursive or conceptual and because every historical epoch prior to that of Hegel is incomplete. The tragic individuals who achieve world-historical status by embodying a specific stage of the Absolute cannot *know* (although they may prophesy) that their thoughts are a necessary part of the Whole. Hence, at the core of their being they must remain dissatisfied. Satisfaction in the full and serious sense depends upon logic, in the genuine form of the Hegelian teaching. History prior to Hegel may therefore be described as *the process of the appearance of logic,* even though it cannot be known as such prior to Hegel (since the "appearance" is in the process of disappearing or contradicting itself at each appearance). The process of the appearance of logic is also, of course, the process by which man's spirit acquires self-consciousness or *appears to itself*. Finally, human history could also be called the process by which God or the Absolute *appears to man*. In these three senses of "appearance," one could call essential human history

24. *Philosophie der Geschichte, SW,* 11 : 49 f.

a *phenomenology,* which means literally "the discursive account of what shows itself." More comprehensively, the essential explanation of human history is a *Phenomenology of Spirit:* an explanation, to repeat, which can be given only after history has been (logically) completed. It is this completion which makes possible the preservation of phenomenology within logic as the human content of the divine categories.[25]

THE INVERTED WORLD

We are now prepared to turn to the passage in the *Phenomenology* which describes the dialectic of the inverted world.[26] Since this is the first text from the *Phenomenology* upon which we focus our attention, I begin with a remark concerning the external organization of the work as a whole. Sections 1 and 2 are entitled respectively "Consciousness" and "Self-Consciousness." The third (and final) section has no general title and is subdivided into four parts: "Reason," "Spirit," "Religion," and "Absolute Knowledge." It is plain that the last section is organized differently from the first two. The most obvious reason for this difference is that the last section does not go *beyond* self-consciousness but considers it as a totality in its attempt to preserve or transform itself into self-knowledge. It is worth noticing here that no special subdivision in the third section is devoted to art, even though in the *Encyclopedia,* "Art" is the first of three moments in the final section entitled "The Absolute Spirit" (of which the other two are "Revealed Religion" and "Philosophy").

Nevertheless, there is no radical difference in the treatment of art in the *Phenomenology* and in the *Encyclopedia,* so far as systematic knowledge is concerned. In both cases art is closely associated with religion; it provides us with an external image of the divine corresponding to the perception of divinity at any given historical period. As an image or representation, art expresses the beautiful shape but not the conceptual truth.

25. Ibid., p. 21.

26. For supplementary commentary, cf. H. G. Gadamer, *Hegels Dialektik;* and J. Flay, "Hegel's 'Inverted World'," *Review of Metaphysics* (June 1970) : 662–78.

It is a "liberating stage, but not the highest liberation itself." [27] As a product of human spirit, art is higher than nature. Since it exhibits only that aspect of spiritual content which can be sensuously expressed, it may be said to contribute to the "spiritualizing" or assimilating of nature. Once nature has been assimilated and the Spirit has achieved the universal or conceptual articulation of its own essence, the work of art is completed. "In all these relations, Art is and remains with respect to its highest destination (*Bestimmung*) for us a thing of the past." [28] This association of the work of art with the past serves to define its great importance in the *Phenomenology*, which is concerned precisely with the triumph of Spirit over nature. Nevertheless, art is connected with religion as a transitional stage; it is not a part of science or wisdom.

The *Phenomenology*, then, is concerned with art in a way parallel to its concern with scientific epistemology. In both cases, man believes himself to be grasping the Absolute, but achieves only a partial "world-view." This part, since it masquerades as the Whole, is to that extent a production or construction: an *image* of the original. The superiority of Art to scientific epistemology is indicated by Hegel in the organization of the *Phenomenology*. In section 1, which corresponds to the natural consciousness, there is no discussion of art, morality, politics or religion in their own terms. Section 1 is almost exclusively concerned with problems of perception, epistemology, and "objective" natural science. In section 2, which corresponds to the acquisition (but not the perfect vision) of self-consciousness, science is treated in the middle of a general analysis of moral, ethical, political or philosophical themes, and now from the viewpoint of the scientist or the self-conscious subject as "observer." In this way, Hegel shows that the significance of objective science lies in the subject; and the significance of the subject is to be found in the complete devel-

27. *Enzyklopädie*, p. 445 (par. 562); *Encyclopedia Wallace–Miller*, p. 297.

28. *Vorlesungen über die Ästhetik*, ed. F. Bassenge (Frankfurt, Europäische Verlagsanstalt, 1955), 1 : 22. For an English translation, see *G. W. F. Hegel: On Art, Religion, and Philosophy*, ed. J. Glenn Gray (New York, Harper and Row, 1970), p. 34.

opment by philosophy of his moral, political and aesthetic-religious experience. Whereas scientific thinking is an expression of human consciousness, it cannot in itself raise man to the level of self-consciousness. Scientific epistemology remains true to the Greek conception of knowledge as a selfless or self-forgetting apprehension of the arithmetical or geometrical form. The transition from the level of consciousness to that of self-consciousness takes place in response to the paradoxes of a radically scientific epistemology, which is closely if not always explicitly associated by Hegel with the *aporiai* of Greek philosophy. The most important specific feature of the "inverted world" passage is to show that Galilean-Newtonian science suffers from the same deficiencies as Platonism.

In the three chapters of section 1, we move from immediate or sensuous certitude by way of perception to understanding. Hegel, of course, means by "understanding" (*Verstand*) the analytical thinking of reflection. The main thread of the argument in the initial section is as follows. Our beginning certitude about the sensed world is, despite its apparent richness, in fact an abstraction: the lowest degree of consciousness. In attempting to make explicit what we intuit, we go beyond the immediate grasp of particular things (*this* and *that*) to the universals of sense-perception (thing, property, one-many), or from "my own" to the *common*. In the process, we lose the immediate consciousness of ourselves as in touch with things of the world, which is replaced by a consciousness of the common or universal, in which "I" as individual awareness am no longer accessible. We can see from a slightly different angle here the aforementioned connection between this stage of Hegel's analysis and Greek philosophy. There is a dialectical process of inversion in the efforts of the Greek thinker to study, and so grasp in discursive concepts, the nature with which he "communes" in the prephilosophical sphere. The scientific definition of nature in Greek philosophy is form, or a geometrically oriented generalization on the "shape" of sense perception. The geometricizing philosopher goes one step beyond the artist, who has already "universalized" the sensuous particular. Whereas nature is itself life, or the unity of form and content, the reflection upon nature, in art as well as in philosophy, separates us from its living or (as we may call it) subjective dimension. The perceiver abstracts from himself, or retreats in favor of his perceptions. But the perception is intrinsically unstable, since it contains in a suppressed form nature as growth, activity, or intelligence.

The inner dialectic of the excitations of perception leads us initially to the understanding (*Verstand*). With extreme concision, Hegel treats the transformation of Greek into modern scientific rationalism, which in turn culminates in the philosophy of Kant. The Greek *form* is replaced by the modern *concept;* this in turn reflects the initially ambiguous shift from nature to subjectivity as the locus of objectivity. The "concept" of scientific epistemology is like the art work in that it is *constructed* by the mind. The concept of the structure common to a multiplicity of particulars is not an abstract or stable universal like its Greek ancestor, but an internal excitation of formal moments, thanks to its "constituted" status as an expression of mental activity. Hegel, thinking of modern science in general and of Leibniz's philosophy of dynamics in particular, calls this concept *force.*[29] Very simply put, this means that, in thinking about the intelligibility of a thing (and so reflecting upon it as related to ourselves who think), we come to understand that its formal structure is identical with its existential, material, or natural *behavior.* (This quasi-conscious reflection thus results in a self-identification of the thinker as external behavior: the "interior" experience of thinking is ignored.) The Aristotelian conception of form as "being-at-work" (*energeia*) is now understood in a radically expanded sense as "activity." To a certain extent, this is concealed by the generalization of the patterns of the activity of force into *law.* The scientific understanding reverts to a certain extent to its Greek ancestor in this mathematicizing of force. But law is not immobile; its inner dialectic is the same as that of the things whose law it is.

The transformation of force into law is a more sophisticated, and also more abstract, version of the transformation of sense

29. Cf. Leibniz's essays *Specimen Dynamicum and Système nouveau.*

perception into forms or Platonic Ideas. It takes place, however, within the context of modern phiosophy and science, or of the Cartesian discovery of subjectivity: the presence of the ego in what it looks at, as we might say. Since law is grasped by *us,* since it is a concept, and thus in the human mind, our grasp of law is at the same time a grasp of ourselves. This is why modern "behaviorism" is in essence an *unconscious reflection.* The common properties of form are reunited with the individual consciousness, which is replaced by a *structure of its own making.* This structure is an unstable amalgam of form, matter, and consciousness; immediate or sensuous certitude is inverted into an "unconscious" objectivity by the effort to grasp it. And this unconscious objectivity transforms itself, by the restlessness of its three components, into modern subjectivism, the inverse of objective or "observing" reason. The three components are continuously losing their identity within an unstable totality: they turn into each other and back again. The next task is to bring stability, not as geometrical or arithmetical, but as the absolute reflection of dialectical excitation.

This is the context within which Hegel discusses the inverted world. As I have tried to suggest, the context is already an *exemplification* of the dialectic of the inverted world. The discussion itself is thus a kind of temporary coming to self-consciousness about the significance of human experience as it has emerged thus far. But as I have also emphasized, the inversion-process here studied will be found at all points of Hegel's teaching. Only at the end point (which is also the beginning of the circle of wisdom) will the inversion process be coequal to self-consciousness, which is then self-knowledge. The dialectic of the inverted world is in sum the same as the contradictoriness of things. Our "natural" inclination is to follow the initial differences of things, already the most noticeable feature of ordinary or prereflective experience. Regardless of the continuity of experience, we can neither perceive nor think it except by "analyzing" or dividing it into its various specific aspects. The shapes of individual things are like joints guiding us to the articulations of the continuity of experience.

These articulations correspond to the *articulateness* of discursive thinking. We cannot think without language, and language "articulates" experience as a discontinuous continuum of *this* and *that*. The analysis of experience, as rooted in sense perception, soon culminates in an emphasis upon its discontinuous or particularized character, which is immediately contradicted by the universality of the concepts of analysis themselves.

One consequence of this analytic process is that the continuity of experience as a natural or "external" reality tends to be replaced by the continuity of the analytic process. Instead of "one world," we have "one method." This is of course not to suggest that the world disappears, or that we lose all existential content with its unity independent of our analytic method. But there is an instability or fluctuation between the world and our method. The effort to affirm the world by analytic thinking immediately transforms the reality or essential significance of the world into concepts or laws: into analytic thinking and its products. The sensuous world is transformed by thinking into the supersensuous world. On the other hand, the supersensuous world is itself derived from the sensuous world, which is consequently the *essence* of the supersensuous world.[30] The sensuous gives substance to, exhibits, renders accessible the supersensuous. But this exhibition, precisely as it succeeds, at the same time negates itself, or results in the inversion of the sensuous into the supersensuous. Conversely, every effort to explain the essence or substance of the supersensuous immediately inverts it into the sensuous. This reciprocal oscillation is the dialectic of the inverted world.

Let me illustrate Hegel's meaning with a well-known example from Plato's *Republic,* the myth of the cave.[31] This passage is of special interest to us because it is the approximate Platonic equivalent to the demonstration of the logical essence of phenomena. In this passage the world of genesis or appearance is represented as a world of illusion. Images of artifacts

30. *Phänomenologie,* p. 113; *Phenomenology,* 193; *Logik,* 2 : 126 ff.; *Logic,* pp. 502 ff.

31. *Republic* 7.514a1 ff.

are cast by firelight on the wall of a cave in which men are imprisoned. The true, actual, or essential world is the domain of Ideas, of things as they stand forth in their truth, illuminated by the sun and not by fires lit by cave-dwellers. But Ideas, as the image of the sun makes evident, are themselves manifestations or appearances ("looks" of things). They are what appears as it appears (the essential appearance). The essential appearance, the essence *of* appearance, is itself an appearance. "Looks" are necessarily correlative to a "looking" intelligence. Ideas or essences are *how things look* or appear to the observing intelligence. But this appearance is transposed to heaven—the heaven of pure intelligence—and therefore designated as invisible to the corporeal senses alone. On the one hand, the Ideas are invisible; on the other, they are the essence of visibility. Let us underline this consequence. The essence of visibility, the visible as visible, hence as most fully or actually itself, is invisible.[32]

Of course, Plato distinguishes between intellectual and sensuous visibility. It might therefore seem that the preceding formulation is based upon an illicit and unacknowledged shift from one sense of "visible" to another. But the question is precisely how the visible in the ordinary sense can show itself in its true or genuine nature by suppressing its ordinary visibility and replacing it by another, extraordinary kind, which is *invisible* in the ordinary, regular, or initiating sense. What has the intellectual "Idea" of a rose to do with the rose in my garden? This question need not be motivated by unphilosophical coarseness. I move from the rose in my garden to the Idea of the rose because I want to understand the rose in my garden. But I conclude by understanding something else, something which is ostensibly both the living rose and altogether different from the living rose.

What Plato calls "intellectual intuition" would be designated by Hegel as a kind of dreaming. Intellectual intuition of the invisible (i.e. of the essence of the ordinarily visible as ordinarily invisible) is necessarily silent. The moment intelli-

32. Heidegger's interpretation of the Platonic Ideas is closely related to this Hegelian dialectic.

gence begins to speak of what it has intuited, it describes the things of this world (the rose in my garden). It describes the things of the invisible world, in the extraordinary sense of "visible," entirely in the language of the things of the visible world, in the ordinary sense of "visible." The description itself, as words, concepts, or formulas, is not visible in the same sense as the things it describes; the concept of a rose is not a rose. But that description is constructed from elements of the ordinarily visible world, and is itself a resident of that world. Intellectual intuition, taken as a faculty apart, or as a nonsensuous "eye" looking directly into the nonsensuously visible, cannot speak (a nonsensuous language) because it has nothing to say. It is looking into pure emptiness, which is to say that it is itself pure emptiness, or a phantom generated by the intelligence as resident in the ordinary world, a self-deception by which intelligence alienates itself or loses its ordinary residence on behalf of a phantom residence. In this deception, intelligence says to itself: "Yes, I saw the supersensuous Idea, only, as supersensuous, it does not present itself to language, although it is the condition of language, which, however, speaks always the idiom of sensuousness."

The point of this example is certainly not that Hegel denies the legitimacy of the effort to understand conceptually the rose in my garden. His point is rather that the concept and the rose are not in two separate worlds but are two moments of the same world. Until we understand this "sameness" as the "gateway" from one moment to the next, or as the structure of absolute reflection and so the life-pulse of the Absolute, our effort to "analyze" any particular will lead to a self-contradictory dualism. To grasp this world is to invert it into a "Beyond" (*Jenseits*); the effort to dwell in or explain the Beyond leads immediately to its inversion into this world. In modern philosophy, this dilemma is still present in the notion of law as a mathematical exposition of force, which is thus different in nature from force itself. Analytic reflection upon the "inner" reality of external appearance here corresponds to the previous effort to rise from this world to the Beyond by intellectual intuition. The intelligence is not satisfied by the very apprehension of experience as discontinuous, as *this* and *this*, which is a necessary consequence of the initial sensory orientation. It seems to discern a pattern in the behavior of *this* and *this*, or to distinguish *this* from *that* as defined by behavior of a particular kind, differing in each case. But the difference incorporated in particular statements is itself the expression of a common pattern or essence: difference as such.

The interior essence is now conceived as the process of external differentiation, namely, force. However, we cannot grasp force conceptually except by penetrating once more into *its* essence, which we define discursively as *law*. Law, so to speak, is the "interior of the interior" of the world of appearances. Our new effort to understand the rose leads first to the notion of force as pure differentiation. This is already altogether different from our starting point, the rose. The rose is negated or inverted from its initial condition as a specific difference into undifferentiated difference qua difference. But this is not the end of the story. The conception of force at which we have now arrived is too indeterminate to be discursively intelligible in the language of (non-Hegelian) science. The undifferentiated must again be negated or inverted. However, instead of returning to the rose, or to the things of this world, we are transported into the domain of mathematical formulas or laws. In sum: the effort by the mathematically oriented scientist or epistemologist to explain the phenomenon (the rose in my garden) leads him, unknown to himself, into the Absolute, which he inadequately conceptualizes as "force." The inadequacy of this concept is shown by the further passage of the scientific epistemologist out of the Absolute and into the domain of mathematical concepts. The domain of thinking is detached from the domain of being; differently stated, the two are separated by a failure to understand force as the identity-within-difference of the concept and the phenomenon. Instead, the epistemologist attempts to define force *as* the concept, and in an insufficiently analytic because nondialectical manner. Hence, force is "forced" into the straitjacket of mathematical laws. It rebels by enacting the dialectic of the inverted world.[33]

33. *Phänomenologie*, pp. 112–15; *Phenomenology*, pp. 191–95.

This point is sufficiently difficult that it deserves a restatement. The general conception we have of force is embodied in law, or as I have put it, in the "interior of the interior." But law is marked by a double dialectic. First, there is the difference between a law and its phenomena; second, there is a difference between laws as such and the multiplicity of individual laws. By "law as such" I mean the pure concept, the essence of law. All (non-Hegelian) rationalist explanations of phenomena attempt to subsume diverse phenomena under regular patterns of behavior, which are in turn further generalized into mathematical equations or in expressions modeled upon mathematical formalism.[34] The rationalist believes himself to be achieving ever-increasing clarity with respect to the diverse phenomena of experience, precisely to the extent that he turns away from these diverse phenomena to their common essence or structure.

If we carry this tendency to its logical extreme, the result is the pure concept of law which is, as it were, so pure as to be empty of the phenomena whose essence it purports to convey. The pure concept of law conveys nothing beyond the assertion of the law-like character of phenomena. We recall that the essence of law, its universality, is *difference as such*. But difference as such is indistinguishable from the empty interior of phenomena. Like the interior, like force as active emanation (and dissolution), difference as such is visible only as *this* or *that* difference. It is visible only as the difference embodied in a specific law, stating explicitly that *X* is rendered necessary by virtue of *Y*. The pure concept of law, in short, is an essence which can be grasped only by articulation or inversion into its opposite: a particular case (or a particular formulation of generality). The assertion of identity (even in so peculiar a case as the identity of pure difference) is equivalent to a negation of identity, or to an assertion of diversity. At the same time, we must not forget that identity is the same as difference qua difference. Simply stated, one identity differs from another, or

34. A possible exception might be claimed on behalf of Wittgenstein's "language games." Hegel would undoubtedly reply that these are not "rational." Games are either conventions or pseudonyms for laws.

preserves its self-identity, by virtue of the general property of difference. *Identity as such is indistinguishable from difference as such.*[35] And this is the result of our analysis of reflection.

The dialectic of the inverted world is the representation within the *Phenomenology* of the reflection process, albeit not yet understood as absolute reflection in the dual sense of logical circularity and self-consciousness. The unintelligibility of the *Phenomenology* apart from the *Logic* is equivalent to the lack of stability (in the Hegelian sense of circular excitation) in self-consciousness, or in the historical process which is consciousness appearing to itself.

35. *Phänomenologie,* pp. 116 ff; *Phenomenology,* pp. 197 ff.

7 The Unhappy Consciousness

Consciousness as the Struggle for Recognition

The *Phenomenology* is the story of the connection between logic and appearance as that connection appears to the human spirit. As a "story," it is both a description and an interpretation. There can be no distinction between the two, since Hegel accepts and develops the Kantian return to a teleological conception of the world. The "facts" of history can be understood only when measured against the goal of history altogether. There are, furthermore, two different kinds of interpretation in the *Phenomenology*. The first and most comprehensive is provided by Spirit, in the form of Hegel's recollective monologue, which is spoken from the standpoint of the Absolute, or *sub specie aeternitatis*. The second is that of the human spirit, interpreting itself as it unfolds within historical time. The duality of the science of appearing spirit thus corresponds to the duality of the eternal and temporal. So long as that duality is not completely understood, we remain within the domain of the second kind of interpretation. As is evident from the organization of the *Phenomenology*, Hegel makes further articulations within the stage of appearing spirit. So long as spirit is merely conscious, it does not experience its separation from the world. In general, the spirit is assimilated into the objective world, but possesses no explicit interpretation of itself as so objectified. The unsatisfactory or aporetic nature of the "world-view" of consciousness both separates spirit from the world and thrusts it back upon itself. Self-discovery or self-consciousness is thus accompanied by a radical homelessness. The loss of the world or home, however, makes it impossible for spirit to preserve or coherently interpret itself to itself. Spirit, so to speak, floats over the waters of the void: it is in one sense a god, but more fundamentally, an impotent god. In this homeless condition, spirit lacks an "objective correlative"; it can only dream and suffer. This is the condition which Hegel describes as *the unhappy consciousness.*

In my opinion, the condition of the unhappy consciousness is necessarily coextensive with the development of self-consciousness toward wisdom. In what I have called the third section of the *Phenomenology,* that is, the chapters devoted to Reason, Spirit, Religion, and Absolute Knowledge, we find the unhappy consciousness manifestly present in the chapter on Spirit, in both the lengthy discussion of alienation and the analysis of the travails of the "beautiful soul." One might quarrel over whether the unhappy consciousness is still present at the stage of religion. My own view is that, wherever wisdom is absent, there we find the unhappy consciousness. The resolution of the quarrel thus turns upon the exact knowledge of Hegel's attitude toward religion. All that we can say with certitude is this: whether or not Hegel was personally religious, wisdom is for him conceptual, never representational. In order to be wise, it is necessary to assimilate religion into the concept. Whether it is also necessary to be religious, we may leave here as an open question. This issue obviously cannot be resolved on the basis of Hegel's conventional assertions of faith, since it has nothing to do with his private convictions. The truth of the religious experience is a logical truth: I leave it at that for the moment.

A more important consideration in the present context is the connection between the unhappy consciousness and *the struggle for recognition.* Since self-consciousness originates as a historical or temporal condition in conjunction with a loss of the world as stable dwelling, it is marked by a struggle to reappropriate the world: this is the fundamental meaning of the effort to "master nature." Human history, properly speaking, begins with the discovery of self-consciousness as a condition of war. We recall that the first two sections of the *Phenomenology* cannot be understood in a simply historical or chronological sense: only the concept as a Whole is history. In the early sections, Hegel dissects figures of consciousness, albeit in an ontological rather than a psychological sense. Where there is no separation from the object, there can be neither subjectivity in the genuine sense nor ontological unhappiness. This separation is coincident with the origin of human history in the serious sense of the term. But it is not always recognized as such. It is often difficult to keep straight Hegel's ontological analyses as independent of, or more comprehensive than, his historical examples. In what follows, we must bear in mind that consciousness is unhappy as conscious of itself, for so long as it lacks a comprehensive interpretation of, or has completed, its experience of itself. I therefore regard it as necessary for the entire process of human history, prior to its completion, to be marked by the struggle for recognition in one form or another. But this view is not fully supported by Hegel. In the *Encyclopedia,* for example, Hegel says:

> The struggle for recognition and submission to a master is the *appearance* in which human living together goes forth as a beginning of *states.* The *force,* which is the ground in this appearance, is thus not the ground of *right* (*Rechts*), although it is the necessary and justified moment in the transition from the *condition* of self-consciousness sunk in desire and particularity to the condition of universal self-consciousness. It is the external or *appearing origin* of states, not their *substantial principle.*[1]

In my opinion, Hegel is not consistent in his development of phenomenological experience. His general description of it is such as to render it equivalent to alienation or homelessness: in logical terms, the moment of absolute reflection is not grasped by self-consciousness as the gateway between eternity and temporality. Within that description, however, he distinguishes between the prepolitical and the political in such a way as to suggest that the struggle for recognition is no longer present in a legally constituted state. Of course, one could easily resolve this inconsistency by distinguishing between the struggle for recognition and the unhappy consciousness. That

1. *Enzyklopädie,* p. 352 (par. 433); *Encyclopedia Wallace–Miller,* pp. 173 f.

this is untenable follows immediately from a consideration of such phenomena as the war of conflicting world-views or the struggle of intellectuals for recognition within the state.

The question of the presence or absence of the struggle for recognition is not restricted to political societies prior to the ostensible embodiment of absolute wisdom. It is at bottom identical to the question whether Hegel succeeds, in his own terms, in the reconciliation between theory and practice. I shall return to this question later. It is present here as the background to Hegel's explicit treatment of three closely connected themes: the unhappy consciousness, the master-slave dialectic, and alienation. In the present chapter, I shall give a brief analysis of these three figures of self-consciousness. In the process of discussing the first figure, it will be necessary to say something more about the structure of self-consciousness in general.

The Dialectic of Master and Slave

From the standpoint of the natural consciousness, which takes its bearings by the object as given to sense perception, the effort to grasp this object in thought leads to the puzzle of the inverted world. And yet, it is the recognition of this puzzle which raises the human spirit from the level of consciousness to that of self-consciousness. I now recognize myself as inseparable from the form or essence of the object, even if at first this inseparability has the negative consequence of separating me from the object as *objective*. This negative consequence takes two main forms, both variations on the defeat of consciousness by the object, even as this object is incorporated into consciousness or transferred from objectivity into subjectivity. Either I repudiate the significance of the objective world and take solace in my spiritual independence, or I deny the capacity of subjectivity to find permanent significance in the objective world of which I am myself an insignificant resident. In both cases, represented within the history of philosophy by Stoicism and Skepticism respectively, I am torn apart within myself, or marked by the unhappy consciousness.

As I mentioned above, Hegel represents dramatically the

discovery of the self in his famous analysis of the master-slave relationship.[2] This relationship is a figure intrinsic to human consciousness, and no more a historical "event" than the transition from the "state of nature" to a political society in pre-Hegelian political philosophy. At every stage of history prior to its completion (assuming that to be possible), each human being is at once master and slave, Stoic and Skeptic, or the living unity-within-difference of the inversion process which we studied previously with respect to the sensuous and supersensuous realms. Needless to say, some individuals express more of the master than the slave in their nature (compare here Schelling's doctrine of the balance between the subjective and objective components in both subjects and objects). One man is predominantly a Stoic, another a Skeptic. But these individual "types" are intrinsic to the nature of human spirit altogether. To study them is to study the existential versions of the logical moments of position and negation, which undergo unstable resolutions within the deeper unity of the negation of negation.

We begin with Hegel's observation that, thanks to our recognition of the dialectic of inversion, the object turns into consciousness: "Through this reflection, it has become *life*" (135; 22).[3] When we understand that the objects we desire, whether in a corporeal sense or through the pursuit of knowledge, are within our consciousness, or that they are modes of life, then we understand that what we desire is alive in the sense of possessing consciousness. The desire for satisfaction is a desire for complete self-consciousness. It is implicitly a desire for the Absolute Spirit as the unity of desire and object. This is Hegel's "Christian" reinterpretation of the Platonic doctrine of Eros. The process of self-discovery, or of the assimilation of the object into the subject, is at first necessarily a rediscovery of the dialectic of the object, only now in terms of sub-

2. The standard commentary on the master-slave dialectic (to be criticized in the text) is by A. Kojève in his *Introduction à la lecture de Hegel*.

3. Numbers in parentheses in the text refer *first* to the German edition of the *Phänomenologie*, *second* to the English translation. See chap. 1, n. 19 for full references to both.

jectivity. We have already seen that the initial human phenomenon of desire is marked by the labor of negativity. The human spirit develops by a process of opposition to the external object. The object is posited by me as the *objective* of my consciousness or desire (which is intrinsically intentional or even teleological). But this act of position is at once an act of negation: I proceed to assimilate the object desired. In the primary case of the body, I *eat* it. The negation of the object is thus its preservation as a mode of my consciousness: in one sense or another, it is part of my satisfaction. One could therefore say that the negation of the object gives significance to it and to the subject, which has been satisfied in *this* objective way.

The process of negative assimilation, which continues throughout human history and is the engine of progress, *produces* as well as consumes. This is evident from the fact that to negate *P* is not to annihilate it but to reproduce it as non-*P*. The negative activity of spirit continues in the sense described until all objects (every essential value of *P* and non-*P*) have been produced and assimilated. In other words, it continues until man has satisfied his desire by producing the objective world as the complete actualization of his own subjectivity. He thereby identifies himself with God. Having satisfied his desire (essentially: human or empirical history, and so production and assimilation, continues, but not in the same sense), man may now devote himself to thinking the thoughts of God. So too Aristotle says that we turn to theory for its own sake, after the needs of the body have been satisfied. Man does not leave the objective world; on the contrary, he is now fully at home in it and for that reason able to think divine thoughts, that is to grasp the world as the thinking of God. This is the final confirmation of my previous remark that at every stage of human history, man desires self-consciousness.

Man's satisfaction depends, then, upon his being at home in the external world. In logical terms, the process of satisfaction is a dialectic of identity (the ego) and difference (the non-ego or object), of same and other. In phenomenological terms, man's sameness and otherness is decisively exhibited in his encounter with other men. I shall first summarize Hegel's account of this encounter and then return to a closer analysis of the most difficult point. According to Hegel, I become radically conscious of myself in another consciousness.[4] The other desires what I desire; thus he is both the same as and other than I, even as I am the same as and (since I posit my satisfaction in the external object) other than myself. This discovery of myself in the other occurs therefore as a challenge and not simply as satisfaction. I see myself in the other as external to, even as a rival of, myself. Therefore I must assimilate him in order to preserve my identity or sameness. However, my identity or sameness itself depends upon the preservation of the moment of otherness. I am not genuinely myself except as "externalized" in the object which is not inanimate but is itself self-conscious. Otherwise the object would not reflect *me;* it would lack human significance. The human significance of the object is therefore rooted in *intersubjectivity.* Inanimate objects acquire value because they are desired by subjects. In desiring an object which is also desirable to another, I really desire the *desire* of the other object. I want him to recognize or submit to my desire, but without simply disappearing. He must continue to be present in his submission as subjective evidence of my otherness, and so as part of my self-consciousness (which is an identity of identity and difference). He must be "assimilated" in such a way that he preserves his identity within my own, albeit as subordinate to my desire (and this moment of subordination, of course, is transformed into mutual recognition in the final reconciliation of self and other within the just state). Since, however, his needs are the same as mine, recognition is initially the struggle for recognition. The intersubjectivity of self-consciousness manifests itself as war rather than peace. In logical terms, I discover myself as self-contradiction (141–43; 229–31).

There is a sameness and otherness in the individual within

4. This is a "Christian" or "private" revision of the Greek (Socratic) notion that man finds or understands himself within the *polis.* Cf. Augustine's *Confessions* as well as such post-Hegelian writers as Kierkegaard and Buber.

the medium of self-consciousness. Hegel begins with an analysis of otherness (since this is primary in the development from consciousness to self-consciousness). Satisfaction or completeness exists initially as independence. My desire for security is rooted in self-certitude. I can count on myself; my perceptions and my desires are mine, and so they cooperate with each other. However, the presence of another "I," making the same claim to independence, challenges my own. I cannot count on the other individual. So long as he is independent, I am alienated from myself; I cannot be certain of my own truth or value. Since my independence turns upon my ability to negate or assimilate whatever I desire, I must risk my life in a struggle with the other for mastery of desire. My goal, however, is not to kill him but to reassert my independence within the medium of self-consciousness by forcing him to recognize me as independent. I struggle not to kill but to prove my manhood, to show that I am independent enough to be prepared to die. If I cannot negate all other objects, I will negate myself. This assertion of the primacy of independence is the existential expression of the priority of freedom to "being" in the sense of objectivity. But the autonomy of the individual does not depend, as Kant and Fichte claimed, upon conformity to a moral law, which is mine precisely as expressive of the "next" world or "Beyond." On the contrary, morality and freedom depend upon the production of *this* world of intersubjectivity, as initiated in the war of each against each. We see here Hegel's affiliation with Machiavelli and Hobbes (143–45; 231–34).

The dialectic of the master and slave is a mythical representation of the historical recognition of the self in its relation with others. I do not mean by this remark to deny that the dialectic has empirical historical forms. But self-consciousness cannot "originate" as an empirical historical event. If this were Hegel's meaning, he would contradict himself in a dialectically unfruitful manner. In order for me to "recognize" myself in the visage of another self, I must first know myself, or be conscious of myself. So far as phenomenological experience goes, there can be no explanation at all of self-consciousness.

Hegel's meaning, which does not become clear until after we know the logic, is that I can recognize myself in the other because we are both instances of the self-consciousness of Absolute Spirit. The structure of my relations to the other is the externalized version of my "relations" to myself. And these interior "relations" are the expression of the Absolute. We can establish this interpretation by returning to the *Phenomenology* for a more careful analysis.

According to Hegel, self-consciousness is at first a simple genus for itself; it "covers" itself as its only instance or object (138–40; 227–29). Hegel is of course not using the term *genus* here in a strictly analytic or mathematical sense. The problem of the class which includes itself does not arise because there is no determinate structure here, but only activity. Every attempt to analyze this activity leads to the separation of reflection. But analysis is a consequence of the activity of self-consciousness, which possesses the structure of absolute reflection intrinsically or prior to analysis. One could say that the phenomenon of alienation (and so too the master-slave struggle) arises from the propensity of self-consciousness to make an analytic self-interpretation. This propensity, if it is carried through completely, leads finally back to the self, and in the special Hegelian sense of the identity-within-difference of the finite (analytic) and infinite (absolute) self-consciousness. The analytic propensity takes the existential form of the desire to incorporate external objects. Its goal is true self-certitude. In analytic terms, part of the self is encountered *outside oneself;* the desire to assimilate the desire of the other is thus an effort to grasp analytically the preanalytic or indeterminate structure of absolute reflection.

We have already seen the rhythm of this process. I "negate" the other by appropriating the object of his desire (self-satisfaction or freedom). In this satisfaction, I experience myself as secure; but my security is "negatively" related to the other whom I have assimilated. He must therefore be reestablished, created, or posited anew, in order to serve as the "other" within my own self-consciousness. The other, so to speak, is both *P* and non-*P*. In Hegel's own words, the first stage is the pure undifferentiated ego. The ego is posed, but as undifferentiated, it is negated; in itself, or initially, the ego is the mediation of position (Being) and negation (Nothingness). This mediation shows itself "immediately" as Becoming, or in terms of the present passage, as desire, which is thus the mediation of the previous mediation. The ego desires itself as reflected in the other (Hegel calls this "doubled reflection"), and this is negation of negation, or the desire to assimilate while preserving what one assimilates. Let us note carefully that this process is not solipsistic; my capacity to recognize myself depends upon recognition from the other as external to me. The "interiorizing" of the other is possible only on the ground of his otherness: hence the *identity-within-difference* of self-consciousness. Recognition "is a self-consciousness for a self-consciousness. Hereby is it so in fact for the first time, for herein for the first time arises for it its unity with itself in its being-other" (140; 227).

In the passage I have just analyzed, Hegel does not say that individual self-consciousness is generated *ex nihilo* but rather that genuine self-consciousness (as opposed to the simple or undifferentiated genus) arises as a reciprocal act of recognition by two pure egos that their desire or negative actvity is the same. Each serves as the "external" or "objective" for the other, while each remains "internal" or "subjective." The most one could say is that Hegel is extremely unclear whether this "intersubjective" process produces self-consciousness or whether it is a development of an already present, albeit generic, version of self-consciousness. My exposition of the logic contains reasons for assuming the latter of these alternatives. Certainly it is only in this manner, for which there is a secure Hegelian basis, that we can make sense out of the discussion in the *Phenomenology*. There is no doubt that for Hegel, contrary to Fichte and Schelling, the individual acquires self-consciousness in a stable way only in and through external experience. At no point does the Hegelian ego detach itself from external experience in order to return to itself by an act of intellectual intuition. Despite his great emphasis upon negative activity,

Hegel never follows the *via negationis.* This is also evident from the fact that self-consciousness is "stabilized" only in the family, and thus in the state. But the externalizing and "politicizing" dimensions of the stabilization of self-consciousness are in fact externalizations of the generic ego or Absolute Spirit. Interpreters like A. Kojève, who assimiliate Hegel's logic into the *Phenomenology* or provide us with an "anthropological" account of Hegel, *drop the generic ego or universal Spirit.* Thus Kojève, for example, is faced with the impossible task of generating finite self-consciousness from the struggle for recognition.[5]

The victor in the struggle for recognition is acknowledged as master of the slave's desire. The slave works to satisfy not his own desire but that of the master. To that extent, he has been "objectified" or reduced to the status of a *thing.* Not altogether, however; since the master recognizes himself as such in and through the submissive recognition of the slave, each is an essential moment in the self-consciousness of the other. The independence of the master from the things of this world is now mediated by the work of the slave. The master enjoys the fruits of the slave's labor. This enjoyment is "pure" in the sense that the master does not work himself. Things are therefore insubstantial for him. They lack independence in themselves and also because, as not produced by the master, they do not directly express his own independence. For the slave, of course, things are indeed independent, not because he cannot transform them through work, or because he has not produced them, but because he does not enjoy the consequences of his work. He neither consumes the work nor validates his independence by having produced it. The slave works for another; therefore, things are genuine obstacles to his own enjoyment or independence. But since these things, as produced by the slave, embody his own essence, he becomes an obstacle to him-

5. R. K. Maurer, *Hegel und das Ende der Geschichte* (Stuttgart, W. Kohlhammer Verlag, 1965), correctly criticizes Kojève on this score (pp. 152 ff.) but does not himself explain the status of self-consciousness in Hegel.

self: the slave is divided from his own essence. The process of externalization, which characterizes all human activity, is in the case of the slave alienation (146; 234 f.).

We come now to the crucial transposition in the master-slave relation, which is an excellent illustration of the dialectic of the inverted world. As dependent upon the slave, the master's self-consciousness is slavish or inessential, and precisely as dominant or essential. As that upon which the master depends, the slave comes to recognize his own independence, and precisely as dependent. Each is the opposite of himself; each is implicitly the other. We see here with great clarity how the master and the slave are related as position and negation, or identity and difference. In historical terms, made notorious by Marx's version of the transformation of worker into free man, the master becomes the slave and the slave the master.[6] For Marx, of course, master and slave are social classes, to be abolished by the consequences of the transformation process or revolution of the proletariat (under middle-class leadership). After the revolution, there can be neither masters nor slaves; Marx is, so to speak, hyper-Idealistic in his return from objectified being to human freedom. But the situation is rather different in Hegel, for whom master and slave are aspects of human consciousness, and only secondarily members of society. Even at the completion of history as alienation, in the just state which embodies the intersubjective identity-within-difference of its citizens, there will be degrees of independence, represented generally by the difference between the wise and merely religious citizens. For reasons to which I shall return in my conclusion, I doubt that the master-slave relation would be entirely absent in the "post-historical" situation. However this may be, despite Marx's talk of having stood Hegel on his head, it is the speculative logician who is more realistic than the "realistic" metaphysician of economics.

The slave dissolves his inner determinations in the acid of absolute fear. He therefore experiences himself as pure negation. As afraid of everything, he possesses nothing, and so is

6. Cf. the so-called Economic-Philosophical MSS of 1844.

negatively independent of everything. The slave returns to the condition of pure negative activity. He recognizes himself not as Absolute but as human or independent within his reification or enslavement. As Marx puts it, the proletarian, stripped of every human determination (even his reproductive functions serve only to produce more slaves), recognizes in himself nothing but pure humanity. Absolute fear or pure negativity is also self-consciousness, and of a peculiarly significant kind. In Hegel's striking phrase, which again reminds us of Hobbes, the fear of the master is the beginning of wisdom (148; 238). Fear brings the slave to consciousness of himself as required to work in order to survive (since his absolute fear is also fear of the Absolute, that is, fear of death). Through work, the slave rises from the disintegrative to the productive and self-productive consequences of negativity. Work is more substantial than the pure satisfied desire of the master. In making things himself, the slave substantializes himself in the products of his labor.[7] Work improves fear, the "substance" of intersubjective (and so political) existence, in a way similar to Aristotle's observation that art completes nature.

Work disciplines fear into self-consciousness: physical labor is the external correlative to the work of conceptual thinking. Fear internalizes and vitalizes work, or as Hegel says, it internalizes absolute negativity. In the process of work, or the making of particular determinations, the self is thereby freed from all particular determinations. It becomes free not by discarding these determinations but by recognizing them to be both the same as and other than the self. Freedom, in short, is the making of the self in the activity of producing the world. The world is not produced by sheer imagination or mere subjectivity, of course. Hegel is referring to man's appropriation of nature, giving it the significance and so subjectivity which it lacks in itself, by the ordinary modes of human activity like science, art, or politics. I have already spoken of the Hobbesian element in Hegel's interpretation of fear. We

7. For an interesting Marxist-Hegelian analysis of Kant in this connection, see G. Lukács, *Geschichte und Klassenbewusstsein*.

may also compare Hegel's analysis with that of the most interesting philosopher of the post-Hegelian doctrine of historicity. It seems that for both Hegel and Heidegger, dread, essential or ontological fear before finitude, death, or pure nothingness, originates the process of human self-discovery. But whereas for Heidegger the self discovers its finitude as bounded by *Nichts,* the latter is assimilated by Hegel into the self, which thus becomes both finite and infinite, or, differently stated, a logician of totality instead of a spectator of *Nichts.* For Heidegger, at least in his later period, self-discovery turns upon the capacity to free oneself from the contingent determinations of work. The doctrine of *Gelassenheit* is an effort to overcome the separations of reflection, or to "let Being be" in its integrity prior to the work of cognition. Self-discovery is thus strangely like the self-disappearance of classical Greek theory. For Hegel, "Being" is an empty abstraction until such time as work differentiates it or actualizes its possibilities. In this sense, Heidegger is a "Greek," whereas Hegel is a "Christian." But Hegel's Christianity is gnostic or Averroistic, and in that sense, more Greek than the Greeks, to say nothing of Heidegger (148–50; 237–40).

Stoic and Skeptic

We have now arrived at the threshold of history in the proper sense: the war and work of self-consciousness. This is the history of the unhappiness or homelessness of the human spirit. The unhappiness, of course, is not unmitigated. Thus the dialectic of the master and slave might also be called the dialectic of enjoyment and work. Man must learn how to enjoy his work; and this is possible because man is already in his proper dwelling, even if not yet fully master of it. "Homelessness" does not refer to an impossible longing for heaven, but rather to the desire for satisfaction on earth. Since this desire is itself defined by alienation or reflection, it is painful. History, as the education of the race in the enjoyment of work, is thus the odyssey of the unhappy consciousness. The immediate result of the master-slave dialectic, which frees the master from labor, is to make the worker unhappy with the fruits of his own labor. The slave becomes a Stoic. According to Hegel, Stoicism is the first philosophical response to universality. The Stoic is the first man to respond philosophically to both aspects of human life, enjoyment and work (or theory and practice). Self-consciousness, we recall, originates in dread before death. The consequence of this dread for the slave is work. At first, the slave conceives of himself as an instrument of the will of the master, and so as dependent upon him, but also as limited by the objects of the external world, even by those which he himself produces.

The slave is alienated from his own essence as it is contained in the products of his labor. But from slavery emerges Stoicism, or the rejection of the situation of alienating labor as *unreal*. The Stoic turns inward to his own thoughts, which he now regards as his genuine work. He finds within these thoughts the freedom which he is denied as a slave in the external or historical world. At this point, we must try to understand how Hegel conceives of the difference between Stoicism and Platonism, from which the former is derived. In general, the Socratic tradition, or the philosophy of the aristocratic city-state, does not take work seriously. There is of course a certain difference between Plato and Aristotle, which led Kant to say, in rejecting Plato as a fanatic, that "the philosophy of Aristotle is, however, work." [8] Kant, of course, was referring to conceptual labor. Hegel shares the Kantian preference for Aristotle in a way; nevertheless, for him, the Platonist and the Aristotelian both lack the genuine experience of human labor. Their flight from the sensuous to the supersensuous comes too soon. This flight lacks the negative moment of physical labor, and so cannot be dialectically transformed in such a way as to reappropriate it. One could also say that Hegel implicitly criticizes the Greek conception of nature. For the Greeks, *physis* is alive and divine, yet divided within itself in such a way as to prevent man from achieving a conceptual unification of it. Although Spirit is present in the Greek

8. "Von einem neuerdings erhobenen vornehmen Ton in der Philosophie," in *Werke, Akademie Textausgabe* (Berlin, Walter de Gruyter, 1968), 8 : 393.

physis, it remains alienated from itself, lacking self-consciousness, and so it is finally inaccessible to man. Hegel's "nature" is fundamentally connected to the modern scientific notion of *res extensa.* Since "extension" is for him the *externalization* of Spirit, it can be reconciled with consciousness through the medium of work: the mastery of nature is possible for modern man, but not for the Greeks. Thus what seems initially a defect of the modern conception of nature turns out to be an advantage (in Hegelian terms).

Platonism is the philosophy of masters, the consolation of the philosopher-king in daydreaming about the work of his slaves. The result of this daydreaming is not merely a loss of external reality but a loss of the self. As we have seen, the self-consciousness of Platonism terminates in the cancellation of self-consciousness. To put the same point in a different way, the presence of physical labor, the moment of difference within mental freedom, and the moment of unity in the Stoic are all exhibited in the transformation of the Stoic into the Skeptic. Platonism avoids this transformation in its own person (although it deteriorates historically into a variety of historical schools) by the disappearance of the self-conscious philosopher into the "death" of intellectual intuition. Needless to say, reason is more cunning than Platonism. Philosophical death leads neither to beatitude in the world of Ideas nor to absence of self in the thinking of divine thought, but in fact to the dialectic of the Stoic and Skeptic. These two are not so much historical personages as interrelated moments of the unhappy consciousness, which arises from the internal instability of Platonism.

We might almost say that the Platonist dies because of his refusal to work. The Stoic is born in an incomplete but nevertheless genuine human experience of work, and gives rise to the Skeptic as the virile expression of his own incertitude. Stoicism and Skepticism coexist as do mastery and slavery. Differently stated, whereas Platonism is the repudiation of work by a master, Stoicism is the denial of its significance by a slave. As a slave, the Stoic retains the experience of work in a way that the Platonist cannot. The result is the collapse of the Platonist's attempt to harmonize the One of Parmenides and the many of Heraclitus. The Platonist disappears into the One or *Nichts* of Parmenides. The fires of Heraclitus (which may be compared to the forge of the smith as the instrument of art or mastery of natural diversity) burn more genuinely in the bosom of the Stoic than they did in the Platonist. Therefore Hegel says: "Obstinacy is the freedom which makes itself fast in its individuality, and remains *within* slavery; Stoicism however is the freedom which comes immediately out of slavery and back into the *pure* universality of thought." Stoicism rises above obstinacy by a return to Platonism. However, as a universal form of the World Spirit it could arise "only in the age of universal fear and slavery, but also of universal formation" or interior education. It arises after the fall of the city-state and the growth of the empire. The universality to which it rises is no longer that of the Platonist, but a universalization of historical experience, as Platonism was not (153; 244–45).

Stoicism, then, is the first effort of the slave to transform himself into a master, but by *dreaming:* he remains within the horizon of Platonism. The essence of the Whole is for him thought separated from life; it is the concept of freedom, but not freedom itself. In other words, the thought of the Stoic is form without content. The Stoic incorporates the results of his work into his thought in a negative sense only, by denying its significance. Hegel refers to this as an "incomplete negation." The content of the real world is preserved only as "determination as such." This means that the content has been transformed into formal structure, or "food for thought" but not for the body. The Stoic believes himself to have escaped from external or physical reality by ignoring its concreteness or details, by preserving it merely as a kind of determination in general. The Skeptic, on the other hand, completes the negation of the world initiated by the Stoic by actually working out the determinations of the world in the negative work of analytic thinking. The Skeptic *reflects,* without, of course, being capable of absolute reflection. In this sense, "reflection" is not empty daydreaming but a working out of the content of the dream. *Skeptic* means "one who investigates" or "looks for," and so, one who has not yet seen the "looks" of things. Hence the connection in the history of philosophy between Skepticism and empirical science. The effort to negate the world at each step requires us to take seriously external objects; and this is a necessary stage of Hegelian as well as of scientific wisdom in the empirical sense (154–55; 246–47).

Skepticism *realizes* the dialectic of master and slave. "It exhibits the dialectical excitation which is sensuous certitude, perception, and understanding" (*Verstand*). This realization, however, remains negative (155; 247). The Stoic gives no significance to the object. But the significance given to the object by the Skeptic is negative: the Skeptic shows in deed that the object has no significance. Since the object is a product of his own work, however, the Skeptic also demonstrates that he himself, the worker, has no significance. The Skeptic destroys the significance of thinking as the Stoic does not. The diversity of the Skeptic is therefore dissipated into the same empty negativity as the unity of the Stoic. We see again the dialectic of the inverted world. The rise of the Stoic produces Skepticism; the assertion of Skepticism produces Stoicism. In Hegel's language, the Skeptic fluctuates erratically from self-identical negator to a contingent particular which is itself negated by negation in general (157; 249). In this case, the negation of negation is too general to rise beyond the level of the Stoic. Again we are caught in a seemingly vicious circle. As Hegel says, the conversation of the Skeptic is like the quarreling of youths who contradict each other in order to obtain the joy of remaining united within the process of contradiction (158; 250). This "joy" is of course the bitter resignation of the unhappy consciousness. And the quarreling youths are Skepticism and Stoicism, the latter as assimilated into the former, thanks to the greater labors of the Skeptic. The unhappy consciousness, or the essential structure of European history until Hegel, is thus the recognition by Skepticism of its internal scission. European man, caught in the dialectic I am now describing, is a nihilist whose consciousness is alienated from its essence.

The unhappy consciousness, as Hegel later remarks, is a preliminary version of self-estrangement or alienation (346; 506) and is a midpoint between the classical religion of art and modern self-consciousness (525; 755). As I have already indicated, I regard the unhappy consciousness to be coextensive with pre-Hegelian history. If this is a fair interpretation of Hegel, the remarks just quoted do not necessarily contradict them. Taken as a specific historical figure, one could say, the unhappy consciousness emerges explicitly in the conflict between Stoic and Skeptic. Since these figures recur throughout the total experience of consciousness, or are permanent features of Spirit in its course of appearing to itself, no problem of interpretation need arise. Another general observation should be made at this point. The unhappy consciousness is often associated specifically with the Hebrew religion and historical experience. In view of the pagan origin of Stoic and Skeptic, this is clearly an oversimplification. Furthermore, the "unhappiness" of Christian self-consciousness (at least from a Hegelian standpoint) is evident in its identity as *conscience,* which is inseparable from the experience of sin, and so the feeling of *guilt.* The unhappy consciousness surely has pagan, Jewish and Christian forms, and modern as well as ancient variations. For example, Hegel further defines the unhappy consciousness as pure thought that *feels* itself to be an individual. He refers here to "a musical thinking" which feels but does not conceive itself as a stranger to itself (163; 257). One thinks immediately in this connection of the German Romantics of Hegel's own epoch.

In its Jewish manifestation, the unhappy consciousness renders man the slave of God. The individual derives his certitude and satisfaction from obedience to the divine Word, and so from doing the work of the Lord. But the effective absence of the Lord renders his Word ineffective in this world. The Jew is commanded to do justice, but is condemned to injustice. Hence the work of unification (= salvation) is the work of self-destruction: "The consciousness of life, of its existence and deeds, is only the grief over this existence and doing, for there is here only the consciousness of the opposite from its essence, and its own nothingness" (160; 252). In its Christian form, the unhappy consciousness is the result of the death of Christ, or the loss of God from his existential identity with man. God becomes once more the *deus absconditus* of the Hebrew religion, a "Beyond" which can be achieved only in hope and prayer, that is, in dreams, or in the imaginative representations and mediations of the Catholic church (161–63; 254–57). Identification of man with God in Catholicism is what Hegel calls "formal particularity" (162; 256). In attempting to transform himself into the unchanging God, man succeeds only in becoming a particular form. And so, as in the previous example of the Skeptic, man is subject to dissolution by the same temporal process he seeks to negate. In other words, man is not reunited with Christ via the mediation of the Church or priest, but neither by prayer or cult, as has been forcefully maintained by a recent commentator.[9] The true reunion with God, the true assimilation of the meaning of Christ, is the conceptual or scientific grasp of the Absolute Spirit. Without such a conceptual grasp, the individual is subject to cancellation or separation from God by the historical process, which brings images and cults into being and vitiates them as well.

It is essential to understand that when Hegel criticizes prayer or devotion (*Andacht*), he is not referring merely to Catholicism. Lutheran prayer is no different from Jewish or Catholic prayer with respect to the crucial point: the relation of the individual to his object is not one of *pure thought* (163; 257). Prayer is a "musical thinking," however necessary it may be from the human standpoint. Furthermore, if the individual search for permanence terminates even in such a representation of God as that of an incarnated Christ who has died on the cross, the result is "an object of immediate sensuous certitude," or an image which has disappeared and which causes the searching believer to disappear as well (164; 258–59). The grave of Christ is thus the grave of individuality, because of its inability to rise above the level of transient immediacy. The grave of individuality, however, is immediately trans-

9. E. L. Fackenheim, *The Religious Dimension in Hegel's Thought* (Bloomington, Indiana University Press, 1967). This is one of the best studies on Hegel in English.

posed into the absence of individuality, or the "Beyond" of the inaccessible and supersensuous God. We have to understand that God is *not* a dead man. Thus Hegel interprets the Crusades, or the search for the sepulcher of Christ, as the experience of the lack of actuality of Christ's actually unchanging essence. Only by this experience, namely, the recognition that there is no grave of Christ, or at least that this grave has no transhistorical meaning, do we find the actuality of the unchanging individual in the universal truth of the concept (164; 258–59).

As a consequence of the experience of the Crusades, modern Europe is born: a Europe based upon work, the work of the slave seeking to rediscover his master. This is Hegel's spiritual explanation of the significance of modern science or the mathematical conception of reason. In these pages (164–67; 259–62), Hegel is summarizing the subsequent sections of the *Phenomenology*, understood as the essentially Protestant version of the unhappy consciousness. Stability is present only as the continuous process of changing particulars. By work, man shares in stability, but in such a way as to express himself negatively, that is, as the transformation of particulars. The negation of objects continues to result in a negation of the negator. This process will not yield an affirmation until the final pages of the *Phenomenology*. Meanwhile, the worker's essence is *the other*, understood either as the absent master or more generally as the alienated world, the "Beyond" which provides power for work but not satisfaction. The worker's labor seems to go *beyond* himself; he is thus creating his master (by tending to his needs), and even the world from which he has become alienated. We are now in the presnce of what Marx will later restate as the four-fold alienation of the worker from the product of his labor, from the act of production, from himself, and from other men.[10] This leads to self-degradation, irresponsibility, and the reification of the self which is parallel to, if not identical with, the reifications of reflective or analytic science (167–70; 262–65).

In sum, the process of reification, or the brutalization of

10. *Frühe Schriften, Erster Band*, ed. Lieber-Furth (Darmstadt, Wissenschaftliche Buchgesellschaft, 1962), p. 569.

man as worker, is the obverse of the modern doctrine of individualism. By the cunning of reason, man passes through the purgatory of "industrialization" not to the heaven of communism but to the experience of his unity with the Absolute as the consequence of laborious suffering. The human spirit passes from the "musical, abstract moment" of feeling, via the immediate self-forgetfulness of work and enjoyment, to a thankful rediscovery of the self, a "return of consciousness into itself, and indeed, into itself as the actual truth within it" (168; 262–63). But this is to anticipate the conclusion. Prior to the rediscovery of the self, the self must lose itself in degradation and suffering, necessary consequences of work as opposed to daydreams.

Alienation

Throughout this chapter, and indeed, throughout this study as a whole, I have had to make use of the term "alienation" in a variety of contexts. I trust that the contexts have served to prepare the reader for a systematic analysis of the term, to which I now turn. Stated with etymological simplicity, the term "alienation" means "becoming another." This translation, however, is in itself too simple to convey Hegel's thought. Since the Absolute is a process of self-manifestation by differentiation, one could say that every moment of Becoming is a case of the Whole "becoming another" (without thereby ceasing to be itself). For example, in the *Philosophy of Right,* Hegel discusses alienation in the context of the connection between right and private property. The person manifests himself in his work; this is *externalization* (*Entäusserung*). Private property is rooted in the fundamental characteristic of externalization: I show, or rather incorporate, my essence in the fruits of my labor. The connection between right and private property is first visible in the body, which is itself the externalization of the spirit. If I transfer my property to another, or surrender my right by a contract, then I have *alienated* what was not merely "mine" but in a real sense "me." Of course, my actual self or personality cannot be alienated in the sense that I have a *right* to express my will. Needless to say, this right is abrogated in slavery of the political kind, and in a deeper sense, within the master-slave relation. So far as the contractual transference or "alienation" of property is concerned, this is a legitimate phenomenon upon which political life obviously depends.[11] In this section, we shall be concerned with alienation in the deeper sense, as an expression of the unhappy consciousness.

It is not possible, at least in the *Phenomenology*, to distinguish sharply between Hegel's use of "externalization" and "alienation." To take the decisive example, God becomes other than himself in creating the world, or as the Father in generating the Son. Hegel sometimes (as in chapter 7 of the *Phenomenology*) refers to this process of externalization by the word normally used for "alienation" (*Entfremdung*). Nevertheless, I think it would be wrong to infer that, for Hegel, the Absolute (or God) is alienated from itself. Were this to occur, there would be a dissolution in the mediation process of absolute reflection. It seems more likely that God is said to be "alienated" from himself, in the discussion of religion, because Hegel is now using the language of religious representation, and specifically, in the discussion of good and evil, or the role of Satan in the Christian religion.[12] Let us say that "externalization" is the transition from the immediate to the mediate, in which the content latent in immediacy is rendered explicit. "Alienation" takes place only when, or for so long as, the explicit content is separated from a source rendered self-conscious by the fact of separation. Man undergoes alienation when he is separated from the products of his own labor, not by a voluntary contract but by a failure to grasp (in the dual sense of "owning" and "conceiving") the significance or essence of his life as a worker. Alienation is in this sense a characteristic of Spirit, but not of nature. It cannot be a natural phenomenon because, for Hegel, nature lacks self-consciousness (and so history). Nature is the "otherness" or externalization of the Idea in which Spirit is merely implicit.[13]

So much has been written about "alienation" in recent

11. *Philosophie des Rechts*, pp. 53 (par. 40), 56 f. (par. 43), 70-72 (pars. 63, 65 f.), 79 (par. 73); *Philosophy of Right*, pp. 38 f., 40 f., 51–53, 58.

12. *Phänomenologie*, pp. 537–40; *Phenomenology*, pp. 770–74.

13. *Enzyklopädie*, p. 200 (par. 247); *Encyclopedia–Miller*, p. 13 f.

years that an elaborate account of the history of the term is now unnecessary.[14] I limit myself to a few essential remarks. Let us say that externalization is the process of work or the substratum of alienation as a special form of work. Man loses himself in his work in order to find himself within that work. Hegel thus revises the Christian notion of *alienatio mentis,* itself related to the Greek *ekstasis,* or the process by which man leaves himself altogether qua finite mind, in order to achieve perfection through union with God or in the selfless vision of pure forms.[15] Within the modern tradition, the idea of alienation may be said to have four more or less distinguishable lines of ancestry: the scientific, political, aesthetic, and epistemological. The scientific and epistemological, taken together, amount to external reflection, which we have already analyzed at sufficient length; I shall therefore say only that Pascal's quarrel with Descartes is of considerable interest in this connection. The famous fragment 84 of Pascal's *Pensées* interprets the new scientific revolution as man's loss of self; more specifically, modern man is lost between two infinities which result from his loss of faith (the infinity of nothingness) and his belief in science (the infinity of space or extension). A recognition of this dilemma plunges man into an *eternal despair,*[16] or what we may call a despairing for eternity: this is a clear manifestation of Hegel's "unhappy consciousness."

A somewhat longer comment is in order with respect to the political and aesthetic sources of alienation. Without searching for the complete pedigree, we may say that the decisive figure for Hegel in these two cases is without doubt Rousseau. One might object that, in the case of aesthetics, Diderot is of greater explicit importance in the *Phenomenology*. The reply to this objection, I suggest, is that Diderot stands for *nihilism* rather than alienation, or for the complete disintegration of

14. Cf. H. Popitz, *Der entfremdete Mensch,* 2d. ed. (Darmstadt, Wissenschaftliche Buchgesellschaft, 1967).

15. Cf. N. Rotenstreich, "On the Ecstatic Sources of the Concept of Alienation," *Review of Metaphysics* (March 1963).

16. *Pensées,* fr. 84 (Paris, NRF, 1954), pp. 1,106 f. Cf. chap. 6, n. 19, above.

the modern European "man of letters" who is the final negative consequence of Skepticism. Rousseau's aesthetic alienation is more significant, or has greater positive content, because it is closely connected to his political teaching, which was of extreme importance for Kant and Fichte as well as for Hegel. Rousseau accepts the Cartesian conception of nature (by way of Locke and his French disciples), but turns to classical political philosophy in an effort to repair the damage done by modern nature to the human spirit. This mixture of ancients and moderns is evident in Rousseau's use of the term *aliénation* in the *Social Contract,* to designate the necessary and complete departure of man from the dangerous freedom of the state of nature into a political society marked by the universal will, which combines safety and egalitarianism.[17] Rousseau's conception of political virtue, although heavily dependent upon classical sources, is compromised from the outset by his acceptance of modern science. Political (and in that sense historical) life is thus the sign of a permanent self-estrangement or division in the human spirit between freedom and morality (which is in turn a dialectical mixture of justice and utility). This shows Rousseau's superiority to Diderot, for whom there is no morality and only a negative sense of freedom. Rousseau's spiritual division is thus an essential preliminary version of the schematism of German Idealism. The separation between freedom and morality is overcome when the universal will is revealed as Absolute Spirit.

For Rousseau himself, the situation is as follows. Since man is by nature both cunning and marked by desire, the human forms of satisfaction of desire, or virtue as well as vice, have a natural origin. However, the process by which these forms develop is the history of the human spirit, the history of the quarrel between virtue and vice which both draws man into political life and leads him away from it. The city is necessary for the development of man's highest faculties. But this development occurs only in conjunction with the development of luxury, and so, vice.[18] Whereas every citizen is "alienated"

17. *Du Contrat Sociale* (Paris, Garnier, 1954), pp. 243 f., 255 f.
18. Cf. chap. 6, n. 15.

from nature by the fact of his citizenship, the dualism of nature continues to function within the bosom of political life. Certain citizens, such as Rousseau himself, who understand the roots of this natural dualism, are driven out of full participation in political existence, yet are unable to do without the city altogether. In a deep sense, the Greek philosopher finds his happiness by transcending the city in theory. In Rousseau, the notion of the artistic temperament or aesthetic sensibility replaces the notion of philosophical theory as the highest human perfection. The philosopher, despite or even because of his theoretical nature, can live in the city and benefit from conversations with his fellow citizens. But men like Rousseau, who find their happiness in the "reveries of a solitary promenader," and who, unlike Socrates, prefer the country to the city, or the conversation of plants to that of men, are doubly alienated. They cannot exist within the city as virtuous or unselfconscious citizens. And yet, they cannot engage in reveries unless they are self-conscious, or products of the city.

Rousseau prepares for German philosophy, and so for Hegel, by his doctrine of the universal will as anticipation of the Absolute Ego or Spirit, which achieves freedom by an assimilation of, or reconciliation with, morality. If analytic science is the truth of beings, the union of morality and freedom contains the significance of the truth of science. From a Hegelian standpoint, then, the Absolute is present in Rousseau as the "universality" of will (whether so recognized by Rousseau or not). In contemporary, non-Marxist doctrines of alienation, as for example that of Heidegger's *Being and Time,* every vestige of an accessible Absolute, whether divine or human, except perhaps for *Nichts,* has been obliterated. Alienation thus becomes a permanent feature of finite and radically temporal man. Instead of being told to seek Hegelian satisfaction, contemporary man is directed toward *resoluteness:* courage replaces wisdom, justice, or temperance as the highest virtue. The result is a curious mixture of elements from previous teachings. Stoic resignation without wisdom, the contingent world of Christianity without God, a radicalized version of

Hobbes's doctrine of fear without the security of geometrical reason.

In the *Phenomenology,* alienation is both a recurrent theme and a characteristic of a special transition in human experience. The experience of alienation acquires its central historical role in the decay of the Greek city-state and the emergence of nations and empires. The Greek city-state is the expression of consciousness at what Hegel calls the level of ethical substance (whereas "moral" refers to the private or social sphere as opposed to the political, even though existing within the state). The city-state is founded by divine law, but in such a way as to give precedence to the community as a whole rather than to families or individuals (except, of course, in their political *personae*). The consequences of the ensuing instability or conflict between the political whole and its parts (the city and the private citizens), are crystallized in Greek tragedy, of which Hegel's favorite example is Sophocles' *Antigone*.[19] In this play, the two sons of Oedipus, Eteocles and Polyneices, perish at each others' hands in a war for the dominance of Thebes. Creon, the king, orders that Polyneices, who had returned from exile to lead the invading force, be neither lamented nor buried as the religious rites demand, but left exposed to the elements and scavenger beasts. Antigone, the sister of the two warriors, refuses to obey what she regards as a sacrilegious command, thereby placing her private religious obligations above her political duties. The play closes inevitably with the deaths of Antigone and Creon's son (her fiance), and wife. Of the various uses to which Hegel puts *Antigone,* we can mention only the most comprehensive (336 ff.; 490 ff.).[20]

Subjectivity is not yet present in the Greek world, since God has not yet revealed the identity-within-difference of Christ as both divine and human. There is a separation between the universal and the particular in the Greek citizen which makes him an unstable individual. This instability, or the conflict between the divine and human law, dissolves the universality of

19. For criticism of Hegel's interpretation, cf. G. Müller, *Sophokles. Antigone* (Heidelberg, Carl Winter Verlag, 1967), pp. 10 ff.

20. See n. 3, above.

the city-state, but the result is not a genuine form of individuality. Instead, as Hegel puts it, universality is reproduced at the level of particularity: "The universal splits apart into the atoms of absolutely many individuals; this perished spirit is an *equality,* in which *all* are valid as *each,* as *persons*" (342; 498). In other words, with all his faults, the Greek citizen possesses an unstable unity of universal (divine) and particular (human) spirit, which renders him an individual in the genuine sense of the term. Men like Themistocles, Pericles, Sophocles, and Plato are not just equal or anonymous atoms in a homogeneous society, but for so long as the aforementioned unity prevails, they are outstanding instances of spiritual activity, combining universal validity and individual personality. Unfortunately, the genuineness of Greek individuality is transient. In political terms, the Greek city-states are divided both against themselves and against each other. They are not held together by the force of an adequately developed self-consciousness. Hence their continuous revolutions and wars, which exhibit on the public level the instability of the most spirited individuals.

The war of individuals can be resolved only by contracts or human laws, enforced by the most powerful, who guarantees the rights of those who submit to his rule. In an important sense, the transition from city-states to empire exhibits the struggle for recognition of the master-slave dialectic. There is also a separation between the principle of legality (the emperor) and the instances of the law (the citizens) which reminds us of the contradiction in modern scientific epistemology between law and its instances. The destruction of universal ethical substance produces an artificial "substantializing" of the individual in the form of "legal rights." But the citizen gains these rights by submitting his will to that of the emperor. He is thus lacking in genuine subjectivity or self-consciousness. The "legal" individual or person is the political expression of Skepticism. The content of the person is accidental, nonessential restlessness, held together only by a form which has itself arisen through the negative activity of the destruction of the city-state. The *person* (a legal term, also used in a technical sense by Kant) is rendered stable *by the universal lack of significance of his individual life.* But this in turn is a consequence of the analogy between the legal person and Stoicism. Having lost the community of individuals (however unstable) of the city-state, the citizen retreats within himself. The ethical significance of political existence is gone; the individual becomes assimilated into the whole or "reality" in his capacity as abstract legal entity or *person* (343–44; 501–02). The term "reality" thus suggests that man has been "reified," turned into a thing defined by law rather than into the living source of law.

Hegel is of course speaking now of the citizen in the Roman empire; we shall soon see what implications are present here for modern European man. The Roman citizen provides us with the political expression of the origin of the dialectic between Stoic and Skeptic, which was previously shown to give rise to the unhappy consciousness of European man. Pagan, Jew, and Christian are alike moments in this dialectical process. All have been sundered from their essence. All respond to this loss by projecting a supersensuous and so transpolitical "Beyond" with which they seek to identify themselves, in imitation (or anticipation) of the genuine unification of universal and particular in the concrete individual. This imitation of individuality is doomed to failure and brings unhappiness to those who attempt it. But the consciousness of unhappiness is at the same time the engine of negativity which drives men to work and thereby finally to overcome their unhappiness. This process of work is *alienation.*

The Stoic identifies his interior daydreaming with the Whole. This Whole, however, is at once solipsistic and contradicted by the dreams of other solipsists. The Stoic, in asserting or "positing" himself, at once negates himself. He splits apart like an unstable atom into a multiplicity of equal duplications of the original Whole, and the result is Skepticism. The Skeptic finds his "wholeness" in the negative process of the reciprocal contradiction: the result is modern "individualism." The connection with modern science is evident from the character of scientific method, which derives its unity from the process of negating each antecedent result. In political terms, whereas reality is now understood as the totality of persons under the master of the world, or the emperor, the *content* of reality is contingent and self-destructive. The emperor is himself merely a formal imitation of God (and an anticipation of the modern scientific method). He is a "hidden god" who can hold his subjects together in a negative manner only. The absence of intimate connection between form and content produces extravagant and even insane variety.

Hegel draws an implicit comparison between the excesses of "individuals" within the Roman empire and the struggle of disorganized intellectual experience in modern Europe. The Republic of Letters is a modern version of the Roman empire. A formal concept of equality is in both cases contradicted by the conflicting individual interpretations of the content of equality. The arbitrariness of the emperor toward his subjects as persons is assimilated into the relationships of the persons, qua citizens of the Republic of Letters, with each other. God, essence, or spiritual unity is an empty formal concept. Hence each individual believes himself to be "free" to express a private (and therefore contingent) interpretation of the Whole. The person therefore becomes estranged from himself by his own activity of intellectual expression, because this activity itself originates in a separation between person and essence or universality. The result is at once alienation and *culture,* or the cultivated formation of what is today known as the "alienated intellectual." This point, which will be developed further in the next chapter, when we discuss Hegel's analysis of the Enlightenment, also shows clearly the influence of Rousseau.

In theoretical terms, the alienated intellectual is a product of the disappearance of the Whole. As one might put it, the Platonist awakens from his daydream to find that the Whole is an opinion, since the logical conception has cancelled itself through internal contradiction. "One man's opinion is as good as another's." In political terms, the modern cultivated individual is an image of both emperor and citizen in the Roman empire. Each individual is abstractly equal to every other individual, but at the same time, each is master of the world of his spiritual labor. Again, just as the emperor is the separated essence of the world of citizens, so too the modern individual is separate from the world of his labor (347; 507). Work, however, is externalization. The world is not simply a daydream, but (as incomplete) an "image" of the worker's dreams which has been imprinted onto immediate actuality. The culture (*Bildung*) of the individual is his image-making (*bilden*) but at the same time his estrangement from what he has made. The individual is alienated from his own formation (*Bildung*) or form: modern culture is a disjunction of essence and accidents. As Hegel puts it, Spirit has shaped a double world: the actual world, and beyond it, a consciousness of its essential actuality in the alienated consciousness of the world-maker (348; 510). In other words, the individual consciousness is alienated not merely from its world (of which it is the essence), but from itself as essence.

The multiplicity of cultivated individuals stands to the absent spiritual essence as does the multiplicity of worlds to the individual image-maker. The Whole falls apart into a multiplicity of alienated instances of self-consciousness, themselves separated from a "Beyond" of essential consciousness which is not actual but an object of *belief* (349; 511). Hegel is thinking here once more of Kant and Fichte, or the conception of a cognitively inaccessible God who actualizes himself in the manifold of individual consciousness, each instance of which is separated by its very existence from what it instantiates. Hence the significance of Hegel's frequent use of the word *person,* which is common also to Roman law and Kant's ethical teaching, with reference to belief in a "Beyond." At the same time, the Kantian teaching is a necessary passage to the reunion between individual and universal consciousness, although it leaves that reunion in an infinitely distant future.

The Kantian teaching, taken as a transition to Hegel, must be opposed to the general significance of the modern Enlightenment in its eighteenth-century version. There is for the Enlightenment neither "Beyond" nor genuine individualism. Instead, the Enlightenment reunites the individual atoms of human spirit in historical actuality, now conceived as the expression of universal will or the universal self. Rousseau's doctrines of the general will and the social contract, decisive for the Enlightenment, thus repeat the defective relationship between universal and individual which characterized the Roman empire.[21] The loss of individuality is accompanied by the substitution of *utility* for goodness (especially in the doctrines of the British empiricists, which were very influential in France). The conflict between individuality and universality produces the French Revolution, or the destruction of the historical actuality in which the human spirit had found its last unstable reunion. The French Revolution culminates in the Terror, or self-destruction of its own leaders (a phenomenon not unknown to our own century); it is the practical counterpart to the theoretical nihilism of Kant and Fichte. But this does not mean that Hegel rejects the revolution as altogether bad. On the contrary, it sets the stage for the negation of negation in the person of Napoleon, "the World Spirit on horseback." [22] The French Revolution prepares the way for the harmony of theory and practice represented by Hegel and Napoleon. Thus Hegel says that Spirit relinquishes the ruined home of "the land of culture" (France) and moves to "another land, in the land of moral consciousness" (Germany). There it will find absolute freedom, but not until Hegel has recovered the universal essence of the individual from its supersensuous home in a Kantian heaven (349–50; 512–13).

21. Cf. *Philosophie des Rechts,* p. 80 (par. 75); *Philosophy of Right,* pp. 58 f. The "social contract" theory makes the individual prior to the state (and so intrinsically insubstantial).

22. *Briefe* (Hamburg, Felix Meiner Verlag, 1961), 1 : 120 (13 October 1806).

8 The Enlightenment

Culture and Chatter

The Enlightenment is for Hegel the culmination of European history understood as alienation. Hegel's analysis of the Enlightenment is rather different from the procedures of contemporary historians. Whereas we tend today to emphasize the political consequences of the Enlightenment, understood as a period of scientific Skepticism or an intellectual attack against religion of the older, dogmatic sort, Hegel defines the Enlightenment as *an internal conflict of faith.* The contemporary student emphasizes the role of the intellectuals in the Enlightenment as contributing to the emergence of modern liberalism and the democratic state. Hegel, on the contrary, studies the Enlightenment as a religious crisis in which reason repudiates faith through ignorance of its intrinsic identity with what it rejects. The political character of the Enlightenment, while obviously important, is not central for Hegel because, unlike contemporary liberals, he sees the activity of its intellectuals as the last form of spiritual disintegration. As I indicated at the end of the last chapter, it is true that Napoleon represents the practical incarnation of World Spirit, or the negation of the negation of the terroristic dissolution of the French Revolution. But Napoleon is scarcely the political representative of Enlightenment liberalism. Beyond this, however, the political solution of the crisis of nihilism is a *consequence* of spiritual activity, not a cause of that activity. The road to Napoleon is, properly speaking, neither political nor scientific (in the Enlightenment sense of the term), but ethical, cultural, or aesthetic. These terms derive their special significance from the quarrel between philosophy and religion. It therefore makes sense to study Hegel's interpretation of the Enlightenment in conjunction with his discussion of religion.

Let me try to elaborate upon this thesis in such a way as to show the subordinate role of politics in Hegel's *Phenome-*

nology. The Enlightenment is essentially a moral effort by man to find significance in his work. Even though that work is decisively shaped by the tools of mathematical and experimental science, the Enlightenment is not primarily scientific. Science does not *enlighten* man. It is man who must enlighten himself about the significance of science, or perform the "absolute reflection" by which the scientific object is assimilated into the spiritual activity of the scientist. Second, the phenomenon of culture (*Bildung*) is a quasi-moral consequence of the decay of political unity. Culture is a substitute for morality. Morality cannot justify or preserve itself in the absence of intersubjective community. This is not to say that politics guarantees unity, but rather that political unity depends upon the proper spiritual condition. As I suggested previously, this means that the political implications of the Enlightenment, understood as quasi-morality, are negative. Culture is intrinsically unstable: it leads to solipsism or nihilism on the one hand, and to political revolution on the other. The nihilistic condition of atomized cultured "individuals" leads to a political revolt against culture in an effort to unite these atoms into a common political reality.[1] The war which is implicit in culture as the relativity of taste is then made explicit by the overthrow of culture: by the negation of negation.

The final section of the *Phenomenology* is divided into four chapters: Reason, Spirit, Religion, and Absolute Knowledge. Neither here nor, obviously, in the *Logic*, is political thought or practice an independent topic. In the *Encyclopedia*, the discussion of political themes is the second of three divisions of the final section entitled "The Philosophy of Spirit." These three divisions are called: "Subjective Spirit," "Objective Spirit," and "Absolute Spirit." Within the first division, there are three subsections, of which the second is called "The Phenomenology of Spirit." In other words, politics is discussed in conjunction with morality as the Objective Spirit, which is united with the Subjective Spirit in the Absolute. We must also notice that, in the last division of the Philosophy of Spirit, the

1. I cannot help thinking of the remark attributed to the Nazi Alfred Rosenberg: "Whenever I hear the word 'culture,' I reach for my pistol."

three subsections are called: "Art," "Revealed Religion," and "Philosophy." These subdivisions seem to correspond to the last three major themes of the *Phenomenology*. I have already discussed Hegel's change of mind concerning the place of the *Phenomenology* in his system. Here we should see that the subordination of politics to philosophical science is a constant feature of the Hegelian science of wisdom. In the language of the *Logic,* the transition from the Idea of the True to that of the Good takes place in a chapter called "The Idea of Knowledge," which is itself the transition from "Life" to "The Absolute Idea."

In view of the marked tendency by some of the best students of the *Phenomenology* to exaggerate its political significance, and specifically because Hegel is often studied by Marxists as a preparation for Marx, it seems necessary to underline the subordinate role of politics in the economy of Hegel's thought. The exaggeration of the Marxists has given rise to a countervailing but equally exaggerated tendency to see Hegel as primarily a religious thinker. But politics and religion have a secondary status in Hegel's doctrine. "Secondary" is high enough, to be sure; we must not diminish the importance of politics and religion, but establish the proper perspective. Hegel's perspective is fundamentally Greek, and specifically Aristotelian. He never deviates from the Aristotelian conception that theory is higher than practice. Even Plato, whose doctrine of the unity of virtue suggests at least a tendency to unite theory and practice, makes it clear that the just city is the wish of good men: a daydream.[2] The just city depends for its existence upon the rule of philosophers who have nothing in common with the nonphilosophical citizens. As Aristotle says in the *Politics,* the guardians reside in the Socratic city like an occupying military garrison.[3] Socrates, of course, does not rely upon theoretical persuasion in wishing for a just city. He attributes its possibility to the chance birth of a king who is also a philosopher and to force: the expulsion of citizens over the age of ten. Hegel replaces chance by the

2. Cf. Aristotle *Politics* 1265a17.
3. Ibid., 1264a26, b29 f.

historical process; force is thus *already* a synthesis of theory and practice, or the cunning of reason.

Hegel understands perfectly that the nonphilosophical many will never be persuaded by the philosophical few, if by "persuasion" is meant theoretical discourse. (The Marxist effort to overcome the difference between the few and the many requires the substitution of "ideology" for "theoretical discourse." Therefore, logic can be replaced by economics.) Hence the great importance of Napoleon, the World Spirit on horseback, or the military expression of the Absolute Idea. Plato's *Republic* is a dream because no mention is made of how the philosopher-king will obtain troops to "purify" his city of everyone over the age of ten. Critics of Plato sometimes ask: "Who will guard the guardians?" From Hegel's standpoint, this is liberal romanticism. The more fundamental question is: "Who will purge the purgers?" Purified troops cannot be developed until *after* the city has been purged. The seriousness of this question for actual political life is easily inferred from the simplest reflection on the career of Stalin. To return to Hegel, for him as for Napoleon (to say nothing of Stalin), God is on the side of the big battalions. For Hegel, of course, this means the practical or objective manifestation of the Absolute in the process of civilizing the human race. But the significance of this objective force, understood as the army and institutions of the state, lies within the subjective or self-conscious grasp of religious and philosophical truth. The last stratum of the debate is between religion and philosophy. Since philosophy is the truth of religion, whereas religion is the basis for the self-consciousness of the ethical state,[4] it should be clear what Hegel's priorities are.

Whatever may be the truth about the final reconciliation between theory and practice, theory dominates within that reconciliation. And prior to this last stage, politics is discussed in terms of the world-historical individual whose spiritual characteristics represent any given epoch. Hegel's entire treatment of the Enlightenment follows from his analysis of the "magnani-

4. *Enzyklopädie,* p. 432 (par. 552); *Encyclopedia Wallace–Miller,* pp. 283 f.

mous" or "noble-spirited" man. This man is originally the citizen of the classical city-state. But in a way which we partially studied with respect to the master-slave dialectic, the noble-spirited man of antiquity decays into the mean-spirited modern individual. At the same time, the mean-spirited man of antiquity evolves into the noble-spirited courtier of the feudal and modern state. When the aristocratic master falls from power, he rejects the significance of political existence in favor of his fantasies. As the slave rises in status, he comes to identify the meaning of his life with the court he serves. Nobility, in other words, is defined in terms of the state. However, the noble and mean-spirited men whom I have just introduced are fundamentally two extremes of the same incomplete development. Since wisdom is lacking, both types are united by the attribute of *faith*. The noble spirit believes in the state, whereas the mean spirit believes in himself. This common dimension of faith provides for the subsequent inversion process of the two extremes in the detailed analysis of the Enlightenment.

To begin with, however, we have to study the political aspect of modern individualism, or the connection between politics and culture. In terms of a point made in the previous paragraph, the Greek philosopher deteriorates into the modern alienated intellectual only through the mediation of the non-philosophical nobleman. As one might almost put it, the cultivated individual is the product of the synthesis of Athens and Sparta. The love of truth must be subordinated to the love of honor before the conception of culture can emerge. To the ancient philosopher, the true is everywhere the same; hence the individual who perceives the truth is of little or no importance. Certainly irrelevant is his historical personality or uniqueness: what we may call the spiritual accent of his corporeal appetite. Variety of style, technique, expression, and the like, are altogether extraneous to the assertion of the true as true, whereas they are altogether essential to the expression of culture, which is always particular or historical. Greek individualism is then in conflict with Greek philosophy. The triumph of Sparta over Athens means the assimilation of philosophy into honor, or the debasement of philosophy into culture. The same process of assimilative debasement transforms the Spartan citizen into an Athenian individual. Athenian cultivation leads to a deterioration of Spartan virtue. The love of truth is thus transformed by a dual pressure into the love of one's own, but in a private rather than a political sense. The individual comes to love not the laws of the state or empire but his own discourse.

But this formulation is already too general. Modern individualism did not develop directly from ancient Sparta because of the lack of self-consciousness of the Spartan nobleman. The process by which this nobleman assimilates Athenian philosophy is in a way as long as European history. In the feudal nobleman, however, it is possible to discern the historical consequences of the assimilation. The content of feudal honor is the Absolute in a way radically more visible than it was in classical antiquity. This can be shown as follows. The Spartan lives in silence, which is to say that his life is indistinguishable from his death. This is, perhaps, itself a kind of universality, but rather like the night in which all cows are black. Differently stated, there is a veil of silence drawn over the disputes within Spartan political life, so far as the fundamental relationship between the man of honor and the city is concerned. Political dispute terminates in action, and action terminates in death. Sparta remains true to itself only for so long as it refuses to countenance an alternative to death as the certification of honor.[5] But the modern epoch has its origins in chatter (*Geschwätz*), and so in a reinterpretation of how to certify honor. Instead of dying in battle or exposing himself to the danger of death, the nobleman may express his honor by becoming a courtier (360–61; 527–28).

The court is characterized by a diversity at least with respect to the forms of speech. Like every crucial concept in Hegel, the diversity of speech has good and bad aspects. The silence of the noble warrior, which is consummated in an honorable death, has a kind of dignity lacking in the refined gossip of the courtier. Nor is it an accident that Hegel uses the low term *Geschwätz* to characterize the discursive origins of modern culture.

5. As is so often the case, the Spartan position is articulated by Plato. Cf. *Republic* 3.387d11 ff.

We may see here another residue of Hegel's "Platonism": the high is prefigured in the low. Or what seems to be the high at an intermediate stage of historical development is also the low. With respect to the primacy of honor, the true service to the state is death. At the same time, death is the negation, if not of honor, at least of the state. For if the best men die in silence, the state will fall into the hands of the worst men. The noble servant must therefore enter into discursive competition with the base men; political council must develop into the art of political rhetoric.

We see here a Hegelian explanation for the historical fact that the beginning of modern political philosophy is marked by two crucial features. Self-preservation replaces aristocratic virtue as the basis of political life, and rhetoric assumes a central position in political thought.[6] Virtuous speech is essential speech rather than chatter; but the essences are not accessible to speech (prior to Hegel's logic), and certainly not to political speech. Classical political philosophy, despite its emphasis upon virtue, necessarily speaks to the capacity of the nonphilosopher. To a Hegelian, its speech is therefore essentially silence. This silence can be implemented politically only in death. The honorable death of the noble warrior is the practical imitation of the philosophical death to the things of this world as advocated by Socrates. But honorable and noetic silence will inevitably be violated by those who lack honor and philosophical intelligence. In order to preserve virtue and honor, the noble man must replace death by rhetoric. The good man must become "bad" in order to provide a foundation for political virtue: this is the teaching of Machiavelli's *Prince*. This means that the noble man must necessarily become base, and precisely for the sake of the noble. If virtue is habit, and the best men become habituated to the rhetoric of self-preservation, the result will be a debased interpretation of virtue. Hegel understands and accepts this initially bad consequence because it in turn will be transformed into a higher stage by the cunning of reason. Genuine virtue depends upon intelligence or wisdom, exactly as was taught by the ancients.

6. Consider the importance of Aristotle's *Rhetoric* for Hobbes.

But wisdom in turn depends upon the complete development of the human spirit. The low will not submit voluntarily to the high but must be forced to submit. And this requires the high to learn both the ways and the weapons of the low. At first the high will be "corrupted" by this required education in baseness. But what looks like corruption from a classical perspective is part of the process by which opposites are united and the human spirit travels toward totality. The development of discourse will produce alienated individuals, to be sure; but these individuals are the "atoms" of a completed human nature. The use of rhetoric for selfish or low purposes leads necessarily to the reappearance of the high, but now as articulate or wise. The process by which this takes place is the theme of the succeeding pages of the *Phenomenology*.

Let us therefore be extremely precise in understanding what Hegel means by "chatter." First, he denies the historical or scientific efficacy of silence. Second, he recognizes that the modern epoch begins by a lowering of standards in comparison with the classical conception of virtue. Third, he is fully aware of what we may call the self-contradictory aspects of "high chatter" or cultivated discourse. But fourth, he insists that only by passing through the self-contradictory nature of culture can the human spirit become genuinely articulate. Chatter does not reduce to silence in the same sense as an honorable death. There is an *Aufhebung*, or recognition that incomplete speeches must be replaced by the complete speech of Hegelian science. Finally, chatter is not slavish speech, or not simply slavish speech, but rather the speech of the noble man who enters into dialectical conflict with the slavish man. If the noble man or master becomes thereby slavish, this is not the same, incidentally, as attributing to the slaves the primary role in the development of the human spirit. The wise or genuinely noble man must assimilate the base as part of his wisdom, for only in this way will he be able to subordinate the low to the high.[7] So long as the low remains external to the high, dialectical paradoxes or the "bad infinity" will prevail (361–62; 528–29).

7. Cf. *Parmenides* 130c5 ff: the philosopher must know dirt, etc.

This is the context in which Hegel makes his transition from ancient to modern political life, and thus to the origin of culture, or the Enlightenment as alienation. Man enlightens himself through the process of work, which is also a self-estrangement or loss of self in the various forms of spiritual interpretation. Human work is fundamentally discourse, or "the existence of the pure self as self" (362; 530). In the medium of discourse, the individuality of self-consciousness stands forth as visible or *there* (*Da-sein*) before the other, and so as part of intersubjective actuality rather than a private dream. The transient character of existence is preserved in the universality of discourse, which grasps in the concept the otherwise separated and opposed moments of the universal and the particular (362–63; 530–31). In terms of the present discussion, discourse grasps or reunites the alienated moments of the noble and the mean spirits: it overcomes the separation between the death of Antigone and the speech of Thersites.

The discursive competition between the high and the low, which leads to their reciprocal transformation and reunion, is in logical terms the emergence of the concrete individual and in political terms the birth of the modern state. Let me underline that the essence of the state is discourse or spiritual work; this is quite the reverse of the claim that spiritual work is determined by the state. It is also clear that the aforementioned competition is an instance of the twin dialectics of the inverted world and the master-slave. The absolute monarch is the master, and his noble courtiers or counsellors are the slaves. The courtiers have been rewarded for their flattery with survival and riches: the price they pay is the alienation of their self-consciousness in the absolute power of the state. On the other hand, the absolute monarch depends for his actuality upon the praise and self-sacrifice of his subjects: hence his own independence is alienated within their discursive work. Speech mediates between master and slave, but in such a way as to alienate each from his essence. Both monarch and courtier exist *in praise* rather than in themselves (364–66; 532–35).

On the one hand, then, the absolute state has its existence in the speeches of individual courtiers. On the other, the noble spirit, who became a courtier in order to preserve his nobility or honor, has his actual existence in the rewards given him by the monarch. The actuality of praise, or of the existence of master and courtier-slaves, is not honor, but riches or material rewards. Honor has been replaced by selfishness, the necessary outcome of the modern emphasis upon self-preservation. We may note here the connection between "chatter" and modern economics. The purpose of speech is to sanction the satisfaction of individual desires. Life thus becomes a competitive struggle not for recognition but for material satisfaction. However, I cannot satisfy my private desires without cooperating in a division of labor with my fellow men. The silence of aristocratic honor is thus replaced by a "rationalized" or articulate version of democratic selfishness, but with the necessary consequence that virtue reappears, in a radically more efficient guise, as the mutual satisfaction of desires. This mutuality of satisfaction is in effect the return of recognition: I cannot satisfy myself without recognizing the validity of my neighbor's desires (364–66; 532–35).

Let us be careful to notice that we are still in a transitional or defective stage of intersubjective recognition and mutual satisfaction. The "mechanism of the market" has been established, but it has not yet carried out its historical assignment. In political terms, the universality of the state and the particularity of the courtier have been united in a self-contradictory and external "essence": the wealth of nations. The noble and the mean spirit are thus shown to be identical; the virtues of selfishness have not yet become fully visible. The modern state seems to have terminated in the corruption of all. This connection between free discourse and the free market thus leads to riches in the cultural and material domains, but also to decadence and nihilism. The first stage of the modern epoch, the period prior to the French Revolution, terminates in what Hegel calls *absolute Zerrissenheit*: "total distraction," or still more literally "being torn completely apart" (367–69; 536–38). If I seek my essence in my body, I fall prey to the radical defect of externality. Just as the external is infinitely divisible, so too is corporeal desire infinitely variable. The satisfaction of one desire merely gives birth to another. Every goal is transient, and so the high cannot be distinguished from the low (366–69; 535–40).

Nihilism

In the previous section, we studied the dialectic of culture or the emergence of modern discourse as "chatter," so called (among other reasons) because it signals the deterioration of classical honor (silence). Now we shall inspect the disastrous consequences of cultivated chatter, or nihilism, as well as the modern attempt to "negate" nihilism by a return to silence. The key historical figures in this new dialectic are Diderot and Rousseau. Whereas the content in the *Phenomenology* corresponding to this section and the previous one in fact comes just before the explicit analysis of the Enlightenment, the themes are inseparable. Since the Enlightenment is for Hegel the continuation of the Rousseauean "negation of negation" as exemplified in Kant, we have to grasp the preliminary steps in order to follow his analysis.

We began with the conflict between the noble and the mean spirits, or between honor and self-preservation. In order to survive, the noble spirit (= the classical citizen) must sacrifice his honor and so become indistinguishable from the mean-spirited man (= the modern citizen). Therefore, the struggle between the noble and the mean is replaced by the struggle between the rich and the poor. From the classical standpoint, the distinction between the rich and the poor is in general necessary, but in particular cases obviously contingent. A man who is rich today may become poor tomorrow, and vice versa. But more important, a poor man may have a noble character, although the exercise of nobility is evidently conditioned by the possession of wealth. To take the extreme modern position, however, the distinction between the noble and the base is both contingent and identical to the distinction between the rich and the poor. There is, to be sure, a certain "inversion" in this extreme form of the modern view, or a tendency to think of the poor man as noble in spirit. This tendency, however, is in fact a substitution of Christian humility for pagan nobility, joined to the respect for work which is in a way shared by Scripture and modernity (although it should be emphasized that, in Scripture, work is *punishment*, whereas in the modern period, it is often mistaken for the reward).

The poor shall inherit the earth because they are noble in spirit; it is not poverty that is noble, but working to become rich. Hence the modern simplification of the classical teaching amounts to the contention that universal nobility and wealth are obtainable, provided that we alter our conception of nobility in such a way as to give precedence to the body over the soul. "Spirit" is redefined in terms of the body. The body is accessible to scientific control. Hence the struggle between the rich and the poor may be terminated in the satisfaction of all, thanks to methodological work, or the transformation of Christianity into mathematical science (to overstate somewhat for maximum clarity). The view that I have just sketched is typified by Marxism. Hegel is not a Marxist, but he accepts the modern belief that all men may acquire nobility thanks to the dialectic of desire. Man must work in order to *inherit* the earth, and not merely to survive on its face until death carries him away to his heavenly reward. If work is essentially discursive, it remains true for Hegel that discursive work must be externalized in concrete history, and this means in the body and in bodily riches. The manifestation of the Absolute is in this context identical with the manifestation of discourse in physical labor. This manifestation process is painful and full of contradictions which must be experienced and mastered. "The speech of *Zerrissenheit* is the complete speech and the true existing spirit of this whole world of culture" (370; 540). Hence the necessity of nihilism: man must be torn apart by the diversity and contradictoriness of speech, in order to discover his essential nature as author of the complete discourse.

In considering Hegel's analysis of "cultural" nihilism (with which the student must compare the logical analysis studied previously), it is worth thinking of Nietzsche. Nietzsche inconsistently speaks of a difference between noble and base nihilism, or between what one might call the purifying and the decadent versions of *Zerrissenheit*. This distinction is illegitimate because it depends upon a standpoint beyond the world (excluded by Nietzsche), from which we may judge the noble and the base.[8] Hegel's interpretation of cultural nihilism is more complex than Nietzsche's but also more coherent. In the absolute distraction or disintegration of modern cultural nihilism, there is no difference between good and bad. Nor may one refer to the process itself as simply good or bad, for it is both at once. There is no transcendence of the nihilistic process while it continues. Instead, there is a *logic* of nihilism, a dialectical process by which nihilism develops into the next stage of human spiritual history: "The true spirit is however just this unity of the absolutely divided, and indeed, it comes into existence just through the *free actuality* of this *selfless* extreme itself as its middle" (372; 542). Again, man learns who he is by learning how to talk. One cannot mistake the Faustian motif in Hegel's interpretation of nihilism. But history, as explained by Hegel, will complete the process which Faust was himself unable to achieve.

The transition from pure nihilistic distraction to the eventual overcoming of nihilism lies in the self-consciousness of the distracted or self-lacerated spirit. Whereas Nietzsche attributes the overcoming of the decadent nihilism to the nonselfconscious creativity of noble nihilism, or to a creation *ex nihilo,* Hegel makes no distinction between decadence and nobility. The nihilistic process is *self-conscious* and thereby unified within its diverse moments; it is just this unity which enables spirit to overcome its self-inflicted lacerations. Nihilism is an obstacle posed to itself by consciousness; therefore, the act of posing is already the act of stepping beyond the obstacle posed. By denying the primacy of self-consciousness, or the unity of transcendental apperception, Nietzsche makes it impossible to understand why nihilism should have a noble or creative as well as a base or destructive form. Nietzsche, un-

8. Nietzsche does say that whoever would understand Zarathustra must have one foot beyond life: *Werke,* ed. K. Schlechta (Munich, Carl Hanser Verlag, 1955), 2 : 1074, par. 3.

like Hegel, is a *dualist*. He returns us to a fate which is the detached essence or impersonal force of nature, genesis, or the eternal return of the similar. But this is to guarantee the discontinuity of history, and so to make nihilism the permanent "sense" of human experience. "Creativity" is then a euphemism for chance, or what Nietzsche's own successor in our day calls *Seinsgeschick*.

"The distracted consciousness is the consciousness of transposition, and indeed, of absolute transposition; the concept is what rules in it, what brings together the thoughts which lie widely separated from honesty, and whose speech is therefore spiritual" (372; 543). Whereas Nietzsche insists upon honesty in the sense of commitment to one's historical destiny, Hegel directs our attention away from the honesty of particular commitment to the *consciousness of consciousness*, or to the unity of the spirit that speaks within its mutually inconsistent thoughts. Hegel, so to speak, provides us with a rational interpretation of Nietzsche's nonrational conception of the will to power (which, in strict historical terms, is itself Hegel's Absolute Spirit suffering from a loss of consciousness). The will is a property of mind, self, or consciousness. The effort to interpret nature as will is to a certain extent a return to the Greek conception of nature as divine. But Nietzsche commits the same error as the Greeks; he fails to realize that the divine or spiritual is self-conscious. One cannot explain away self-consciousness as a mistaken interpretation of nature. The interpretation of consciousness as the unconscious is still an interpretation, and an interpretation is the conceptual activity of self-consciousness. The validity of Nietzsche's comprehensive interpretation of nature depends paradoxically upon its invalidity, or upon the perpetual presence of a self-consciousness which makes the interpretation of nature to itself.

Nietzsche lacks a conception of totality because he does not grasp the consequence of the doctrine of perspectivism itself. For Nietzsche as well as for Kant and his successors (including Hegel), it is impossible to separate the sense of an object from the mind that thinks or grasps that sense. But this is the fundamental precondition for the identity of subject and object. The effort to "avoid" the subject-object distinction is possible, in other words, only for a subject, or for self-consciousness. The great problem of modern philosophy is thus inseparable from its great discovery: how to avoid "subjectivism" and "objectivism" without losing self-consciousness. Nietzsche, ostensibly opposed to all forms of the "Beyond," in fact alienates man as self-consciousness from nature as unconscious Becoming. A consistent interpretation of Nietzsche's teaching would lead either to the disappearance of man qua man, or to Hegel: namely, to the recognition that all interpretations are indeed valid, but *each in its proper place*. The task of Hegelian science is to understand what history has already uncovered for us: the "place" of all fundamental interpretations. At the present stage, the consciousness to be grasped is the nihilistic consciousness. But its intelligibility shows that this consciousness is not itself just another instance of nihilistic dissolution. Nihilism is intelligible, and therefore it may be overcome. Indeed, it *must* be overcome; the mind responds inevitably to the intelligible by grasping it. The presence of an obstacle is "food" for the engine of desire in its pursuit of total satisfaction.

Our present task is to understand the consciousness of what I translated above as "absolute transposition." We are in the presence of a crucial instance of the dialectic of the inverted world. In the dialectic of inversion, the assertion of *P* is immediately an assertion of non-*P* as well. But this is equivalent to the axiom of linguistic nihilism that "everything may be said," or to a denial of the principle of contradiction. However, this denial is itself intrinsically the affirmation or assertion of totality. The simplest schema of wisdom is "*P* and non-*P*." Needless to say, this schema is in itself too simple; it lacks the moment of self-consciousness or absolute reflection. The thinking spirit must grasp itself as the *S* which predicates of itself simultaneously *P* and non-*P*. With respect to the consciousness of *Zerrissenheit*, we may observe that it both thinks and does not think totality. On the one hand, it says everything; but on the other, it does not understand the significance of its capacity to say everything. It fails to separate the sense of "everything" from that of "nothing." Consciousness lacks a sense of the higher unity which enables it to conceive of self-laceration. Each discourse is then an exemplification of *Zerrissenheit:* not only is it torn apart from other discourses, but it is in itself lacerated. Speech is the work of spirit. If spirit is continuously discontinuous or self-contradictory, there is no reason to say *P* rather than non-*P,* because the assertion of *P is* the assertion of non-*P.*

Hegel illustrates this situation by a quotation from Diderot's *Rameau's Nephew.* The madness of the musician represents the transposed or inverted consciousness. Speech which says everything and nothing is not mere silence, but rather like a musical composition which mixes together all forms and idioms of song. Music is sound that evokes meanings like transitory shadows; the music of a madman evokes all meanings. One might dare to call it *meaningful meaninglessness.* The total speech of the consciousness of *Zerrissenheit* is like the total music of madness. All notes are struck from the high to the low, but each note lacks integrity or is instantly dissolving into its opposite. What is at first hearing total heterogeneity may thus be characterized with equal justice as monosyllabic sound. The indistinguishability of the high from the low note corresponds to the indistinguishability of the good from the bad, or in terms of the previous discussion, of the noble from the mean spirit. Culture originated in chatter, and the mixture of nobility and baseness in the origin is now seen to have vitiated the consequences. From the standpoint of the sage, of course, this mixture is an essential step in the final reconciliation with reality. But the consciousness of *Zerrissenheit* is not wise: it is rather both wise and ignorant, or *mad,* and so the image of musical mania (372–74; 543–45).

Diderot represents the intoxicated nihilism of prerevolutionary culture. Whereas Hegel does not name Rousseau or quote from his works, he clearly represents the negative response to cultural nihilism. Rousseau is a preliminary version of the negation of negation. In this response, spirit rejects culture and turns inward toward a higher stage of consciousness: the universal self. As Hegel rightly observes, this is not simply a turn away from "spiritually cultivated consciousness" toward "the simplicity of the natural heart," but a spiritual transcendence of nihilism (374; 545–46). Hegel is thinking here primarily of the Rousseau of the *Social Contract:* the rise of the universal self leads directly to the level of "faith and pure insight," or in effect to Kant and his contemporaries. Stated more completely, the spirit, in recognizing the vanity of human culture, turns inward (Rousseau) or into the pure universality of the self as thought (Kant). In the first case, the perception of the vanity of human culture is not accompanied by the perception of rationally accessible divinity. Therefore, the vanity of the human is at the same time the vanity of the self: the result is total alienation. The self repudiates power and wealth, but in such a way as to grant their status as the only accessible concrete objects of human desire. There is, in other words, a cultivated rejection of culture, or the substitution of daydreams—of *confessions* and *reveries*—for discourses. But this is merely to reenact the consciousness of self-laceration: "It *is* the self-dismembering nature of all relations, and the conscious dismembering of the same; only as scandalized self-consciousness, however, does it know its own laceration, and in this knowledge of it, it has raised itself immediately above laceration" (374–76; 546–48). Rousseau's reveries are the mirror-image of Diderot's portrait of manic music. In both cases, all content is negative: "The positive object is only the *pure ego itself.*" This pure ego transforms self-laceration at the human level into the transcendental distinction between the worldly and heavenly self; its object is itself as its own "Beyond."

We are now in the brief section entitled "Belief and Pure Insight," which must be understood as a continuation of the section on the world of alienated spirit. It provides us with the transition from Rousseau to Kant, or in Hegel's general terminology, from alienation understood as culture to alienation understood as Enlightenment. This transition is not so much historical as conceptual. The pure ego which transcends the world of nihilistic culture reflects the divisions of that world within its self-interpretation. The world is present in this ego as a representation (*Vorstellung*) rather than as grasped in conceptual thought. Hegel means by this that the world is separate from the ego as well as present in it. A representation is an image of something external to the representing consciousness. The ego is thus alienated from the world, or grasps it only in an image of what must be repudiated. In other words, rejection is not mastery but slavery. The real content of the ego is a "Beyond" or empty supersensuous dimension of what ought to be, located somewhere beyond actuality. The actual world is nihilistic, but there is no world other than the actual world. Thus the pure ego is alienated both from actuality and from the essential world to which it aspires. Therefore it is defined by the very world it rejects (376–77; 549–50). Hegel calls this stage of the alienated consciousness *religion*. More precisely, it is religion in its alienated form, or the unhappy consciousness. In this stage, consciousness is like the musical mania of nihilism. It contains the totality of worldly forms, but as shadows or *Vorstellungen*. Just as the nihilist prefigures the totality of wisdom, so the alienated form of religion prefigures the genuine or scientific religion of conceptual reason. Consciousness of the total worthlessness of the world is consciousness of *the shadow of totality*. Shadow becomes substance when worth is transferred from the parts or perspectives of totality to totality itself. This cannot take place, of course, until totality is visible in and for itself.

The philosopher desires a rational account of the world, whereas the moralist insists upon the actualization of goodness in the world. The alienated form of religion is characterized by a third desire, namely, for goodness-in-itself, which is neither a rational account nor a worldly actualization. Hegel calls this desire "belief" (*Glauben*). He contrasts belief with pure insight as correlative forms of the ego of pure consciousness. The ego as pure insight repudiates all worldly content as negative, or in effect identifies itself with the (true) world. The ego as belief is directed toward transcendent goodness as content; it is therefore alienated from the world. In the first case, the world is just the process of excitation by which worldly content is disintegrated. In the second case, the disintegrated content is both within and outside the ego. It is within as disintegrated, or in the shadow-form of a representation of what has been rejected. It is outside as rejected, or as the correlative to the representation of what has been rejected, and what therefore motivates the flight of the ego from itself as well as from the world. In either case, whether we understand the ego to preserve or to destroy the world, the result is alienation. To repeat the general result, consciousness preserves the world (as pure process of dissolution) but loses its own essence, since it is incapable of thinking the process of dissolution as the totality of self-consciousness; consciousness itself dissolves or has no content whatsoever. By the same token, consciousness destroys the world (or repudiates all worldly content); but in so doing, it incorporates or identifies itself with the world as *Vorstellung,* and in two different senses. First, there is the nihilistic or actual world which, in rejecting it, consciousness judges or interprets. Second, there is the supersensuous world of belief, which is a projection of consciousness beyond itself (378–79; 552–53).

Hegel then summarizes the moment of belief and pure insight as follows. Belief spiritualizes the world and in that sense has an object—but one which it cannot grasp, of which it has no concept, and from which it is thus alienated. Pure insight, on the contrary, is nothing but concept or self-consciousness: it has nothing to grasp (380–82; 554–57). In the first case, the ostensibly supersensuous world is indistinguishable from the sensuous world because, as lacking a concept, it may be represented in any way whatsoever: we see here the *Aufhebung* of worldly nihilism. In the second case, the identification of the pure self with the world leaves open the content of the world, or gives rise to a "war of geniuses." This war repeats the nihilistic conflict of interpretations of the content of the world. If "I" am the world, then everything turns upon my identity. This identity is not provided by the pure ego (= synthetic unity of apperception), and especially not by a pure ego whose "purity" is discontinuous excitation or negation. Under these continuing conditions of nihilism, the "identity" of the world is determined not by the wisest but by the strongest. Nevertheless, within this nihilistic situation, which is inverted via culture from the state to heaven, there remains a valid if still implicit dimension. By spiritualizing the world, the self understands that it is its own essential object. What remains is to give rational content to self-consciousness understood as both subject and object (382–83; 557–58).

Insight, Utility, and Terror

We turn now to Hegel's analysis of the Enlightenment. The term *Aufklärung* means literally "clearing up," but the reader will bear in mind that for Hegel, there is as much shadow as light in this process. The Enlightenment is for Hegel an aspect of alienation. The human effort to "clear things up" has the initial effect of "clearing them away" or depriving them of significance. This is not Hegel's last word on the subject, but it is his first word, and it provides us with the key to the instability of the process. In Hegel's account, the Enlightenment arises as the negation of nihilism, but one which is necessarily incomplete. The ego turns away from the self-lacerating diversity of cultivated world-views into itself. This inner turn takes two forms. The first is that of pure insight, or conceptualization without content; and the second is belief or faith, or content without conceptualization. In both cases, consciousness is concerned with itself as totality, although in neither case does it grasp discursively or conceptually the significance of such a concern. At first glance, belief and pure insight seem to be opposed to each other, and the Enlightenment might be interpreted as the struggle between these two modes of consciousness. As we shall see, however, the dialectical development of the Enlightenment results in the initial identity of its two sides.

This conclusion is implicit in the first paragraphs of Hegel's transition from nihilism to Enlightenment. Whether on behalf of universal self-absorption or a flight to heaven, consciousness attempts to flee from the dissolute world of culture. But it is a crucial premise in Hegel's teaching that a genuine rejection of the world is impossible. In attempting to reject the world, we define ourselves in terms of the world. We carry the world with us as a shadow-image or *Vorstellung* which is our only real substance, and which, because it is reduced to the status of a shadow, desubstantializes the self as subjectivity as well. The man of faith creates his heaven from fragmented images of the rejected world. The man of pure insight deprives the world or its interpretation of significance, and finds the unity of the world exclusively in his own universal interest. But this interest, even though directed toward the self, is necessarily defined by the world which elicits and shapes it. Faith spiritualizes the world, and pure insight identifies the spiritualized world with the human spirit (383–85; 559–60).

The Enlightenment, then, is not fundamentally a "return to earth from heaven" in the popular sense of the scientific rejection of religion as superstition. We should bear in mind here Leibniz's efforts to reconcile science and religion, as well as retention by such "enlightened" figures as Bacon of a restriction upon scientific publication in their scientific utopias.[9] These themes are assimilated into the eighteenth-century Enlightenment which, as Hegel sees it, is an equivocal identification of earth and heaven, or the identification of man and God. The equivocal nature of this identification is easy to see. A divine man scorns human culture, but a human god has no content apart from culture. The positive dimension of the Enlightenment, its universality of consciousness, is at once its negative dimension. The universality of consciousness is self-conscious only via the assimilation of the negativity of all forms of culture. In the last analysis, the Enlightenment as universal insight is faith in the man of genius. Since there are many such men, the Enlightenment cannot escape from the destructive perspectivism of nihilism. It cannot quite complete its positive task of making explicit the identity of subject and object in the human spirit, which still (as in Kant and Fichte) eludes the concept. All elements of the equation are plunged into negativity, but as an excitation which will produce its positive form from the fecundity of inner motion.

Understood as pure insight, the Enlightenment is an attack

9. See the *New Atlantis*, in *Works*, ed. Spedding, Ellis, and Heath (New York, Hurd and Houghton, 1864), 5 : 411.

upon the stupidity of the masses, the deception of the priests, and the oppression of the despots. It is thus primarily practical or quasi-moral. That is, it is not the expression of a rational political ethic, but rather the transpolitical effort of the universal ego to interest itself, despite the uninteresting character of what it does. The ego "clarifies" itself in its lower manifestations, but as a mixture of light and shadow. As Hegel says, "the communication of pure insight is therefore to be compared with a tranquil extension or diffusion, like a fragrance spreading through the yielding atmosphere" (387; 563). The success of the Enlightenment is due to the community of essence in its warring parts; hence the war is more like peace. But this means that the ostensible enemies infect or turn into each other. The struggle to free religion from superstition by means of reason produces a "rationalized" or denatured religion. Conversely, the attempt to purify religion by reason results in the assimilation of religion into reason. As Hegel rather obscurely puts this, pure insight has no content of its own, and therefore assumes as content the essence of what it rejects as corrupt. In other words, an insight into the insignificance of human activity is an insight into the insignificance of humanity. The negation of error by pure insight is thus an absolute self-negation. In slightly different terms, the "egoism" of the pure ego is the mirror-image of nihilism (387–90; 564–67).

Man can become a god only because of the insubstantiality of the world; in becoming a god, he divinizes the insubstantial world. The Enlightenment teaches that man makes God, but also that this making is a lie. The rational clarification of religion is thus at the same time a "clearing away" of significance from man, who expresses his self-interest by engaging in such false labor. The Enlightenment is then the pure insight into the triviality of the activity of pure insight. As Hegel says, the essence of belief is the spirit of the community (391; 568–69). God lives within the world. If the world is corrupt, so too is God. If the world is empty of significance, so too is God. In other words, the object of belief is the essential character of the consciousness of an age; one might say that men exist *as* what they believe. Whatever this may be, the immediate certitude of belief cannot be doubted. Hegel wishes to indicate in this way the *deficiency* of immediate belief. What cannot be doubted because it is the horizon of doubt itself, cannot be seen, and hence, despite its immediacy, is in fact inaccessible or invisible (391–92; 569–70).

By criticizing and corrupting faith, pure insight criticizes and corrupts itself. The "rational purification of faith" may be summarized in three steps: (1) It pollutes the object of religion to a form of sensuousness by distinguishing it, together with all objects, as other than itself or other than pure consciousness; (2) it makes contingent the grounds of belief by reducing them to the status of external or historical evidence; (3) it vulgarizes the ends of belief by a denial of teleology or eschatology, and the substitution of arguments from self-interest. Pure insight criticizes the good intentions and honest deeds of faith as foolish and unsuitable in the sense of inconvenient. And it does so from a kind of cynical skepticism which we previously identified as the egoist mirror-image of nihilism. Pure insight denies not the goodness but the desirability of the ends of faith. By so doing, *it shows the impurity of its own intentions,* or contradicts its own claim to purity in the sense of freedom from sensuous individuality or mere worldliness (393–96; 571–75). Pure insight now stands revealed as the essence of worldliness, and therefore, as insubstantial as worldliness itself. Faith in oneself as pure insight is thus driven to bankruptcy by the very critique of faith in another.

Hegel next studies the positive significance of the Enlightenment. What is the truth that the enlightened pure insight advocates in place of faith? In effect, pure insight makes a virtue of its vice. Taken in itself, pure insight lacks predicates or qualities. It is a "pure form" in the sense of a vacuum. But this means that it cannot be distinguished from the finite, worldly singulars which serve as its content. Since consciousness qua pure insight arose from the skeptical negation of all content, it is mere negation in itself. Therefore, it has no "transcendental" characteristics. We see here a reference to

Kant's criticism of speculative theory, or the attempt to think the concept without regard to sensuous content. Consciousness has rejected everything but itself, in the effort to purify or enlighten itself; but this makes it inaccessible to itself, or at the mercy of its content. Consciousness is not the synthesis of form and content, but content related to a vacuum, namely, the unknowable God of modern Deism. The result is to reinstitute sensuous certitude, but now as absolute truth rather than as opinion (*Meinung*). In the absence of form, or in the presence of formal absence or vacuity, the sensuous singular is absolutized. But what can this mean? An absolute singular which lacks all form is in itself only whatever it is for another. The thing is defined by its use: the positive doctrine of the Enlightenment is *utilitarianism.* Man returns in a sense to the Garden of Eden, or the natural enjoyment of nature. Whereas nihilism denies the distinction between good and evil, utilitarianism expresses the same doctrine positively by asserting that everything is good, to someone, in some way. Natural enjoyment is restricted only by the "commandment" against too much enjoyment, which turns to pain. Hence the good may be defined as rational cooperation for communal enjoyment, and religion is the expression of the Absolute as pure utility (396–400; 575–80).

Absolute egoism, as we may refer to the positive teaching of the Enlightenment, spiritualizes the world in one sense and reconciles the actual and the rational in another. The defect here is the absence of conceptual structure or form. The mere rejection of the "Beyond" is not an overcoming or reappropriation of it. Instead, negativity is itself defined as the "Beyond." And this is equivalent to the traditional religious failure to assimilate negativity into the concept. Whether the world is "created" out of nothing or hangs in the void, its significance is delimited and hence defined by nothingness. In Hegel's language, the Enlightenment is the negative power of the concept, or the negative unification of subject and object, but not the positive form of that unification. The Enlightenment does not understand that it, too, is faith. The negativity of pure insight is the shadow of the positivity of faith. The two belong together, and this togetherness is the overcoming of the split between faith and knowledge. Until this unification occurs, the conceptual assimilation of particulars is an assimilation into nothingness (400–02; 580–83).

Faith is dissatisfied Enlightenment; Enlightenment is non-selfconscious faith (402–07; 583–89). The truth of the Enlightenment lies in its identification of pure insight as the negativity of pure thought (407; 590). Hegel interprets this to mean that, as altogether negative or other than every particular determination, consciousness is indistinguishable from matter. In other words, the Enlightenment, as the quarrel between Materialism and Idealism, is the internal dissolution of the Cartesian doctrine of substance. Thought and extension cannot be distinguished from each other, as is especially clear in Descartes' successor, Spinoza. There is no difference between Materialism and Idealism until such time as a self-conscious subjectivity manifests itself in place of a dead or invisible substance; this is the process which we have studied in previous chapters. Since the world is an interpretation by consciousness, Idealism is true. But since consciousness is the essence of the world understood as the totality of sensuous particulars, Materialism is true. These two truths cancel each other; in political language, the radical instability of the modern epoch culminates in the French Revolution, which itself begins as Idealism and ends as Materialism: from absolute freedom to terror. Men tear apart their bodies because their minds have been lacerated by the instability of their self-interpretations (408–10; 591–94.)

Hegel attributes the failure of the Enlightenment to its inability to sustain the guiding concept of Cartesian metaphysics, namely, that "in itself, Being and Thinking are the same." Hegel seems to understand Descartes as a proto-Idealist, for whom "thinghood is thought' (410; 594). In his own *Logic,* Hegel says that pure Being is identical with pure Nothing. If "pure Being" is "pure thought" in the Cartesian metaphysics, it is the same as "Nothing," and thereby indistinguishable from "pure matter." The identity of thing and thought at the level of "purity" is too abstract to account for heterogeneity;

"purity" is another word for vacuum or *Nichts* (410–11; 594–96). In the Cartesian teaching, the "heart" of each thing is a vacuum: the negative identity of thing and thought. In the Enlightenment, the vacuum at the heart of things is filled by the concept of utility. A thing is nothing in itself, but whatever our desire defines it to be. Things are defined not by thought but by the "passions of the soul," which means that the soul is defined by its appetites. A thing is then continuously changing: its stability is that of negativity. But the thing does stand forth as the representation or objectification of negativity. In each case of desire, it is a specific thing or form which is desired, and so a specific kind of use. There is, then, still a split between the thing as representation and the essence of the object. The concept of the object is the negativity of pure insight; the object has not yet been united with its concept because negativity alone is ungraspable. Pure insight is not and cannot be genuinely self-conscious (412; 597).

On the other hand, self-consciousness is now certain of its own desires, and in that sense appropriates or unites with the world of material things. Desire, and in that sense consciousness, is satisfied in the concept of utility or the enjoyment of nature. Therefore Hegel can close his long critical analysis of the Enlightenment with what seem in themselves to be words of unqualified praise: "Both worlds are reconciled, and heaven is planted on the earth below" (413; 598). The meaning of these words, however, is contained in the criticism that preceded them. Heaven is planted in the soil of the earth, but the earth remains the unconscious identity of spirit and flesh, which must be resuscitated by the cataclysmic turmoil of the French Revolution, or the self-destruction of desire. In somewhat different terms, the ostensible "Platonism" of the founders of modernity is in an essential respect an *inversion* of Platonism. In order to satisfy the soul, the moderns define it in terms of the body. But this leads to the transformation of reason into an instrument of bodily satisfaction. The soul remains only in the form of what Hegel calls "utility." The useful is defined, not as it is in itself, but as it appears to another. The soul, as useful, is "objective" only in the continuously changing shapes which it assumes from the reciprocal desires of human bodies.

At this stage, man is not defined by what he does but by what he desires or *wills.* And this is the link between Descartes and Rousseau, or more generally, between the beginning of the modern epoch and its end in the terror of the French Revolution. The situation is not changed by the fact that human desire takes the form of speech or culture. As we have seen, "freedom" of speech produces a multiplicity of contradictory world-views. The essence of culture is diversity, or the encouragement of others to express themselves. On the other hand, each expression is an implicit claim to provide a true account of the Whole. Each atomic speaker says "*my* desire," not "desire." The Republic of Letters is in fact a state of hypocrisy, or of war posing as peace. Hence the moral depravity of the cultivated world, which is attacked so persuasively by Rousseau. But Rousseau himself has no rational alternative to the situation he attacks. The only effective solution to the war of speeches is to provide the complete or circular speech, which alone 'tolerates" all others by preserving them in reciprocal relation to each other. Rousseau failed to understand this. Instead, he tried to reformulate the modern doctrine of desire in "idealistic" or spiritual terms. The result is the doctrine of *universal will.*

In order to understand the transition from desire and cultivated speech to the universal will, we must remind ourselves of the significance of Hegel's concept of utility. The tyrannical nature of desire is required for practical reasons to subordinate itself to its democratic aspect. Each man defines himself as desire, and in so doing, he defines the world as objectified in and as his desire. Each man defines the Whole as *his* desire, or as himself. Since others do the same, the ensuing destructive conflict can be avoided only by recourse to the element of universality in the situation: desire as such, or rather, universal desire as expressed in terms of the human body. There is a general agreement that "I will satisfy your desire if you will satisfy mine"; this is the so-called social contract in the Hobbesian form. In this manner, for the sake of self-satisfaction or pure egoism, my desire becomes useful to you, and your desire becomes useful to me. Man as desire is redefined as utility. The recognition of utility as the essence of consciousness frees it from the restriction of objectivity. There is a practical restriction in the form of the social contract, but this contract expresses the theoretical truth that man is pure desire. *Theory is subordinated to practice, itself indistinguishable from production.* There are now only practico-productive limitations to universal self-satisfaction.

The political world is thus the practical expression of the theoretical nature of the self as "Being-for-another" or as defined by the desires of others precisely because of the self's tyrannical desire to be fully satisfied. Men recognize each other (the basis of political life) because they are useful to each other. This recognition of mutual utility is called the "universal will." Rousseau thereby gives a "spiritual" formulation to what is actually still the seventeenth-century materialism of Hobbes (modified by Locke). The doctrine of the universal will is a discourse based upon the restriction of competing speeches. One can therefore understand Rousseau's teaching, less as an attack upon the Enlightenment, than as an attempt to render it stable and coherent. It is as though Rousseau were saying to modern man: "If you genuinely wish to satisfy your desires, restrict your freedom of speech. Since there is no comprehensive or universally valid speech, particular discourses will only conflict with and even cancel each other. Even worse, the truce effected by the doctrine of the universal will is sufficiently unstable that it cannot survive constant verbal analysis. The stability of man rests upon an unstable restriction of instability. But this must not be publicly discussed, or the result will be chaos." Hence men like Rousseau, who understand this situation, must retreat into the silence of reveries. Rousseau's solution to the human dilemma is obviously unsatisfactory, since men cannot be silenced. But this is precisely what Hegel understands by "the cunning of reason." Speech is "free" not by the acts of historical men but in its own essence. This freedom is in fact necessity: the necessity of the concept, or of the Absolute to manifest itself. The short-term results of this necessity are frequently, perhaps always, negative; but in the long run, the result is wisdom (414–16; 599–602).

We have now moved from Hegel's discussion of the Enlightenment to the analysis of "Absolute Freedom and Terror." But there is no radical separation between these two themes. Since the useful is defined by the desire of another, my own essence, as utility, is contingency. This is true of the self as citizen and of political institutions: they may be changed in accordance with changes in desire. The true expression of the universal will, or the generalization of human desire, is *revolution* against all objective restrictions upon universal satisfaction. In political terms, a revolution against monarchy and on behalf of democracy is altogether "justified" by man's radical contingency. Unfortunately, every social and political institution is in one sense or another a restriction upon desire. The desire to implement politically the universal freedom or theoretical equality of citizens leads to the destruction of whatever stands in the path of this theoretical universality. The practical implementation of radical contingency is social and political chaos: the terror of the French Revolution. For it can never be the case that institutions but not men are destroyed. The individual both is, and is dissatisfied by, his institutions. Therefore, he can destroy them only by dying. As Hegel puts it, absolute freedom cannot be achieved by any positive work or deed: "There remains for it only *negative activity;* it is only the *fury* of disappearance." And again: "The only work and deed of universal freedom is therefore *death,* and indeed a *death* which has no inner range and fullness, for what is negated is the unfulfilled point of the absolute free self. It is thus the coldest, flattest death, without any more significance than slicing through a head of cabbage or than a gulp of water" (417–19; 603–05).

The Moral Consciousness and the Beautiful Soul

In the next subdivision of the *Phenomenology,* Hegel discusses the human spirit as it has been "purified" by the Terror or Revolution. In theoretical terms, Rousseau, when reinterpreted by Kant, leads us to moral consciousness or "self-certain

Spirit." The term "certain" (*gewisse*) contains in German a strong echo of the word for "conscience" (*Gewissen*). This term is central for both Rousseau and Kant. Hegel's criticism of Kant is that the appeal to the conscience, in the form of the categorical imperative, is a quasi-mathematical transformation of morality into universal rules, or of spiritual form lacking in content. In the Kantian teaching, consciousness is moral and nature is amoral. This is why Kant attacks eudaimonism, or the view that moral virtue is connected to happiness. Hegel, on the contrary, rejects this ascetic doctrine of pure duty to formal law. As is obvious from his preservation of the modern doctrine of desire, Hegel always admits that the individual has a right to insist upon satisfaction. The individual works toward the rational goal of historical as opposed to heavenly happiness. Socrates is said to have brought philosophy down from heaven into the cities of men. Hegel accepts and revises this by making the state the mediation of desire and obligation.

Hegel is in a way a "Greek" in his criticism of the Kantian thesis that nature is amoral. But this point should not be exaggerated; more cautiously, nature, as assimilated into history, is the "substance" of the state, which is in turn rendered subjective by Spirit or religion. Man therefore finds happiness in actual deeds performed within history; in this sense, man is a "political" animal, since history is essentially political history. Kant cannot separate morality from happiness without transcending the world of nature, which he refuses to do, since his avowed intention is to harmonize Spirit and nature. For epistemological as well as moral reasons, he must insist that sensuousness is *compatible* with morality, while insisting equally upon the opposition between sensuousness and pure consciousness (428; 619–20). The unity of morality and nature both must and cannot appear in nature. The fulfillment of morality leads to a contradiction which seems to rob it of its holy character, to make it unachievable. In order to avoid this, or to account for the requisite harmony of consciousness and nature on the one hand and the harmony of reason and sensuousness on the other, we are forced to postulate a divine legislator. What is *in-itself* is brought together with what is *for-itself*. What must be true of consciousness, yet cannot be true of its human form, is conceived as true of the divine consciousness. I receive my reward of happiness in the divine kingdom of virtuous spirits, for the sake of actions performed in the natural kingdom of human spirits. Therefore, the moral consciousness finds its fulfillment in thought only: in the postulated unity of the divine legislator (428–31; 620–24).

The Kantian moral consciousness falls into the abyss of the emptiness or negativity of its own purity: the "difference" between the noumenal and the phenomenal domains. And yet, Kant's effort to reconcile nature and consciousness is very close to the Hegelian interpretation of the exteriority and interiority of Spirit. For Kant, however, Spirit or the transcendental ego is known only as a "condition for the possibility of" nature and consciousness. This "condition" is neither alive nor dead, neither subject nor substance, but the visible aspect of the invisible or spontaneous "Absolute" which is, as the name implies, all too separate from its own consequences. The hidden or invisible is rendered visible not in a concept but in a *postulate* of what *ought* to be. Consciousness as conscience remains a form of alienation. The self places its significance in moral activity. A moral act can only be performed in the natural world. As such, however, it is subject to natural rather than moral laws. And so, as moral, it is amoral: another instance of the dialectic of the inverted world. In slightly different terms, the self poses its own objective significance in the moral act, and is therefore identical with its own essence. Since, however, the absolute essence of pure morality cannot be externalized or objectified, the moral act is not essential or real in itself, but only via the postulation of self-consciousness. As Hegel puts it, consciousness "pretends" to make by its activity what can never occur in the concrete temporal present. This pretense is a displacement of consciousness, at first into its (unreal) acts, but next in a "Beyond" that lies always beyond the perimeter of activity (432–36; 624–31).

The law of this world (accepted by Kant) is Newtonian mechanics. If moral activity were to fulfill itself in this world, it would negate itself (since morality requires freedom). The moral consciousness pretends that it is in harmony with actuality, and it pretends that its perfection lies in the given finite act as an expression of obedience to conscience. But underneath this pretense is still another pretense. The disharmony of nature and consciousness, and the worthlessness of the finite act in comparison with the true end of the highest good, *make morality a sham.* In order to conceal these results, moral consciousness must then pretend that morality is achieved in itself, as opposed to nature or as purified of all sensuous content. But this is contradicted by the fact of activity; sensuousness is the necessary medium which brings consciousness into actuality. Instincts and inclinations are the engine of moral activity and do not work contrary to it. This engine functions in accordance with natural laws. Once again, moral consciousness is displaced by its dissimulations, or driven from one postulate to another in its search for the *summum bonum.* But each new world is merely the image of its predecessor. There is no progress toward moral perfection, but only toward the *Nichts* or inaccessibility of the end. Moral action is revealed as impossible. We cannot earn our happiness but, at the best, receive it as a gift of divine grace. The real good is thus not morality but happiness or blessedness (436–40; 631–36).

Since morality is impossible or a self-deception, it cannot be wrong to achieve happiness through immoral acts. More accurately, there cannot be any real distinction between "moral" and "immoral" acts, because all activity is a function of amoral nature. The incoherence or lack of seriousness in the self-interpretation of moral consciousness is now manifest. In an effort to define itself as the absolute, consciousness is forced to pose the absolute as outside itself: as the divine legislator. Either morality is nothing but a nihilistic dream, or else, according to Hegel, it must be fulfilled within the "natural" world (as mediated by history), and thus be opposed to "pure"morality. In order to free itself from hypocrisy, the moral consciousness must admit that it was not serious in its interpretation of activity, which leads to the alienation from its own essence. This lack of seriousness is the correlative of taking the world, as the arena of activity, too seriously. The moral consciousness now flees from its representation of the world and its correlative "Beyond." It flees from external reality in these two senses back into itself, which it now interprets as *pure conscience.* In this form, moral consciousness turns to itself as pure universal beauty and becomes the *beautiful soul* (440–44; 636–41).

Hegel, as it were, anticipates Kierkegaard's opposition of the ethical and the aesthetic by showing how the ethical is transformed through its own logic into the aesthetic. The pure conscience is an intermediate stage in this transformation. In order to represent itself as "pure," moral action as subjective self-certitude must be immediate intuition. There can be no interval between the moral agent and the reflexive act of discursive interpretation. The individual act of pure conscience is the content of the universal form of conscience itself, which thus finds itself universally present in all of its deeds. Conscience can act because it is initially silent, whereas moral consciousness as the moral world-view speaks first (or tries to explain its goodness as a postulate of the pure practical reason) and is subsequently silenced (449–50; 649–50). This silencing of moral consciousness is equivalent to a denial of the reality of its activity. Consciousness postulates its significance to lie within its activity. Since it cannot speak coherently of this activity, consciousness cannot recognize itself therein. Furthermore, consciousness cannot be recognized by the other individuals who constitute the world of moral activity, because this world is in fact a mutual deception. Hegel refers to this detachment of the subject from the world of acts and deeds as the transference of objective predicates to the subject (450–51; 650–52).

The subject now knows itself to be subject and object, or an objectively enduring activity. Its own certitude takes precedence over the variety of circumstances and duties characteristic of moral action. Conscience is pure duty; it is free to fill the subjective dimension of pure duty with *any* content, to do anything or to reject anything. For whatever it does must be right: immediate certitude of the self as the highest good cannot be wrong in any mediate determination of itself. Or rather, the conscience is free from every determination: "In this way, conscience is altogether free from every content; it absolves itself from every determinate duty, which claims to be valid as law. In the force of its self-certitude, it possesses the majesty of absolute autarchy" or the power "to bind and to dissolve" (456; 658). This universal dimension of self-certitude is the silent precondition for subsequent meaningful speech (452–56; 653–58).

We have now reached a crucial moment in the argument of the *Phenomenology*. The subject turns inward, or discovers itself as the ground of certitude in every interpretation of the world. Initially, however, this discovery is a kind of silence, and so the inverse of an interpretation. Silent self-certitude is immediately present in moral action. But one silent action is no better and no worse than another. In historical terms, the results of the Enlightenment are a development of discourse to the point of logorrhea and so nihilism. In turning away from discursive nihilism, however, the subjective spirit turns into silent nihilism. This is the moment of the negation of negation. In order to resolve the conflict of silent deeds, spirit must begin to speak again. As Hegel puts it, speech allows the spirit to be for another what it is in itself (456–58; 658–61). Without speech, conscience would not exist for another because all agents would be identical or indistinguishable in the common silence of their respective certitude.

Silence prior to the experience of Western history would be innocence or ignorance. Silence in the midst of cultivated enlightenment would be a surrender to nihilism. Silence after speech has been completed, or all possible interpretations have been offered, is *potential wisdom*. What I am calling here the complete silence of total discourse is the presence of pure spiritual negativity in and as its moments, each of which is both positive (as determinate or asserted) and negative (as contradicted by its opposite assertion). Of course, silence understood as the separation of universal subjectivity from its discursive moments is still radically defective. The self-certain subject must begin to speak *again,* or to justify himself, and therefore in effect to repeat or reappropriate everything which has already been said, in such a way as to demonstrate its own presence (as negative activity) within each and every discourse. This process of discursive recollection requires us ultimately to repeat the entire course of the *Phenomenology,* but at the level of the Absolute, or as Hegel says in the *Logic,* from the standpoint of God, just before he creates the world. We have to acquire the divine standpoint in order to reappropriate or render intelligible the whole speech of phenomenology which we have been studying here.

As Hegel says in the *Phenomenology,* conscience is "the moral genius that knows the inner voice of its immediate knowledge as a divine voice" (460; 663). The explanation or justification of self-certitude is grounded in the immediate knowledge of the self as doing God's will. The justification initially points beyond the self as immediate to God, or to the complete expression of the goodness of the certain self. This means that the justifying speech is initially theology or religion. We are not yet at the level of logic or the Absolute. This is clear from the fact that immediate intuition or self-certitude, in justifying itself, necessarily calls upon a God who is both the self and the completion of, or higher than, the self. Man is still alienated from God (461; 664). The negative moment is still detached from its content because in the process of assimilating that content. Therefore, the absolute certitude of conscience is now seen to be absolute non-truth (462; 665). "It is the absolute self-consciousness, in which consciousness sinks out of view." This is what Hegel means by the beautiful soul. Conscience, in this stage, lives in dread of betraying its silent certitude of its own purity through action and political existence. In order to preserve the purity of its heart, it flees contact with reality. Consciousness longs for activity but is vitiated by its very actualization, like a formless dust that loosens itself into the air (463; 666–67).

The beautiful soul contemplates itself as pure universality, expressed in discourse but unlimited by action. It is the totality of the moments of culture, and thus a recollection of everything that has been done and said thus far, but as lacking in responsibility toward the historical and political world. The beautiful soul is both judge and judged; it is the universal which particularizes itself *as* itself. Differently stated, the individual believes himself to be universal, or to determine the content of action by his immediate self-certitude. But action, or the interpretation of action, is no longer universal. The agent is thus condemned by his own guilty conscience as soon as he acts. Since self-justification is itself an act, the act of justification is at once the act of condemnation. Both action and the failure to act are equally good and evil (463–66; 667–71).

On the other side of the same conflict, the universal element is not action but thought. In fact, the individual conscience becomes aware of its own particularity by an intuition of itself as universal, and so, paradoxically, as other than the universal. The universal is universal as particular: its intuition is determinate, and therefore a (discursive) *judgment* rather than an intuition. I cannot intuit *myself* except by distinguishing myself, or specifying myself *as* thus-and-such. The general form of such an ostensible intuition is thus "*S* is *P*." Judgment is neither merely intuition nor action, but the discursive account of the significance of each other. Hegel expresses this in terms of morality as follows. Every moral act is accompanied by particular motives, such as the desire for fame, love of honor, the pursuit of happiness, and the like. An act from pure duty is impossible, because pure duty condemns every act. The judgment that arises originally from the priority of the universal to the particular now insists that the universal must serve the particular. Hegel refers to this as a "morality of valets" (a phrase later adopted by Goethe). To the valet, no man is a hero, not because there is no hero but because the judge is a valet (466–68; 671–73).

We should be sufficiently familiar with Hegel's dialectic by now to realize that the reference to valets is a preparation for the reconciliation between subject and object, or spirit and external world. Judgment (or the interplay of judging valets) replaces silence (the nobility of the master) or conscience as the medium of universality. In other words, we are now prepared for the labor of conceptual thinking. But this is to anticipate a later stage (471; 677–78). I therefore paraphrase Hegel's meaning as follows. The separation between man and God cannot be overcome by any form of pure morality, whether as explicitly political or as mystical intuition. It will yield only to the labor of the concept: the judgment replaces self-justification. In order to understand God, man must first understand himself. At first, man regards himself as the "image of God," but this is a preliminary and defective formulation. It is true that God is first accessible to man within his own consciousness. But that consciousness is not an image; it is a mode of the divine and so the divine itself. The doctrine of the image, on the contrary, is an eternal mask of the hidden god. To this extent, then, man must "return to the earth," namely, by turning inward and engaging in the laborious process of self-understanding. But this process is identical with a turning outward, or an exhibition of oneself in the concrete political reality of history. Morality must be rendered articulate. This does not mean that it ceases to be moral; on the contrary, discourse is genuinely articulate only if it includes the moral dimension or is teleological. And this is why Hegel develops a logic of *judgment* rather than of propositions. Logic judges practice, and in a certain sense, already explained, posits or constitutes it. The judgment of practice is not the condemnation but the assimilation of the particular. The teleological "cunning of reason" is thus at work even, or especially, in the disputes of valets, who will come to discover their spirituality by the work involved in rejecting it.

The dialectic of nature and consciousness, or the analysis of modern individualism, articulates the various world-views or interpretations of Spirit as actual in human history. In a sense, all the fundamental steps have been accomplished except for the conceptual activity of self-consciousness, which grasps the completeness and hence the significance of what has been accomplished. The modern ego understands itself to be the Whole; it understands the subjectivity of substance. But there is still a dualism within the ego of the universal and the particular (= pure conscience and worldly activity). In religious language, there is still a dualism between God and man, albeit *within* the absolute ego. God has not yet revealed himself in conceptual terms as "the appearing God who knows himself as pure knowing," or the Hegelian version of the Aristotelian divine intellect. Man has not yet conceptually grasped the meaning of the Christian revelation, or the identity of God and man in Christ (472; 678–79). Therefore the next chapter of the *Phenomenology,* devoted to the penultimate vision of absolute wisdom, will be concerned with the structure of the appearance of God to man. This chapter is not "historical" in the sense that it does not mark a new stage in spiritual development. Instead, as I have already noted, it restudies all that has been accomplished from the religious standpoint. Religion is a *representation* of the relation between the universal and the particular. It is therefore couched in the language of imagery, and therein lies its defect. The detachment of the image from the original can only be overcome by the transformation of imagery into conceptual knowledge. This does not, needless to say, lessen the importance of religious representation, but defines it. It would not be altogether inaccurate to say that religious representation is the Hegelian analogue to sensuous content in the Kantian doctrine of conceptual judgment.

Religion

As the conclusion to this discussion of the modern age conceived as "Enlightenment," and so as both shadow and light, I shall analyze briefly Hegel's treatment of religion in the second to last chapter of the *Phenomenology*. It will not be necessary for us to consider the chapter in its entirety. Perhaps the main point for our purpose is that religion, understood as the comprehension in images of the past as divine, emerges from the Enlightenment, which does not suppress religion but prepares it for the final development into philosophy. Hegel, in other words, gives a radical interpretation to an expression commonly employed with respect to the Enlightenment: a *religion of reason.* In order to see what this means, we may pass over Hegel's discussion of natural and aesthetic religions and restrict our attention to his analysis of revealed religion.

In the Greek world, substance (the ethical folk) and subjectivity (individualism) have developed in such a way as to separate the two. Hegel describes this separation as the difference between tragedy and comedy. Within the development of subjectivity, one can also discern a dualism of tragedy and comedy, corresponding approximately to the Stoic and the Skeptic. The Stoic rejects corrupt actuality and tries to make the philosopher a god rather than a statesman. This divine pretention of the Stoic is ironically rejected by the Skeptic, who embodies comic negativity in philosophical form. His laughter at Stoic independence in turn gives rise to the unhappy consciousness: "We see that this unhappy consciousness is the reciprocal side and completion of the in itself fully happy, comic consciousness" (521–23; 750–53). The decay of Greek religion is expressed by Hegel in the striking phrase, *"God has died."* In using this phrase, Hegel obviously wishes to suggest that the death of paganism is an anticipation of the death of Christ. Gods die periodically in history when they lose their vitality: here is another anticipation of Nietzsche. However, for Hegel, the fact of the Christian resurrection, when properly interpreted, is historically final.

When the pagan gods die, they cannot be brought to life. This fact is connected with Hegel's view, mentioned earlier, that the age of art as a developing force is over. Classical art, so to speak, becomes art rather than religion, a representation of the *memory* of the divine rather than a *celebration* of divinity. We "appreciate" the past, which is thus for us no longer the present. And in appreciating or remembering Greek art, we go beyond it by internalizing (*Er-innerung*) what in it was still *externalized* spirit. Greek art is now seen as an inner modality of the human spirit, and not as the external representation of fate (523–24; 753–54). The boundary which Greek art set for spirit is surpassed only by assimilation; and this in turn becomes possible only when Greek art "dies" or loses its hold upon man in the historical present. In this way, Hegel detaches Christ from the Jewish tradition, and presents him as a *necessary historical consequence* instead of as a miraculous discontinuity in human history. The detachment of Christ from the Jews is necessary for the conceptualizing of Christ. The Jews lack *Logos,* and this is related to their inability to externalize the spirit of God in plastic form. The Jews are political slaves; they have no vision (according to Hegel) of God as Spirit present within daily life, but conceive of him only as the unreasonable, jealous, and *absent* Jaweh.

Greek art is rational; with all of its defects, it embodies the anticipation of the unity of God and man in the concrete presence of political existence. Freedom, individuality, political community, and *Logos* are all present in unstable isolation within the Greek world. What is still missing is the conception of Spirit as interiority, and (in terms of our previous discussion) of pure negative activity. The reflection upon or internal appropriation of the meaning of Greek art leads the Spirit to transcend the limits of paganism. Spirit now brings the art work to life as God incarnate in man. The divine Father of Christ is substance as Being-in-itself; his human mother is the actuality of self-consciousness as Being-for-itself. Hence Christ is self-consciousness in-and-for-itself (524–26; 754–56). There is nothing miraculous about Christ because the form of every individual consciousness is Absolute Spirit or God (527; 757–58). "The divine nature is the same as the human, and it is this unity that is intuited" by man (528–29; 758–60).

European history is the process by which mankind assimilates the significance of the resurrection of Christ. The resurrection represents the spiritual significance of the body, or of nature as informed by the Spirit. Until such time as the resurrection is understood conceptually, it remains a representation of the truth. Thus Hegel can praise Christianity as the true religion while at the same time criticizing it: "A deficiency is present in this union of Being and Thought; the spiritual essence continues to be burdened with an unreconciled split between a Here and a Beyond" (532; 763–64). Religion must be surpassed by the raising (*erheben*) of its intuition to the level of the concept, "in order to equate *for itself* its consciousness with its self-consciousness, as this has occurred for us or *in itself*" (532; 764). It is, in other words, not sufficient for Spirit to identify itself with the community of believers or Church.

This alone would debase Spirit to mere historical externality. God and man must be conceptually, and not just ceremonially, identical in the self-consciousness of the sage. Otherwise, the cultic representation of the identity of God and man receives no spiritual confirmation in the genuine, logical sense of the term.

On the other hand, religion mediates between pure thought and self-consciousness. It is therefore the "common determination" of these two elements (533; 765). The sage does not acquire his science by pure thought alone, because this would not enable him to grasp the unity between sensuous experience and essential form. Hegel surpasses Kant by making historical experience the content of the concept. The Christian religion provides us with the indispensable representation of the concrete unity of history and the concept. Since history is for Hegel fundamentally political, this means, as I have previously emphasized, that there is an intimate connection between religion and politics.[10] With all due allowance for freedom of religious conviction, Hegel's final political community is Christian, albeit in such a way as to overcome the split between the kingdoms of heaven and earth.[11] We can illustrate the connection between religion and politics by studying Hegel's treatment of God's loss of self in the creation (536 ff.; 769 ff.). Even while speaking of creation in religious or representational language as an act of love, Hegel makes it clear that "creation is the word of representation for the *concept* itself in accordance with its absolute excitation" (536; 769). In other words, from the standpoint of eternity, *there is no creation,* and hence no "alienation" of God from himself, but rather "externalization" in the logical sense which we have already analyzed. The language of creation, love, sin, and redemption is prephilosophical, and in that sense may be called a "political" version of logical truth. If the wise man

10. Cf. F. Grégoire, *Études Hégéliennes* (Louvain, Publications Universitaires de Louvain, 1958), p. 213; and *Philosophie des Rechts,* pp. 11 f.; *Philosophy of Right,* p. 7 f.

11. *Philosophie des Rechts,* p. 225 (par. 270); *Philosophy of Right,* p. 168.

grasps the conceptual significance of his spiritual divinity in a way which excludes a creation *ex nihilo,* then the religious account of the creation, together with that of man's fall and resurrection in Christ, must be human rather than divine, a human metaphor of the divine.

Consider once more from this angle the story of the Garden of Eden. The act by which Adam and Eve begin human history itself presupposes the existence of human beings, that is, beings capable of distinguishing between good and evil. Whereas history produces self-consciousness, it is already produced by self-conscious beings. The man of faith eludes this circle by avoiding rationalist interpretations, but Hegel's intention is precisely to replace faith by rational knowledge (in the sage). In Hegel's language, the fall of Adam is the beginning of the process by which Absolute Spirit renders abstract essence concrete, by "working out" or "showing" the essential modalities of logic within human history. Man's loss of innocence is the representational or prescientific, and hence human rather than genuinely divine, description of the necessary condition for the immersion of Spirit in its "work." The "fall" of Spirit into the world thus represents the externalization process of the Absolute as a creation or separation which itself depends upon the preexistence of Spirit and world. The fall of man from God is necessarily also the fall of God into man. The objects of the natural world are given significance by the externalization of Spirit as consciousness, which thereby ceases to be itself natural or separate from God and discovers itself as Spirit. And in religious language, this whole process was initiated by Satan, who thereby personifies the pride of the philosophers and so overcomes from the outset the evil within the distinction between good and evil (537–39; 770–73).

Sin is in fact virtue, because it is the principle of spiritual labor: the dialectic of the inverted world. The distinction between good and evil, like that between God and man, is "alienation" only from the religious perspective. No such distinction exists in the Absolute, or in the conceptual grasp of Spirit in the world, but only with respect to man as an incompletely actualized element within the world. The world cannot be genuinely evil because it is a moment of the divine, in a way very close to the doctrine of Spinoza.[12] This does not mean that Hegel denies evil *for man;* to do so would be to deny contingency and empirical history. But evil "for man" is necessary as a consequence of the very finitude of self-consciousness upon which the identity-within-difference of God and man depends. When Hegel refers to the suppression of divine "alienation" by the universalizing of Spirit within the second coming of Christ, he does not mean that the earth and terrestrial history are negated, but that heaven is reconciled with earth (540; 774–75). This in turn means that man has the opportunity to grasp the full significance of contingent history, thanks to a process which preserves contingency.

The separation between God and man is then not "in itself" a division of God from himself, just as the distinction between good and evil has no substance at the level of identity between essence and existence. On the other hand, these distinctions are quite real so far as human consciousness is concerned. Absolute knowledge is "pure negativity" or absolute differentiation. It differentiates into the Whole, which necessarily includes both the separation of good and evil and their identity. In asserting the one, we must be prepared to insist "with invincible stubbornness" on the other. As separate from each other, "neither the one nor the other has truth, but precisely their excitation" is true, namely, the identity of absolute difference, qua difference, with absolute sameness (541–42; 775–77). The same must be said concerning the separation between God and man. Their unity is Spirit in its triune excitation, and not "the judgment and the spiritless *is*," or a finite logical determination of a dialectical totality (542–43; 777–78). In other words, God and man are united in the life of Absolute Spirit, which is also the conceptual activity of (Hegelian) logic, and not a sequence of static or traditional logical propositions. God and man are an identity-in-difference, or the spiritual truth of the One differentiating itself into the continuum of the Whole.

Hegel now restates the previous results in terms of the re-

12. *Enzyklopädie, Vorrede,* p. 10 (see chap. 1, n. 19, above). Spinoza fails to overcome evil, however, because God and man remain separated.

lation between the individual human consciousness and the community or congregation. The universality of self-consciousness is the congregation. The being or essence of man is intersubjectivity. It is not by nature but in his spirit that man becomes a political being, and the "soul" of the state is the congregation. This is to say that Christ is present in man as spiritual universality (the union of consciousness and self-consciousness) in the congregation. The citizen of the just state is a member of the religious and not merely the political community. There can be no separation of religion and politics in the state, although of course there must be a separation of religious and political functions or offices. Even tolerance toward minorities is a political act of the majority as incarnation of Spirit. The congregation, in sum, is a union of free spirits in their common consciousness of God, which thereby functions as the conscience but not as the legal reality of the state. Without any qualifying phrases, then, the church (as an institution) is subordinate to the state. If consciousness is not to perpetuate alienation, it must become actual in this world. The presence of Christ to man is the sanctification of the political community (543; 778).

That this is Hegel's meaning is reinforced by the next two pages, which deal with the overcoming of evil and the significance of the death and resurrection of Christ. As we have already seen, evil is the separation of the individual from God, or the turning inward of man in his identity as natural consciousness. Nevertheless, by turning inward, consciousness interiorizes evil. It thinks or understands and so begins to be reconciled with evil. In religious language, the turn inward is stabilized by a further turn away from one's own (separate) interior, into the spiritual substance of the congregation. This second turn is religious conversion. Similarly, Spirit becomes reconciled with its natural existence through the medium of religious representation. In nonconceptual language, the figure of Christ gives spiritual content to the natural world, and the death of Christ expresses the universality of that content. This is the same as the resurrection of Christ, or the transformation of his individual self-consciousness into the universal self-consciousness of the congregation. "Death is transformed from what it immediately signifies, from the non-being *of this individual* into the *universality* of Spirit, which lives in its congregation, dies and is resurrected in it daily" (544–45; 779–80).

The spiritual passion of Christ is reenacted in the concrete deaths and births of the citizens in the congregation. As always in Hegel, there is no final separation between heaven and the political community. Furthermore, what is represented in the death of an individual man is the overcoming of particularity in knowledge, and not in the transcendence of earthly existence for a celestial paradise. Pure Spirit or eternal thought is no longer a "Beyond" created by the representational religious consciousness. The "return of the Whole into itself" is thus the circularity of the concept, the overcoming of the image of God in the form of a particular person. Not only does the body of Christ die, but the *abstraction* of the divine essence as well (546; 781–82). The unhappy consciousness, in its painful feeling of the death of God, *itself becomes the Whole.*[13] In other words, the entire process of postresurrection history is the assimilation by the human spirit of the universal significance of the death of God as it was stated in religious representation. In order to accomplish its spiritual mission, the human spirit must lose God, just as the Divine Spirit previously lost its own innocence or abstractness in the Garden of Eden (546–47; 782–84).

However, the religious congregation, understood as the subjective substance of the world, is still not free from the form of representation. As religious rather than scientific or conceptual, it is not yet identical with its knowledge of itself as spiritual self-consciousness. It has not yet become fully what it now knows itself to be in essence: Absolute Spirit. Absolute self-consciousness continues to be known in the religious community as *another,* or as a "Beyond" within itself. This "other" (the separate God of orthodox Christianity) has not yet been fully assimilated into the spiritual activity of the self who conceives of God. The satisfaction of the self in God,

13. Cf. the closing sentences of *Glauben und Wissen* with *Enzyklopädie,* p. 449 (par. 570); *Encyclopedia Wallace–Miller,* pp. 300 f.

that is, in its own spiritual work, is still burdened with a "Beyond." And this is expressed in the traditional Christian eschatology as a reconciliation with God which will take place "as a distant event of the future" (548; 784). This reconciliation remains in the heart: it is the *Sollen* or "what ought to be" that provides the future dimension of love. But it is at odds with actual consciousness; the actual is not yet the (fully) rational. Man is not yet whole because he is not yet wise.

Thus Hegel accepts Christianity, but only to transform it into the celebration within the human community of the universal Spirit which acts in and through human experience, and which is expressed in man's interpretation of his own significance.[14] Religion is the enactment via images of the spiritual assimilation of the natural world. But it is not the final comprehension of that assimilation. The distance between the image and the original is overcome only within conceptual wisdom. When, therefore, Hegel says near the end of the *Encyclopedia* that "the content of philosophy and religion is the same," he means that religion is to be assimilated upward into philosophy.[15] Only when this is accomplished does modern history fully *enlighten* the human spirit. The noble and the mean-spirited man pass through the valley of cultivated nihilism, to emerge as the beautiful soul and the pure conscience on the one hand and the valet on the other. If the Skepticism of the valet is too low, the Stoicism of the beautiful and pure consciousness is too high. The justification of conscience as intellectual intuition must be combined with the slavish labor of conceptual discourse in the judgment. In this process of combination (which includes the completion of the judgment in the syllogism of Absolute Wisdom), the human spirit reassimilates its long experience, first in religious representation, and finally in the Absolute Idea.

14. Cf. T. Bodammer, *Hegels Deutung der Sprache* (Hamburg, Felix Meiner Verlag, 1969), chap. 2, par. 12; P. Cornehl, *Die Zukunft der Versöhnung*, esp. pp. 93–159.

15. *Enzyklopädie*, p. 451 (par. 573); *Encyclopedia Wallace–Miller*, p. 303.

9 The Absolute

ABSOLUTE KNOWLEDGE IN THE *Phenomenology*

In the three preceding chapters I have offered an analysis of some of the main points of Hegel's *Phenomenology*. This analysis was intended to show how "the science of appearing spirit" is itself genuinely inelligible only on the basis of Hegel's science of logic. I began this study with the philosophy of history, perhaps the most general way in which to approach Hegel, since it is the "mediation" of logic and phenomenology, using all these terms in the broadest possible sense. A careful dissection of the conception of philosophy of history led us, by way of the notion of "the Whole," to logic. Only after spelling out the essential themes in Hegel's logic did we turn to phenomenology. It is now almost time to return to the *Logic,* in order to bring together again logic and phenomenology in the Absolute. Before doing so, however, it will be fitting to look briefly at the concluding chapter of the *Phenomenology:* "Absolute Knowledge." Although it is only sixteen pages long, this chapter repeats in an extraordinarily concise manner the basic themes of the entire work, and in such a way as to prepare us for the transition to logic, or the first part of the science of wisdom. It might be possible, but it would certainly be inefficient, to elicit Hegel's conception of the Absolute solely from a commentary on this final chapter. Let us instead employ it in such a way as to cast a backward glance at the general structure of the *Phenomenology.*

This structure may perhaps be described as a *reductio ad absurdum,* in which Hegel begins with the traditional versions of rationalism and proceeds to show how each necessarily contradicts itself. The forms of rationalism, by contradicting themselves, are joined in negativity. But Hegel means by "negativity" a pure active capacity of the Absolute to posit forms, or differently stated, subects and objects. The negativity into which the figures of the *Phenomenology* disappear is the absolute reflection explained in the *Logic*. Only when we understand this are we in a position to test Hegel's contention that the *Phenomenology* shows us the circle of wisdom in its historically developing process. This apart, Hegel begins with the analysis of the epistemological "fact" in its various forms. He argues that the "fact" is produced or posed by consciousness, thereby denying the Aristotelian principle that the intellect *conforms to* the preexistent or separate thing. Hegel reinterprets the Aristotelian doctrine of *actuality* to mean that a fact is not "real" or a *res* except secondarily: it is primarily an activity whose pulsation is structurally the same as self-contradiction. A complete understanding of any fact is thus the same as a reflexive comprehension of the principle of contradiction, or the Whole, and the circle of wisdom.

If the object when wholly understood is the Whole, then epistemology, which is based, as we have seen, upon the principle of separation or the primacy of detached monadic form, and so upon the separation of form and mind (even when coactual), is refuted. Epistemology is not simply contradicted, but this contradiction is explained, which is to say that epistemology is raised to a higher and more comprehensive level. Hegel proceeds to summarize the three major stages of modern epistemology in terms of the relation each expresses between ego and thing. The epistemologist attempts to understand the thing or object without reference to the ego, but is forced to make this reference by the very process of explanation. To observational reason, the ego is itself a thing. In the philosophy of the Enlightenment, the thing is a mode of the ego. Moral self-consciousness defines the interior of the thing as pure will or certitude: it in effect claims, without understanding what it says, that the essence or thing-in-itself is the essence of the ego. We move from initial disregard of the ego to disregard of the thing, and finally to a loss of the essential thing *and* ego. Hegel calls Kant an empiricist because he sees in the Copernican Revolution the fulfillment of the lack of self-consciousness in scientific rationalism, even if expressed in a doctrine of subjectivity (551; 791–92). Modern epistemology declares its own bankruptcy (the inaccessibility of essence to reason), but in such a way as to prefigure the correct solution to the problem which it has itself posed. To repeat, all stages of epistemology come together in the *Nichts* (or thing-in-itself), which is also explained in moral or religious, but never in scientific, terms. This is the crucial preparation for Hegel. The significance of the Whole is religious (since morality is a pseudoreligious explanation), but religion is still at the level of representation or image. There is still a gap between what religion "knows" via the conscience and what it can discursively explain. The thing-in-itself is the Absolute (Fichte), and the Absolute is Spirit, or more precisely, Spirit qua development, and so transcendental history (Schelling). It is left to Hegel to present us with the final version of the reconciliation of the three stages of modern epistemology (552; 793).

The transition from epistemology to Absolute Knowledge is one of morality and religion. It is a dialectic between the two, whose middle term or transitional figure is *the beautiful soul.* In the case of morality, the significance of human life is explained as acting (*Handeln*) in accordance with one's duty. But the universal command of duty is contradicted by the "iron" of actual circumstances. So long as reality is independent of conscience, or the particular from the universal, genuinely moral action is impossible. When spirit recognizes this, it inevitably retreats from a separate reality to itself as pure universality, or denies the reality of the particular while defining the Whole as an identity of beauty and goodness in the truth of the self. This is the "beautiful soul." Its function is to unite all moments of spiritual development (previously called "world-views") within self-consciousness, understood as the comprehensive world-view: the world or Whole. The iron of the particular dissolves in the acid of universality. The beautiful soul regards itself as divine, and so as the identity of divine intuition and self-consciousness. The beautiful soul, as pure, has no determinate content. The object of its contemplation is just itself, albeit taken to be pure universality. But this universality is indistinguishable from the *Nichts,* since it lacks every determination. As Hegel puts it, the beautiful soul fades away into empty air. He means by this, however, not that it simply disappears, but that the universal expression of the total significance of spiritual determinations is negativity. What remains to be done is to negate the negation, or to articulate the sense of totality qua negativity. The beautiful soul is thus the pure concept, the identity of interior and exterior, but as an immediate identity, which requires to be mediated or exhibited in its interior structure (553–54; 794–95).

The self-certitude of activity in accordance with duty is thus transformed into the intuition that the self is divine, and the initial explanation of the content or structure of the divine is presented in representational form as religion. Whereas in the beautiful soul there is an alienation between the intuition of self as divine and the content of divinity, in religion there is an alienation within the intuition of the self as divine between the representational and conceptual expression of it. The result is a reenactment of the dualism of good and evil which was characteristic of morality—only now the dualism is not between consciousness and empirical reality, but lies within consciousness itself. The self knows that it is divine or universal, and yet it cannot explain coherently what this signifies. This failure renders the self particular or separated from its own universality: it is therefore both good and bad. Universal and particular, or good and evil, both contradict the unity of consciousness of which, taken as individual, they are aspects. Therefore, they both contradict themselves (since their essence is precisely that individuality of the self-consciousness as a whole). Hegel, in a passage of extraordinary difficulty, expresses this as a double contradiction. The universality of self-consciousness contradicts the individuality of self-consciousness, whereas the universal as good contradicts the particular as bad (555; 796). I would paraphrase this as follows. So long as there is no reconciliation between good and evil, the unity of self-consciousness is torn apart *within itself,* in such a way as to oppose abstract universality and particularity as well as their concrete expressions as good and evil. The battle of good and evil within the individual prevents him from fulfilling the transcendental or absolute significance of his individuality. In other words, *logic and morality remain unreconciled within the religious consciousness, and this leads each to split in half.*

At the same time, however, this double contradiction generates an excitation in which each element of the contradiction loses its separateness, rigidity, or motionlessness. The function of contradiction is not to cancel but to demonstrate the impossibility of coherent partiality or *apartness.* The coherence of life is *a priori* evidence that, despite the dissolutions of analytic or reflective thinking, the world is a Whole. It is finally impossible to understand man as lost in an alien world, because such an interpretation itself depends upon the accessibility of the world to man as interpreter. The human spirit is held together by a grasp of its own interpretations, or what it has done. This is the concept: "The knowledge of the deed of the self in itself as all essentiality and all existence, the knowledge of *this subject* as *substance,* and of substance as this knowledge of its deed" (556; 797). The truth and hence the significance of the world lie necessarily in a self-conscious mind or spirit. And the dialectical structure of that individual spirit is the same as the pulsation of Absolute Spirit. One aspect of eternal activity, in other words, is the actualization of the historical world. In this aspect, the human spirit enacts in terms appropriate to finite and temporal beings the eternal activity of the Whole. When that activity has been completely expressed in human terms, time in the strict sense is completed. But this is because the complete expression of eternal activity takes place in conceptual understanding, which is thus rendered coincident with the Absolute Spirit, or the Whole of which man is the exhibiting part. Man is that part of the Whole which is able, under the form of time, to coincide with the Whole by way of achieving an equivalence between his self-consciousness and that of the Absolute, so as to transcend time, which continues in the modality of nature and finite or nonscientific spirit (556–57; 797–99).

We have already discussed the problem of time in Hegel and will refer to it again in the last chapter. Our task here is to summarize, not to criticize. Spirit as eternity is the annulment of time, yet its preservation in and as history. The "form" of time, or eternity, is pure negative activity, whereas the form of time as history is human discursive labor, or the developing explanation of pure negative activity. This is what Hegel means when he asserts that experience is the process by which substance comes to be what it is *in itself*. Spirit becomes self-conscious of itself as the identity of subject and object only by temporality or the course of human history. Since the Absolute cannot know itself to be such until after what it is in-itself is joined to what it is for-itself, and since this juncture is history, it must be the case that, prior to history, the Absolute is incomplete. If so, then God is incomplete prior to his creation of the world. The universal is incomplete until it is united to the particular in the concrete individual. The transformation of the "in-itself" to the "for-itself," or of substance to subject, "is the circle that returns into itself, which presupposes its beginning, and which accomplishes it only in its end" (559; 801).

One is tempted to infer from all these formulations, together with the results of our analysis thus far, that Hegel's "Christianity" is in fact a strange kind of Aristotelian gnosticism. History completes eternity, but eternity is already complete as the process which generates history: this is not just the "eternal return of the similar" but a return of thought thinking itself. Stated somewhat differently, *God becomes man in order to become God.* This is Hegel's heresy, and the aspect of his doctrine which, like his historicizing of eschatology, has no counterpart in orthodox Christianity. And so Hegel says: "Before spirit completes itself *in itself,* as World Spirit, it cannot achieve its completeness as self-conscious Spirit" (559; 801).

We may pass by Hegel's excessively condensed recapitulation of the history of modern philosophy from Spinoza to Schelling. The result is science, again, not bare logical formulas, but a knowing which "unfolds . . . in this aether of its life" (562; 805). Spirit has now returned to the beginning from which it set out on its journey, because, when everything is known, thought becomes circular. Spirit is now certain of its freedom and knowledge, both being confirmed by existence, or by the impossibility that anything should arise that is not already a moment of wisdom (563; 806). Nature and history are the externalizations of Spirit in space and time respectively. This externalization contains contingency, to which Spirit is reconciled, however, by the knowledge that what happens by chance is unnecessary to the process of self-knowledge. The spatio-temporal matrix is the continuum of self-differentiating Absolute Spirit, regarded merely as the abstract framework of the two modes of externalization, corresponding to nature and history. This is the meaning of Hegel's remark that history is the externalization of Spirit itself, or a negative which is the negative of itself. Within history, Spirit as pure interiority assimilates nature or pure exteriority, and the result is neither nature nor history, but Spirit in-and-for-itself.

Spirit as in-and-for-itself is self-contradictory or negates itself in two senses. First, as for-itself, Spirit is an object or externality. But as in-itself, Spirit negates or incorporates the object. Second, the incorporation of the object is in turn negated or exteriorized as a new form of spiritual existence (564; 807–08). Even after the achievement of wisdom, then, history continues to produce forms afresh, as if for the first time: just as each new philosophical fashion is totally convinced of its own "originality." Nevertheless, continuity is preserved by the memory of what has happened, either in the spirit of the living sage, or as recorded within the pages of Hegel's books. Even when wisdom seems to have disappeared, it will return, because Spirit is eternal and can never be destroyed or halted in the dialectical necessity whereby each partial manifestation develops into the Whole.

The Living Concept: Critique of Analysis and Synthesis

We are now ready to return to the *Logic*. To some extent, this will require us to continue in our summary of what has already been accomplished. But we should be able to add to our understanding of Hegel's sense of "concept" as a reflexive or self-conscious grasp by subjectivity of itself as subject-object.

Hegel, as we have seen, takes the Christian doctrine of God as a basis for revising the Greek conception of knowledge. The content of Spirit is "free Spirit itself." Form is the same as thinking, or is posed by the process of thinking itself, which means that the forming activity of intelligence is higher than, because the principle of, specific forms in the original Platonic sense.[1] This does not mean that man "creates" the natural world by thinking it. In thinking the world, man comes to understand and thus to identify with the Absolute Spirit or self-conscious activity by which the world has been formed. Hegel's doctrine of the Absolute is a radical development of the everyday experience of self-consciousness as the medium within which we unite body and soul by means of rational discourse. The "world" is an interpretation, but not a Nietzschean perspective or relativistic *Weltanschauung*. It is the consequence, complete or tending toward completion, of the absolute reflection upon the fact of existential self-consciousness. Thus every individual is a microcosm or a "mode" (in a way even a Leibnizian monad) which exhibits the Whole, not as an image of it, but rather as the Whole in and for itself.

The development of self-consciousness into self-knowledge is therefore the same as the acquisition of knowledge of the Whole. Since the Whole is the unity of nature and spirit, or the complete expansion of the existential unity of body and soul, one might expect Hegelian knowledge to take on a "practical" or "existential" cast. On the contrary, however; Hegel criticizes "existential" interpretations of wisdom on the very ground that they provide no knowledge, or substitute "feeling" for conceptual analysis. For Hegel, *knowledge is of the form*. But this does not leave him open to the criticism of Schelling and Kierkegaard that he attempts to deduce life from the concept. Hegel rather allows the concept to develop from the self-consciousness of the living and thinking individual. If one looks to the Hegelian Absolute in an effort to justify the aforementioned criticism, one finds instead that the concept qua Absolute is already, that is, eternally, alive. Only within this context can we understand the fact that Hegel's logical ex-

1. *Enzyklopädie*, p. 437 (par. 552); *Encyclopedia Wallace–Miller*, p. 289.

position moves from quantity to quality, or from "Becoming" as a spatio-temporal matrix to "genesis" in a sense which includes the living organism.

The statement that knowledge is form must then be properly qualified in order to take into account the points just stated. All forms are for Hegel essentially one; and the principle of unification is the principle of contradiction, understood as absolute or pure negative activity. Pure negative activity is noetic self-consciousness: the Hegelian "synthesis" of Greek and Christian doctrines. The complete analytic comprehension of form is therefore also and necessarily a comprehension or knowledge of the "self" in its absolute sense of *formator*. This is why knowledge of the Whole may be called "the Absolute Idea," rather than requiring the fuller "knowledge of the Absolute Idea." The latter, as Absolute, *includes* the moment of self-knowledge. Let me now restate this general conclusion in terms of the structure of the *Science of Logic*.

The Whole completes or develops itself at the transtemporal level of absolute activity in a way which is reflected by the essential epochs of human history, but also in the process of the development of individual self-consciousness. For example, philosophy is the activity which seeks to acquire a conceptual understanding of the essence of Being. Obviously, within this activity, Being is the starting point, and the essence must be apprehended in a preliminary manner before we can conceptualize it. Thus the three books of the *Logic* are called "Being," "Essence," and "Concept." In the book on the "Concept," we assimilate all that has gone before, by studying the activities of thinking (subjectivity) and of the natural world (objectivity), in order to see how they are united in the Idea. The Idea itself develops internally, through the stages of life and knowledge (of the true and the good), into the Absolute Idea. This process of development is the overcoming of all fundamental dualisms: subject-object, ideal-real, finite-infinite, soul-body, possibility-actuality, and so on. In the Idea, all relations of the understanding (*Verstand*) are contained "in their *infinite* return and identity." [2] This last and

2. Ibid., p. 183 (par. 214); *Encyclopedia–Wallace,* p. 355.

most comprehensive stage of Hegel's *Science of Logic* provides man with practical satisfaction by reconciling him to his earthly dwelling, and the mode of reconciliation is the theoretical resolution of alienation. The political resolution of alienation is a consequence of the theoretical resolution, not its precondition. What Hegel emphatically calls "the *infinite* return" is the mark of the circularity or completeness of his wisdom. It is therefore the final justification of God, or the explanation of the logical significance of history as the appearance of separation and unending labor. In this overcoming of all dualisms, the Idea is what Hegel calls "the infinite judgment," or the self-conscious concept in which both subject and predicate contain totality.[3] As infinite and circular, the Idea is both complete in itself and the free manifestation of reason within nature and human life.[4] Human life is now a rational actuality. Nature and the human spirit are now accessible to scientific comprehension.

The last stage of Hegel's logic is thus the peak of the entire science of wisdom. We must now try to grasp the main features of the development of the Idea. First, some preparatory remarks are in order. In the book on "Being," Hegel studied the abstract structure of the Whole, or the continuum process of Becoming. This book, as I have said, corresponds *approximately* to Greek ontology as still present within Newtonian science (cf. pp. 106 ff. above). In the book on "Essence," Hegel shows how the inadequacies of a mathematical ontology lead to the period of modern philosophy from Descartes and Spinoza to Fichte and Schelling. The internal instability discussed in the first book as "measure" or the unity of quantity and quality is transformed in the second book into the instability of essence and appearance. In somewhat different terms, mathematical ontology cannot account for subjectivity or the consciousness of the mathematician. Modern philosophy tries to supply this account, but at the price of a dualism between subject and object, appearance and reality, or essence

3. Ibid., pp. 184 (par. 214), 196 (par. 242); *Encyclopedia–Wallace,* pp. 357, 378.

4. Ibid., pp. 196 f. (par. 244); *Encyclopedia–Wallace,* p. 379.

and existence, which leads to the same collapse that characterizes Greek philosophy. The "measure" of mathematical ontology is replaced by the "thinking ego" of Descartes, but thinking remains mathematical.

The ego is thus incapable of thinking or explaining itself, and this robs its thoughts of all value. In other words, Hegel describes here in logical terms the process we studied in the *Phenomenology* as the collapse of the modern epoch into subjectivism and nihilism. At the same time, Hegel shows that the period beginning with Schelling and ending with himself may be called a "negation of negation," or the transformation of nihilism into absolute wisdom. Hegel works out the contradiction in modern philosophy, to "resolve" it not by removing it but by preserving or assimilating it within a more comprehensive, and indeed final, explanation of the contradictoriness of things. This explanation is completed in the third book of the *Logic*.

The Idea is the "adequate concept" or objective truth about the formation process of the Absolute. In traditional epistemological language, it is the adequacy of the concept to the object. But Hegel's "Idea" is not the expression of a "correspondence theory" of truth, because the adequacy of the concept arises from its coherence with the object. For Hegel, to think the truth is to be "in the truth," or still more sharply, *to be* the truth. The Idea is not just what God thinks, or what we think in thinking God's thoughts: it is the identity-within-difference of God's and our thinking. As the truth, the Idea is thus unconditioned. It is the Whole: there is nothing outside it, not even the *Nichts* (since every attempt to posit something outside the Whole amounts to a positing of it within the Whole). The Idea is the activity of forming "things" (*res*), whether subjective or objective, and so it is the actuality (*energeia*) of what we ordinarily call "the real world" (*realitas*). To say that "the rational is the actual" is to say that the essential truth of reality is living and self-conscious Spirit, grasping itself in the concept as Idea. As Hegel puts this, the objectivity of the actual is measured by its concept. Mathematical measure is then brought to life, or identified as the measurer. The concept is the soul or life of actuality; its life is to be rational, purposive, or spiritual (2 : 407–09; 755–56).[5]

The Idea takes on three forms. The first, corresponding to the immediate (incompletely actualized) Idea, Hegel calls "life." The concept, as the identification of Thinking and Being, is "knowing." Knowing is a mediate (the second) form of the Idea, or a process of explicating the modes of the identification of Thinking and Being which, when completed, is the "Absolute Idea" (the third and final form). Knowing thus presupposes living. In terms taken from the *Phenomenology,* life is primarily characterized by desire, and thinking emerges from the process of attempting to satisfy desire. In the *Logic,* we are not concerned with natural life (or the natural consciousness), but with the life of the Idea. Natural life becomes spiritual or "ideal" when it is assimilated or mastered by Spirit. Nature, we recall, is the externalization of the Idea. Now the Idea must reclaim or recollect its exteriority. In order to avoid any possibility of misunderstanding on this sensitive point, I again emphasize that, in this process, externality or nature is not "annulled" in the sense of being turned into "mere thought." Instead, externality is understood. Spiritual life is a higher, more comprehensive stage than natural life, but it contains nature as its exterior dimension. Hegel, having brought together subjectivity and objectivity in the spiritual life of the Idea, turns next to a deeper analysis of the process of "bringing together" these comprehensive opposites (2 : 415–16; 762–63).

Life, as understood in the *Logic,* is "absolute universality in and for itself." It is everywhere present as unity within the various manifestations of living being. But this unity is not a static Parmenidean One. Since living things are composed of fluid determinations (or since every determination is a negation), life is a negative unity. It is both indeterminate (as everywhere the same) and determinate (as the force which shows its sameness by posing and negating determinations or

5. Numbers in parentheses refer *first* to volume and pages in the German edition of the *Logik, second* to the English translation. See chap. 1, n. 23 for full references.

differences). In this sense, negative unity is a "self referring to itself and existing for itself" (2 : 417; 764). Hegel means by this that the principle of life, or the identity of indeterminateness and determinateness, always presents itself as a self, a living soul or individual. The dynamics of the soul are the same as the dynamics of God, because the soul is "God's breath." All living things (not just man) are part of the same life (cf. 2 : 435; 780). But only the human soul is capable of acquiring self-consciousness by understanding its dynamic identity with God: here Hegel combines Spinoza's mode with the Leibnizian monad. In principle, every human soul can think the Whole; in practice, this can be done only by a few. The difference between principle and practice, exactly as in Aristotle and Spinoza, has to do with the difference in *corporeal* perfection, as for example in the quality of desire.

I pass by Hegel's analysis of the dialectic of life in terms of chemistry (chemism) and mechanics (mechanism). Suffice it to say that, in the process of human reproduction, Hegel sees an assimilation of the chemical and mechanical aspects of life into *purposiveness*. Stated in logical terms, the individual is taken outside himself in his desire to reproduce. The child represents the unification of subject and object (the ego together with the non-ego or body of one's mate). As the mediation or assimilation of both parents, the child is their immortality.[6] Hence it is also the individual who unifies the universal (the genus of life) and the particular (the parents). The child thus provides us with our transition to the "Idea of Knowledge." This stage emerges from life as genus. The genus is life "as such" or the Idea relating to itself as Idea (2 : 429; 774). More simply, the child is the individual consciousness which, in understanding itself as genus or principle of life, expressed in or as a self-conscious individual, is on the way toward understanding the principle of life essentially or logically. "Genus" is not a static logical form but must be understood etymologically as that which *generates:* it is the living, purposive, intelligent, and intelligible Idea. In sum, the child is the posing of a new moment which presupposes

6. This doctrine goes back to Plato's *Symposium*.

the origin or returns to the genus even as it stands apart in individual form. Human reproduction is the existential manifestation of the pulsation-process of absolute reflection.

In conventional terms, the genus is the essence. But what is the essence of man? According to both the pagan and Judaeo-Christian branches of the tradition, it is his soul, or the principle of life. Hegel's innovation, for which we have now been prepared, is to identify the soul as the concept instead of separating the two. As has sometimes been said, Hegel unites ontology and logic. The soul as concept grasps itself as the identity between Being and Thinking. Therefore, in thinking beings of any kind, we are led to think about thinking, and so to thinking as the activity which *identifies* or gives form to beings. This takes us on to the soul in the sense just designated: to Spirit. Only in this way can we make sense out of ordinary experience. Hegel thus reverses the procedures of traditional metaphysics by moving from the concept to the soul (but not by "deducing" life from the concept, as I have already pointed out). Traditional metaphysics begins with the soul as an empirical particular and not as the concept. It can therefore never rise from human existence to the level of essence: it never acquires a concept of soul at all.

Hegel illustrates his criticism of the traditional metaphysics of the soul by way of Hume and Kant. Hume starts from empirical consciousness, from the "representations" or appearances of consciousness, and fails to find the continuity of the self in their discontinuity. But this failure is guaranteed by Hume's equation of knowing and thinking with the discontinuous appearances, which are ultimately sensuous images of Greek determinate form. Hume never suspects that the principle of these discontinuous images is "negative unity," or a formation process rather than a form. Kant in a way recognizes negative unity, which he places in the empty "I think" accompanying each (still Humean) appearance. But the emptiness of the "I think" as a logical condition of cognition shows that Kant, like Hume, denies that self-consciousness is a mode of cognition within experience. It has no objectivity. As the mere form of thinking, it is known only via the thoughts that are its predicates. It is conceived exclusively as the subject of judgment, and as a subject which, even though accompanying or thinking and hence synthesizing the object, is itself always *beyond* the object, or never accessible in and through the predicates constructed by categorial thinking (2 : 430–35; 775–80).

As we saw a moment ago, the genus is universal life, the "interior" of the Idea corresponding to the individual thing (*res*) or "exterior" of the Idea. The truth of life as absolute negative unity is the assimilation of all individuals within the genus or Absolute Spirit. The individuals are like the modes in Spinoza's substance, which is itself transformed into the living activity of divine (or transcendental) subjectivity.[7] The interior shows itself as that which appears universally within individual souls. It is the process of Becoming, only now understood to be alive. The "Idea of Knowledge" is the process of acquiring the conceptual structure of, and so identifying with, the process of Becoming in the comprehensive sense, as that process is in-itself (= the objective world) and for-itself (= the subjective world). The process of knowledge is divided into two parts, corresponding to the Idea of the true and that of the good. We note in passing that for Hegel, there is no Idea of the beautiful (2 : 435–39; 780–83). Beauty is the *appearance* of truth.

Hegel begins his discussion of the Idea of the True by connecting it with "impulse" (*Trieb*), a Fichtean term for the working of the ego that has something to do with the Platonic doctrine of Eros. The Platonic Eros, however, is separate from its object (the Idea), whereas the impulse of post-Kantian German philosophy produces its own object. For Hegel impulse, or the root of natural desire, is also the inclination toward overcoming the split between subject and object, to project the subject into the object and thus to assimilate it "backward" into the subject as source of the initial impulse. As we have seen, Hegel sometimes illustrates this process by

7. "Subjectivity" in this sense is not to be confused with the "subject" as opposed to or detached from the object. It is the principle of the subject-object genesis.

the example of eating and digestion. In the present context, of course, the external or natural object serves as the occasion for the projection by impulse or desire of its spiritual sustenance: the concept of the object. The process by which the impulse toward truth conceptually digests the object is called *analytic knowing.*

It will be helpful to contrast Hegel's "analysis of analysis" with the contemporary use of the term. "Analysis" today is at first glance empiricism plus mathematical logic. Within the analytic movement there are two general schools, which may be initially distinguished by their relative emphasis on one or the other of the two components. Despite a certain internecine quarreling between these two schools of analysis, it is clear that together they constitute a distinct mode of philosophizing, especially in contrast to other contemporary schools or movements, to say nothing of their attitude toward the past. One may wonder why the analytic movement does not rather quickly decompose into an unstable dualism of "matter and form" (empirical data plus logical calculi). The answer seems to lie in the crucial importance attributed by contemporary analysts to *language.* Language for them mediates between form and content in a way corresponding to the unknowable substance of modern philosophy, but as modified by the German doctrine of the Absolute Ego. The empirical or natural object acquires its essence or significance from logical categories; one could almost say that the objectivity of the object stems from these categories of discursive understanding in a sense reminiscent of Kant. However, instead of embedding the logical or objectifying categories within a transcendental ego, contemporary analysts derive them from a linguistic capacity which is not finally subject to analysis because it is the condition or horizon of analysis. The analysis of the examples of linguistic use, or even of whole languages or clusters of languages, is not the same as the analysis of the linguistic capacity per se. And when the linguistic capacity is itself subjected to analysis, the limitations of reflection quickly impose themselves; the tools of analysis already presuppose the capacity to be analyzed.

The limitation of reflection in the Fichtean sense of the term enters sooner or later into the contemporary analytic enterprise in its various forms. But Fichte, unlike the contemporary analysts, was aware of the need to explain the limitation of reflection itself by recourse to the transcendental or Absolute Ego as the ground of discursive thinking. It would perhaps be going too far to say that contemporary analysts are unaware of this issue, but they seem to regard it as outside the perimeter of legitimate investigation, or to be replaceable by a vague notion of linguistic capacity which, although empirically certifiable in a weak or general sense, is not reflexively accessible to the tools of analysis. From the Hegelian standpoint, this is to reduce logic to empirical contingency or to generate it from an "invisible source" in the Heideggerian manner.

In a previous chapter, we considered the problem of the "invisibility" of logical connection or formal structure as the contemporary legacy of the traditional problem of the separation of substance from its attributes. In this context, the issue may be given a more general formulation. The logical empiricist defines the correct perspective for the analysis of experience by the assertion of his principles (and we may pass by the "ordinary language" analyst who would regard this assertion as unwarranted: a lack of principles or logical doctrine is not a mark of increased self-consciousness). Let us say such an assertion amounts to the postulation of an axiom system *A*. Since this act of position is either a pure creation *ex nihilo,* or else justified by prephilosophical and so preanalytic considerations, it can immediately be contradicted. Given the assertion of two axiom-systems *A* and non-*A,* there is no external basis by which to choose between them, other thaan usage, convention, or nonrational taste.

No doubt some claim would be made that one axiom system is more "fruitful" than another. To this, one could reply initially that logical calculi are selected by philosophers as tools for analyzing experience, not discovering or generating it. Mathematical "fruitfulness" is not the same as empirical fruitfulness, although obviously the former can stimulate us to experience in new ways. However, even if the consideration of fruitfulness is decisive, an appeal to "fertility" is an appeal to a nonanalytic "value judgment" which may be quite reasonable but which requires a kind of justification other than logical deduction. Logical empiricists never point to specific logical techniques or arguments to justify their entire program. They are rather the contemporary representatives of Cartesian rationalism, or an aspect of the modern Enlightenment. In Hegelian language, they *believe* in reason and certify as cogent those arguments which bolster their faith. The unity of religious and logical elements in this faith may be suggested by the observation that the contemporary analyst has no doctrine of negativity but only a syntactic theory of "negation." He continues to obey the Parmenidean injunction against referring to *Nichts*. But this means that the "non-" or difference between the two opposing axiom systems *A* and non-*A* is in the last analysis a verbal convention, a question of how we define linguistic signs, or a dependence upon a syntactic operation the significance of which is itself dependent upon linguistic conventions. In short, as we have seen previously, a failure to account for *Nichts* not only dissolves logic but is equivalent to the religious withdrawal before the invisible ground of contingent existence. The consciousness of the logician is a product of the loss of self-consciousness.

Hegel's "analysis of analysis" is substantially along the lines just sketched. As Hegel sees it, analysis begins from a subjective immediacy of concept and object: it assumes as known that which is to undergo analysis. This assumption is not itself analyzed; hence it is equivalent to an *intuition*. The object is marked by what Hegel calls an "abstract universality" or an immediate identity of its properties. That is, the object is intuited as immediately identified by properties which are both ostensibly immediate *and* the consequence (so far as their significance is concerned) of analysis. The analyst does not concern himself with the logically prior *synthesis* by which these properties were "mediated" into the object. He analyzes the given object into its immediately accessible conceptual determinations. This is not to exclude the likelihood that the analysis may itself be highly complex and of great technical ingenuity. The complex technical analysis must be certified by the standard of the given, but the given is regarded as an essential consequence of analysis. And this is a vicious circle. The analyst both *poses* and *presupposes* his conceptual determinations. Of course, if he were self-conscious, or understood the dialectical implications of this circularity, it would lose its viciousness and develop into the Hegelian logic. As things stand, however, the determinations are "appearances" of a thing-in-itself, whether the Kantian *noumenon,* the unknowable substance of British empiricism, or the twentieth-century "how we speak." The thing-in-itself is the initial abstract identity of the object, and it is opposed to the differences (properties or predicates) of the object. There is no account of the identity of identity and difference, or in short, of the activity of the transcendental ego or its doctrinal analogue (2 : 442–45; 786–89).

The object of analysis oscillates internally or is self-contradictory. This characteristic, which is the starting point of Hegel's dialectical logic, leads to the self-negation of analysis in the sense of a distinct and comprehensive philosophical position. As we know now, the Hegelian solution to the viciousness of the circle of position and presupposition lies in the recognition of subjectivity as the source of the contradiction, which is nevertheless also intrinsic to the object. But this is to say that analysis is *synthetic* because it arrives at properties which go beyond the results of analysis itself. We move necessarily from the immediately given form to mediation. Hegel means to say that synthesis combines the abstract universal properties obtained by analysis, and the result is a concrete object. But this is also the defect of synthesis; it constructs the object from the *results* of synthesis. Synthesis, as a method, is the correlative to analysis and shares its fundamental defect of an absence of self-consciousness. The "methodologist" in general does not explain himself, the source or *Logos* of his method. In the given case, he does not see that the individual properties which he combines into an object themselves emerge from formal, discrete, and hence arbitrary syntheses of elements produced *by analysis.* At bottom, synthesis is indistinguishable from analysis because the object is constructed externally from static or analytic components. There is no internal, dialectical development of the object. The object is not alive or understood to be formed by its Idea, which is also the Idea of thinking or self-consciousness. Instead of the harmony of subject-object, we have the "reification" of Being.

From Geometry to the Good

Analysis and synthesis (which originate as methods in Greek mathematics) are empirical or contingent because, like any abstract technique, they lack self-consciousness. This leads Hegel to criticize *division,* or the attempt to classify objects which have been obtained by analytic-synthetic techniques. The method of division or classification, which lies at the heart of scientific rationalism, has its roots in the Platonic conception of *diaeresis,* or "division and collection in accordance with kinds." In the *Sophist,* perhaps the most important example of *diaeresis* in action, its adepts proceed to employ the method on the basis of considerations which furnish it with significance but are external to its application.[8] Yet they tend to identify *diaeresis* with rational or scientific thinking. This leads to one of two results. Either the intentions of the methodologist are ignored, including those which enable him to see, within the application of the method, *what to do next,* or which fork in the given division will be "fruitful." Or else "intending" or "deciding what to do next" is itself interpreted as an application of *diaeresis,* a "sorting out" of the possibilities or "dividing" of the alternatives. In Milton's phrase, "reason is but choosing," and choosing is dividing. Both results are vitiating, as can easily be seen. To ignore intentions or purposiveness is to deny the rationality of employing the method of reason. On the other hand, if intending is dividing, then every specific decision is the consequence of a prior division, and an infinite regress ensues. There is no "Whole" but only an unending

8. There is a difference between the *Sophist* and the *Phaedrus.* In the latter, Socrates introduces *diaeresis* in conjunction with philosophical rhetoric or the knowledge of how to argue *ad hominem:* this requires knowledge of human nature. This context is absent from the *Sophist.*

series of "parts." In short, there is no basis for validating division per se, and reason becomes an external mechanism of indeterminable significance. Instead of the Idea, we have method.

One could also say that if division is rational at all, a complete *diaeresis* must be implicit in each instance of division. As we have already observed, the identification of a "part" depends upon our apprehension of the "Whole" to which it belongs. If the Whole is to be determined by the identification of the parts, then we have either begged the question or fallen into an infinite regress. This problem seems to be insoluble for Platonistic rationalism, which inevitably deteriorates into Stoicism and Skepticism, and eventually into the empiricist versions of anaylsis and synthesis. The Hegelian solution is that, regardless of where we begin to divide and collect, an exhaustive (because dialectical) study of the contingent part will ultimately produce the Whole as a consequence of the instability of the "part" itself. *The part grows into the Whole.* Analysts and synthesists (hence diaereticians) either presuppose the Whole without knowing it, or presuppose an unknowable Whole. Hegel's claim, which we studied closely earlier, especially in chapters 4 and 5, is that every position (= part) is, or returns us to, its presupposition (= Whole), and we grasp conceptually the identity-within-difference of the two by the exhaustive study of the process of "return" (2 : 450–64; 793–806).

As the final step in his discussion of the Idea of knowing, Hegel turns to the *theorem*. In the case of the theorem, we move from the particular (an indeterminate or undefined instance) to the individual (or specific formal assertion). There is a close connection between a theorem and a definition. "The definition contains only one determination; division contains the determination as opposed to others; in individuation, the object is divided within itself" (2 : 464; 806). In other words, the theorem demonstrates the structure of the individual object (which is a "kind" or genus), or spreads out the elements of that structure before our eyes. Division contrasts two internally articulated structures but does not spread out the elements of those structures. Definition gives a pervasive but nevertheless abstract or summary account of the structure; it shows the elements but not the conceptual process by which they are demonstrated.

Hegel's example of theorem-reasoning is geometry. This is because, in geometrical construction, the proof of the theorem shows the elements of the structure "growing" into the object. The movement of the formal structure is the same as that of our constructive thinking. The triangle is both particular and individual: *this kind* of shape, obtained by these steps (2 : 469; 811). However, one might say that theorem-construction proofs in geometry are too perspicuous, too immediately persuasive. It seems that the process of constructing the proof, and so of both "laying out" and showing the unity of the properties in the object, follows automatically from the theorem itself, in accordance with the rules of geometry. This is analogous to the situation in abstract logical deduction. In using the techniques of analysis, synthesis, and division, we forget ourselves, or the working of Spirit within the deduction. The same is true in the case of geometrical thinking. The steps of the geometrical construction make sense only relative to the end of the proof. There is an intentionality or purposiveness to thinking which directs the deductive-constructive capacity of the mind in its stepwise procedure from the theorem as postulated to the theorem as the last line of the proof. We cannot move from the first to the last step without knowing "in advance" what we are doing, what it is that we wish to prove. But this "movement" is not studied by geometrical thinking. Let us say that this thinking *geometricizes* the movement of thinking itself: thinking reifies itself. Again, consciousness negates itself as consciousness.

Hegel is of course not criticizing geometry as a branch of mathematics but as a paradigm for all scientific reasoning. For example, in Kant's epistemology, we know the object by constructing it, since we know only what we make. In Hegelian terms, the Kantian knows *what* he has made (the "geometrical" structure) but not the object. We know the object only when we grasp the process of construction as an externalization from an interior which is just the interior of thinking itself. The "interior" or thing-in-itself is a "product of thought" (*Gedankending*). This does not mean that it is an illusion, but rather that it is the intelligibility of the activity of intelligence. His failure to grasp this point makes Kant a kind of empirical Platonist for Hegel. Forms are constructed from appearances or show us how things look to us, thanks to our own activity. But the "looks" of things render the things-in-themselves invisible: we cannot look "behind" (or "beyond") the appearances. These appearances are defined as empirical, but they are in fact subjective, that is, how we appear to ourselves in the course of responding to invisible stimuli. At the same time, we conceive of "looks" (how we appear to ourselves) in terms of intuition of spatial determinations. Again, we geometricize by geometricizing cognitive thinking.

To return to geometry, it, like algebra, deals with the finite object of understanding (*Verstand*). There is no dialectical development of abstract spatial relations or determinations, and so, no negativity or contraction in the sense of assimilative growth from part to Whole. As a "synthetic finite science," geometry makes its objects by an analysis of experience in accordance with arbitrary (nondeduced) principles or axioms. This means that the axioms are both made (as arbitrarily posed by us) and not made (since they are not the consequences of constructive techniques of demonstration). Geometry is self-contradictory but incapable of recognizing or benefiting from this fact. There can be no deduction of the principles of geometry from a higher, more comprehensive, or dialectical logic. When contradiction appears, as in the post-Hegelian effort to formalize or systematize geometry and algebra, it is as a limitation upon rationality. The non-systematic character of finite (nondialectical) sciences means that, despite their formalist intentions, or rather because of them, these sciences are subjective in the pejorative sense. They are, as we may say, the skeleton of the "scientific world-view" (2 : 472–77; 813–18).

So much for our analysis of Hegel's criticism of the deductive method employed by mathematically oriented science.

The effort to know objective substance terminates in subjectivism. Substance has been transformed into subject. The individual knows himself to be a subject, but he does not yet know that the objective world, which he experiences as external to himself, is essentially the same as his interiority or consciousness. In historical terms, this stage corresponds to Descartes. The Cartesian *ego cogitans* awakens from its Platonic daydreams and, aided by the new mathematics, desires to master nature. But the ego does not yet understand the "nature" of desire. It both separates mathematics from desire and makes mathematics an instrument of desire. The result is an instability or incoherence which we have now studied in several different ways, and which underlies, or rather is identical with, the dualistic, antinomic, or self-contradictory structure of modern philosophy.

Hegel concludes the dialectic of the Idea of knowing by a discussion of the good. We recall that, in Platonism, the Idea of the good is both the principle of knowledge (or of the other Ideas) and itself unknowable (or not quite an Idea). This is *the* classic example of the problem of reflection, or the internal division in traditional rationalism between science and the *significance* of science. In the present context, we can say that Plato discerns or "prophesies" (correctly) the ultimate unification of theory and practice, but in such a way as to guarantee their separation. The unknowability of the good means that we cannot know the goodness of the Ideas, or the sense in which they differ from their geometrical and arithmetical prototypes. We remain, so to speak, at the empirical level, in which desire shows itself as already divided into the theoretical and the practical. The theoretical aspect poses the subject as an indeterminate universal facing the particularized world of desire: for example, Kant's "I think. . . ." But the practical aspect poses the subject as an actuality facing actuality. In a quite literal sense, the activity or work of practical desire is the mainspring in the process of mastering or assimilating the external, natural, or objective world. Desire or impulse is "unselfconscious" about its self-centered consciousness. Unobstructed by theoretical presuppositions, it throws itself upon the world in order to satisfy itself. Hence it regards itself as actual and the world as nonactual.

Whereas satisfaction is for Plato a dream, for the practical impulse of the modern subject, the world is a dream. This last result is itself a consequence of the Platonist division between form and content, or the supersensuous and the sensuous domains. But desire is now master of form, which thus becomes construction or "making": poetry instead of theory, to use the terms in their Greek sense.[9] For the modern man, who understands himself as radical desire, the world is a dream until we shape it in our own image (as we like it). It then ceases to be a dream and acquires (our own) reality: bear in mind here the doctrine of world-views. In the modern epoch, the impulse of the individual to complete or satisfy himself in an external world is the "Idea" of the good. And this is now higher than reflective knowledge of the world, because it combines the universality of knowledge with the achievement of individual freedom. In short, the good must be enacted externally in the mastery of the world which is also a production of the world. Only then is it to be reincorporated into spiritual satisfaction or systematic knowledge (*Wissenschaft*). The good is no longer an Idea even in the ambiguous sense to be found in Plato's *Republic*. We may call it "Kantian" to this extent: the good is now *activity*.

More precisely, it is a Cartesianized version of the Kantian good. The world has to be projected or made, and then reappropriated spiritually, conceptually, or subjectively. But Cartesian appropriation is an infinite process, known as "scientific progress" (although Descartes himself evidently believed that it would be completed in a finite time). Kantian appropriation is infinite as scientific and historical (or political) progress, and finite as the determinate horizon of the transcendental ego, whether as epistemological or moral agent. In both cases, the good is cognitively inaccessible. We have therefore a

9. Cf. M. Theunissen, "Die Verwirklichung der Vernunft. Zur Theorie-Praxis Diskussion im Anschluss an Hegel" *Philosophische Rundschau, Special Supplement*, 6 (1970), esp. pp. 52, 56 ff., 74, 77.

"bad infinity" of finite goods which necessarily contradict each other and so are no good. The good is thus indistinguishable from the bad. This vitiating dualism can be overcome only by the unification (or identity-within-difference) of theory and practice, or the completion of the good not as a daydream but as the Idea of knowledge. This is what Hegel means when he says that, in degrees of completeness depending upon the stage of world history, the rational is the actual.

What we therefore require is the cognitively accessible recognition that the practical Idea *contains* the moment of the theoretical. This is not, again, to give scientific precedence to practice over theory. Theory completes itself by the process of growth called "practice." Hegel calls the process of the growth of practice into theory (and vice versa) the "syllogism of activity" (*Handeln*). The middle term of this syllogism is the good end, at first immediate (external activity), then itself mediate or the middle as the instrument of external activity. That is, the good end, at first subjective, objectifies itself in the activity of carrying out its intention. The world, understood as "world-view" or the intention of the ego, is thus negated by this process of objectification. But there follows a second negation, or negation of negation. The good end, or intention of the ego, is interiorized, reincorporated, or "recollected" in the concept. In short, human consciousness, having exhausted all of its possibilities, is now able to comprehend the excitation pattern of negativity, or (in the persona of Hegel) to develop dialectico-speculative logic. The "exhaustion of possibilities," in each case a negation, is converted as a totality into a negation of negation, or actuality. Man is now implicitly satisfied, or at home in the world (2 : 477–83; 818–23). We have reached the last stage, the Absolute Idea.

The Absolute Idea

The chapter on the Absolute Idea in Hegel's *Logic* is less than twenty-two pages long. The philosophical significance of this statistic is that, once we reach the last stage in the pursuit of wisdom, there is no further transition to a higher level but only a development which is at the same time a recollection of what has been accomplished. Differently put, there are no subdivisions in the last chapter of the *Logic* because in it dialectic has been transformed into speculation. Dialectic is the process by which understanding is converted into reason.[10] As we now know, the process is one of self-contradiction or negation, which produces a negation of negation or an assimilation of the contradictory positions at a higher level. But there is no level higher than the Absolute Idea. All the contradictions have been "spread out" before us. It only remains for us to think them together, or in short, to think the Whole. Hegel calls this thinking *speculation.* Of course, speculation includes dialectic, since the Whole emerges precisely from the eternal activity of the parts. The Whole is itself contradictory or, as the negation of negation, it obviously includes negation. Nevertheless, the thinking of the Whole is speculative rather than dialectical. The term "speculation" has a bad reputation among contemporary philosophers because they reject the notion of "the Whole," at least in the sense given it by Hegel. "Dialectic," on the other hand, is not altogether despised, partly because of its Greek resonances and partly because of the nonspeculative dialectics of Marxism.

This helps us to understand a point I made previously about the primacy of theory within the union of theory and practice. Hegel was not a Marxist. True, the Absolute Idea is the identity-within-difference of the theoretical and practical Ideas. The theoretical must actualize itself in the domain of practice if it is not to remain a daydream. The sage is not just a spirit but also a body; he is not just a sage but also a citizen. Therefore his satisfaction, even if primarily theoretical, must be acquired and expressed in both domains. But we must not fail to see that wisdom is *Wissenschaft,* a knowing or thinking of the structure common to subjects and objects, and of that structure as the pulsation of divine or Absolute Thought (which is not itself a structure).

This is why Hegel ends his *Encyclopedia* not with a quotation from the New Testament but with the passage from Aris-

10. *Logik,* 1 : 6; Logic, p. 28; *Enzyklopädie,* pp. 102 ff. (par. 79 ff.); *Encyclopedia–Wallace,* pp. 143 ff.

totle's *Metaphysics* describing god as "thought thinking itself." [11] Wisdom is speculation: the Absolute thinking itself, albeit within its individual manifestations as wise men, of whom the first in human history is Hegel. Speculation in man comes after the completion of theory in practice, whereas in God it is perpetual. Thus, by achieving the level of speculation, man identifies himself with God, or dwells in eternity, but in an eternity which includes temporality. To this extent, Hegel's eternity is *temporalized*. Individual men (and sages) continue to be born and to die, but the reconciliation of eternity and temporality is accessible to the human race for so long as its sages possess and understand the Hegelian teaching. I add that this wisdom cannot be dependent upon the preservation of the Prussian monarchy, or any other version of the rational regime. Having achieved his reconciliation with temporality, or "completed" history by understanding it, the sage finds his satisfaction even in corrupt regimes, knowing that each man finds satisfaction only as a citizen of his own time. This satisfaction is not impaired for him by local defects, because he knows their necessity (or the necessity of contingency) and does not seek to repair them in a heavenly "Beyond" or utopia.

There are, to be sure, different aspects of the Whole. For instance, Hegel says that "the Absolute Idea alone is Being, nontransient life, self-knowing, and it is all truth" (2 : 484; 824). But it is all of truth in and for itself. As true "for-itself," it possesses self-consciousness or personality. Hegel means by this that the Absolute Idea is God, but as dwelling or *incarnated* within each human, whose personality is defined in either religious or philosophical terms by the presence within him of divine Spirit. Hegel conceives of the incarnation not as peculiar to Christ but as a feature of human existence. The resurrection and the logical process of double negation are both "structurally" the same as the human reproductive process.[12] There is no God apart from the congregation. The congrega-

11. *Enzyklopädie,* p. 463; *Encyclopedia Wallace–Miller,* p. 315; *Metaphysics* Λ 1072b18–30.

12. *Phänomenologie,* pp. 344 f.; *Phenomenology,* pp. 502–504. Cf. pp. 226–27 above.

tion is the "soul" of the state, which is in turn a "citizen" of world-history.[13] Since world-history is the procession of the Absolute in time, practice is, even though coordinate with theory, assimilated into speculation. The sage, in knowing the Absolute Idea, knows absolutely, and in that sense is God by remaining himself. Therefore he knows the essential structure of world-history as a Whole, since "every determination" is contained within the Absolute.

What remains to be thought, then, is not content but the "universality of the form" of thinking itself: method (2 : 485; 825). Whereas nondialectical, mathematically oriented rationalism begins with a discussion of method and so becomes finally identical with epistemology, Hegel ends with a discussion of method and so becomes finally speculative. Speculation is the completion of analysis and synthesis. Hegel's method is therefore not "epistemological" in the traditional sense of the term. The epistemologist constructs a tool for the construction of knowledge, the existence of which tool presupposes the possession of knowledge.[14] Each such tool or method already expresses a world-view and may be contradicted by its opposite. For Hegel, however, method is just the process of contradiction, or "the excitation of the concept itself" (2 : 486; 826). Hegel's "method" is thus a harmony of the traditional and Kantian positions. Whereas the inquiring spirit "constitutes" its objects, the "excitation" of the concept responds or conforms to the object as it is in itself. Since the concept is the mediation of Being and Essence, its excitation is the same as that of the object. Therefore "method" is nothing other than *the life of the Whole.* It is "the highest force, or rather the only and absolute force of reason, and not only this, but also its highest and only impulse to find and to know itself in everything through itself" (2 : 486–87; 826).

Hegel turns next to the question of the beginning of logic. Since we have already studied this process at some length, I can limit myself here to a summary of the main point. When

13. *Philosophie des Rechts,* p. 288 (par. 340); *Philosophy of Right,* p. 215 f.: states are citizens in world-history, which is the "world-judge."

14. *Phänomenologie,* pp. 63 f.; *Phenomenology,* pp. 131 f.

every logical determination has been developed, the further exercise of spiritual activity as negation amounts to a cancellation of the last step: the assertion of the Whole is thus at once a "return" to the beginning. Since negation is also preservation, the Whole is also contained within the beginning. We might paraphrase this by saying that the sage *remembers* the totality of his wisdom as he completes it, and so can never step "beyond" it but must rather begin to think it again. From the standpoint of eternity, the assertion of the Whole is a negation in the sense that it denies the last form of separation within the Whole. But it is also an affirmation, or negation of negation, as the assertion of wholeness. Why, one may ask, does activity not cease at this "last" step? Hegel's reply is that the Whole is a Whole of parts: the parts remain parts within the Whole, which is a self-differentiating, and not a Parmenidean, One. Each part expresses its nature as part by continuously enacting the dialectical process through which it develops (or is "reflected") into the Whole. No part can be understood except by understanding the Whole. Whereas the process of developing into the Whole takes place within Spirit, and not in history (since otherwise history would dissolve or be indistinguishable from the Whole as One), Spirit *is* the Whole.

The assertion of the Whole is therefore a "negation" of the Whole as itself a negation of antecedent separations. The Whole is negation of negation, or the absolute reflection of contradiction. It is therefore both immediate and mediate. The "pulse-beat" of the Whole poses it, or exhibits it as structured (and so mediated), thanks to an activity which negates what has been posed, or assimilates it into its source. The return of the Whole to the source is the necessary condition for the continuous posing of the Whole in the "next" pulse-beat. This is the temporality of the Whole. But with respect to the Whole qua Whole, no distinction of "next" is possible: each pulsation is the same as any other. This is the eternity of the Whole. Since eternity and temporality are the same process of negative excitation, a comprehension of the logic of this process is equivalent to the reconciliation between man and God, and is Hegel's replacement for "intellectual intuition." The Whole as immediate is mediate; there is nothing in heaven or on earth that does not already contain mediation.[15] The "difference" between eternity and temporality is then not an "abyss" or alienation, but the expression of the structure of the Whole as pure negative activity. This is why Hegel says that absolute negativity is the unity of subjectivity and soul (2 : 497; 836). It is the unity of man and God.

The dialectical method of mediation is also visible within the structure of the ordinary logical proposition. The copula mediates *S* and *P,* and does not function simply as a static syntactic mark of the rigidity of logical being. *S* is both itself and, as *P,* not itself. *P* is both itself and, as the predicate of *S,* not itself. Therefore "*S* is *P*" is both itself and "*S* is not *P.*" Nothing is gained by distinguishing between identity and predication, since in fact each is contained within the other. Every term can be identified only by being distinguished both from itself ($A = A$) and from every other ($A \neq -A$). The activity of logical judgment is thus not intelligible in terms of static propositions. For the same reason, as Hegel explicitly warns us, the dialectical judgment cannot be genuinely grasped as a triplicity of moments (2 : 498; 836). Truth is not "a motionless third, but even as this unity it is an excitation and activity that mediates itself with itself" (2 : 499; 837). The Whole is thus both identity and predication by virtue of its character as negation of negation.

Just as mediated beginnings are moments leading back to the comprehensive beginning of the circle of mediated immediacy, so the individual sciences may be regarded as circles within the circle of dialectic. Speculation is the synoptic conceptual grasp of this comprehensive circle. It is a grasping of itself as the science of logic (in the sense of *Logos,* which thus includes the logician). The possession of the science of logic leads then to the thinking of the individual sciences, or to their reappropriation from the comprehensive standpoint of logic. One could almost say that, for Hegel, logic is the philosophy of science. But Hegel's philosophy of science is retrospective or recollective, because it is not concerned with em-

15. *Logik,* 1 : 52; *Logic,* p. 68.

pirical discovery (the task of the particular sciences themselves), but with the "conditions for the possibility of knowledge," to use the pertinent Kantian expression. It is quite true, as has often been suggested, that Hegel attempts to complete, in a radically new way, Kant's transcendental philosophy. The completion of science is "absolute liberation" or the achievement of absolute freedom in the sense desired by Fichte and Schelling (2 : 505; 843). Spirit is now complete, and so "resting in itself," although as thinking, it is "excited." This is Hegel's solution to the fundamental problem of the entire philosophical tradition. Hegel returns man to his origins, and thereby to salvation or satisfaction, by answering the question first posed in Plato's *Sophist:* How can Being or the Whole be both at rest and in motion?

10 Conclusion: Intuition and Alienation

Summary Remarks

It is now time to bring this introductory study of Hegel to a close. I need not attempt a comprehensive summary; to a certain extent, the preceding chapter has served that purpose. In the following pages, I should like first to offer some general reflections which may assist the reader toward formulating his own reappropriation of Hegel's science of wisdom. I will then conclude with a necessarily circumscribed statement of what seem to me the most fundamental objections to Hegel's teaching.

No doubt the major obstacle in the path of a sympathetic study of Hegel is his extraordinarily difficult language. This difficulty is a direct consequence of the audacious claim which Hegel makes on behalf of his "science of wisdom." If we begin by rejecting both language and claim, we run the risk of falling victim to a provincial version of the Skepticism which Hegel identifies as the fundamental disease of traditional philosophy. In our own century, philosophers claimed to conduct a revolution against traditional thought, and especially against its difficult and often "meaningless" language. One cannot avoid noticing that quite often the "new" mode of philosophizing has brought with it language as difficult as anything from previous epochs. This is also true of so-called ordinary-language philosophy and, more generally, of the contemporary "analytic" schools, about which I have already had something to say. These schools may all be described from the Hegelian (or Kantian) standpoint as *transcendental,* because all are engaged in an effort to justify rational discourse.

The term "transcendental" referred originally to those ontological principles like *entity, being, one, true,* and *good,* which "go beyond" or cannot be described in terms of the categories of Aristotelian logical explanation. Since the transcendentals are the ultimate principles of discursive thinking or predicative logic, they can only be grasped by an intuitive, or in any case metalogical, mode of thinking (and speaking). The transference of the term "transcendental" to the Absolute Ego as the principle of subjectivity is obviously connected to the Christian (and Neo-Platonist) conception of God as Spirit or Mind, the "source" or "ground" of the transcendentals of objectivity. German philosophers from Kant to Hegel in effect interpret the Parmenidean identification of Being and Thinking as subject rather than substance. To be is to be thought or posed by a principle of subjectivity which is not itself a being, whether in the subjective or objective sense. One could therefore say that metalogic is initially the study of transcendental subjectivity. This entails the development of highly technical "metadiscourses" on the one hand, and on the other, an appeal, implicit or explicit, to the subject of discourse. The explicit appeal is today best seen in phenomenology, at least to the extent that phenomenologists retain the Husserlian concern for transcendental subjectivity. The analytic philosophers, however (and those phenomenologists who have evidently been influenced by the analytic movement), make an implicit appeal to a transcendental subjectivity in what amounts to a rendering absolute of discourse itself. As we have seen, this appeal is often masked by a kind of "Aristotelian" rejection of self-consciousness as a principle. But the result of this rejection is unfortunately linguistic conventionalism. The more self-conscious analytic philosophers become, the more they turn to the study of Kant. This turn is a tacit or explicit recognition of their origins, or of the horizon of their doctrines, which are in individual (and crucial) instances normally of Greek origin. If Kant is taken in his own terms, and not as a pseudocontemporary, then we have already returned to the battleground of Hegel's teaching. The best way for the contemporary philosopher to see the "relevance" of Hegel is for him to understand his own descent from Kant, as well as the fact that Hegel's teaching is a radical criticism of Kant.

In my opinion the greatest advantage to be derived from the study of Hegel is a detailed comprehension of what it means to try to "give an account," not of this or that, but of anything whatsoever. Hegel forces us to see the inadequacies of our local prejudices, even or especially if we give them imposing titles like "world-view," "conceptual framework," or "linguistic horizon." If we ourselves are cognizant of the limits of our viewpoint, and in fact insist upon limitation as a necessary structural feature of any viewpoint whatsoever, then Hegel in effect tells us that we are lazy or shortsighted. He forces us to think through the conception of limitation and provides us with new conceptual tools for this labor. Hegel claims that to "think through" limitation is to overcome it: not to deny or ignore limits, but to master them comprehensively by a discursive account of the horizon of limit. We can even say that Hegel explains, like no one before or after him, the "spaces" between the limits of conflicting viewpoints. More precisely, Hegel gives us a new and vastly richer understanding of negativity than we have previously received.

There can be no doubt that Hegel's account of negativity is extremely difficult, and that every effort to state it with rigor and accuracy brings us face to face with problems for which there may be no solution. My contention, however, is that there are advantages of an order of magnitude greater than the difficulties to be obtained by an assiduous and dispassionate study of Hegel's logic. It is especially urgent for us today to learn this logic, because the perplexities of contemporary philosophy, which are not really different from the *aporiai* of traditional philosophy, have been grasped and analyzed by Hegel with a skill that, for me, exceeds that of any other thinker. This is not to say that Hegel has "solved" these *aporiai*. My own feeling, however, is that Hegel's teaching is superior to those that succeeded it. No prudent man would suggest that Hegel's is the last or most comprehensive possibility for Western thought. Nor am I implying that mathematical should be replaced by dialectical logic. Dialectical logic is an *interpretation* of the philosophical significance of mathematical logic. Perhaps it is the wrong interpretation. But I know of no better ones now in currency. It seems to me, then, that Hegel stands between us and any future possibility of progress in philosophy.

Let me try to formulate Hegel's main thesis in such a way

as to illustrate the previous suggestion. Philosophers, with all due respect for their differences, have always attempted the same thing: to explain, or at least to identify, the principles of all things.[1] In Greek philosophy, these principles are form, matter, and mind. But the Greeks did not think it possible to deduce any two of these principles from the third. They assumed a Whole, and a totally accessible (or rational) Whole, but explained it in such a way as to suppress or divide it into cognitively inaccessible principalities. Hence their quasi-principle or substitute term for the Whole, *nature,* is from the outset divided against itself, even though intended to provide a standard of truth and goodness. The Neo-Platonists and Christian Scholastics present variations on Greek themes, with one innovation: the Whole is now understood as a creation or emanation from the highest principle, the Neo-Platonist One or the Christian God. Since both are discursively unintelligible, the result is dualism. The Whole loses its essence or significance and is reduced to appearance or accident.

Modern philosophers attempt to resolve this problem as follows. First, the scientifically oriented thinkers either deny the Whole or define it as an implicit dualism of matter and space, or of motion as the significance of matter in space. The result is either materialism or "mathematicism": number is the essence of motion, and space is either forgotten or assimilated into matter. Or else they admit a dualism of mind and matter, which they define as separate substances or as attributes of one unknowable substance. This unknowable substance is a disguised reference either to mathematically determined motion or to the "hidden God" of Christianity. The result is an unstable relation between Materialism and Idealism. Eventually, philosophers attempt to overcome this instability by an effort to define substance as a "third" which is neither thought nor extension but the principle of both: for example, *conatus,* monad, the Absolute Ego. Hegel's Absolute Spirit is the last

1. This point has been regularly made by Heidegger. For a statement in a context pertinent to Hegel, see *Schellings Abhandlung über das Wesen der menschlichen Freiheit* (1809) (Tübingen, Max Niemeyer Verlag, 1971), p. 102.

comprehensive version of the effort to explain the Whole by identifying its first principle as conceptually accessible. Hegel explains thought and extension (subject and object) in terms of the first principle of the sameness of their excitation or formation process. God, man, and world are preserved and assimilated into a rational Whole. Any step "beyond" Hegel would seem necessarily to be a step "beneath" him, to some earlier explanation of the first principle, or else to an outright abandonment of philosophy as a rational enterprise.

For reasons like this, I have suggested that our way to the future, *if there is a future for philosophy,* lies through the reassimilation of Hegel. If contemporary problems are traditional problems expressed in new dialects, then we are in fact, if not self-consciously, contemporaries of Hegel. One could therefore say that the first step in understanding Hegel is to follow the advice of the Delphic Oracle and "know ourselves." Hegel does not present us with a "new" teaching in the same way that an artist creates a new poem or statue, unique yet one among many by virtue of its uniqueness. In our time, the notion of "creation" or "originality" has been subjected to a degree of vulgarization that deprives such terms of all serious meaning.[2] Hegel reminds us of what, thanks to Nietzsche, we have forgotten. According to Nietzsche, the philosopher of the future will not refer to "truth" but to "my" truth or "my judgment." [3] We can learn from Hegel that, if philosophical truth is *mine,* then there is no truth, but only opinion (*meinen*).[4] Hegel does not claim to provide us with a new opinion but rather to explain the truth about the old opinions. In the idiom of contemporary analytic philosophy, Hegel shows us what we mean when we say anything whatsoever. In the idiom of existential or fundamental ontology, he shows us the significance of the assertion that man is "the shepherd of Being" or the claim that Being gives itself to man in thinking, that discourse is "the house of Being." Being gives, shows, or un-

2. *Philosophie des Rechts, Vorrede,* pp. 5 ff.; *Philosophy of Right,* pp. 3 ff.

3. *Jenseits von Gut und Böse,* in *Werke,* ed. K. Schlecta, 2 : 605 (par. 43).

4. *Phänomenologie,* pp. 58 f.; *Phenomenology,* pp. 129 ff.

covers itself in human discourse, and Hegel's science of wisdom is the account not just of discourse but of the humans who speak.

To submit oneself to the study of Hegel is thus to take oneself with great seriousness. We are today too exhausted by the consequences of having previously forgotten Hegel to begin lightly the infinite labor of mastering him (and ourselves) anew. Irony, skepticism, and a sense of the Absurd are today the fashions which permeate even the study of the professional philosopher. To think of oneself as professionally engaged in conceptual analysis from nine to five and an ironical wink of fate at all other times is of course to admit implicitly that philosophy is meaningless. It is already evident, however, that thoughtful persons are fatigued with fatigue, or about to pass through the negation of negation which Hegel tells us is a necessary preface to a new affirmation. If the new spirit of affirmation is nothing more than an "optimistic" return to the post-Hegelian repudiation of reason, it will evaporate into "pessimism," or another epoch of universal darkness masquerading as universal enlightenment. The renewed interest in Hegel among members of the philosophical community may allow us to hope that, with all our difficulties and for all our world-historical fatigue, Spirit has not yet departed from this gray patch of the Whole.

Hegel and Intellectual Intuition: A Critique

This completes my exposition and defense of Hegel. I want now to offer a reasonably full exposition of what strikes me as the central technical deficiency in Hegel's teaching. The following pages should be read in conjunction with a reconsideration of my remarks about the Whole in chapters 2, 4, and 5. If I can succeed in making a persuasive case with respect to this deficiency, the reader will be able to discern how it underlies most of the important criticisms that have been made against Hegel. Such an exposition should then stand as a fair sample of a full-scale criticism of what needs criticizing in Hegel's science of wisdom.

My objection turns upon Hegel's attitude toward intuition (*Anschauen*). Stated simply, Hegel seems to reject outright the

Platonic-Aristotelian doctrine of the intellectual intuition (*noēsis*) of determinate form. Despite the obviously approving citation of *Metaphysics* 12.7, at the end of the *Encyclopedia*, "intellectual intuition" is for Hegel invariably the doctrine of Fichte and Schelling: the immediate grasping by the ego of itself as transcendental, or as the unconditioned condition of all determinations of being: as the ultimate identity of finite determinations in the Absolute. Such an intuition is for Hegel a merely subjective postulate, lacking in determinate content, or "a night in which all cows are black." [5] Hegel's critique of intellectual intuition (apart from which his citation of Aristotle makes no sense whatsoever) is partly a consequence of of the process, culminating in Kant, whereby noetic intuition is replaced by sensuous intuition. This process is closely connected with the effort to preserve metaphysics in a new form by rendering subjectivity both objective and rational.[6] The subject intuits visible form in the individual; this form is spatial or "sensitive," and not intellectual in the Greek sense. Sensitive intuition is the immediate precursor of the transcendental aesthetic in Kant; it is the principle which brings unity into the phenomenal world, and in that sense produces the Whole as a function of the transcendental subjectivity. Sensitive intuition in man thus imitates the intellectual intuition in God, by which he spontaneously produces the noumenal world. Divine intellectual intuition, or the direct apprehension of things as they are, is in the Kantian teaching impossible for man. The imitation of intellectual by sensitive intuition is the sign of a dualism, or separation of human from divine subjectivity. Fichte and Schelling attempt to overcome this separation by their doctrine of intellectual intuition.[7] Unfortunately, the ascent to divine unity is empty of all

5. *Logik,* 1 : 61; *Logic,* pp. 75 f.; *Phänomenologie,* pp. 16–20; *Phenomenology,* pp. 76–81; *Differenzschrift,* pp. 5, 32 f.

6. For an excellent account of this process, cf. A. Baeumler, *Das Irrationalitätsproblem in der Ästhetik und Logik des 18. Jahrhunderts bis zur Kritik der Urteilskraft* (Darmstadt, Wissenschaftliche Buchgesellschaft, 1967).

7. For Schelling's doctrine of intuition, see X. Tilliette, *Schelling: Une philosophie en devenir* (Paris, J. Vrin, 1970), Vol. 1, *Le système vivant 1794–1821,* pp. 96 ff.

content, since content is determination, or the consequence of a "fall" from unity. This emptiness is the result of the activity of intellectual intuition, which is not merely spontaneous or productive but which conceals itself within its determinate productions by our very effort to understand or "see" it. Whereas for Kant man is not God, for Kant's successors, man is as it were the unselfconscious exhibition of divine creativity. Hegel claims to render man fully self-conscious, and so to recognize his divinity. But this is accomplished by the rejection of intellectual intuition.

In the Neo-Kantian doctrine of Fichte and Schelling, reason (*Vernunft*) cannot grasp itself theoretically but only practically. The subjective activity of spontaneous production can be *felt* but not thought; the finite ego is driven to pose determinations and assimilate them in a process for which there can be no end. Instead of a logical account of the totality of subjective activity, that is, a reconciliation of the transcendental ego and its objective productions, there is a striving to continue such activity forever. The end becomes an "ought" (*Sollen*) or infinitely alienated essence of a process which, thus separated from its goal, loses all sense and value. This doctrine of Absolute Idealism is characterized by the typically modern restlessness associated with the Faust of Goethe's epic. It is finally misleading to refer to Hegel's own teaching as "Faustian," since his purpose is to overcome such restlessness not in resignation but in the conquest of infinite striving by infinite wisdom. The excitation of Hegel's Absolute Spirit is circular, or the harmony of infinity and finitude: it is not the "bad infinity" of perpetual dissatisfaction. One could say that Hegel achieves satisfaction by "unmasking" intellectual intuition as the totality of its productions. There is then no indifference point of perfect unity, separate from or concealed by the interrelated determinations of the phenomenal world of understanding (*Verstand*). This world, which is the resolution of the classical separation of "Whole" from "All," is itself understood, or rendered fully rational, by dialectico-speculative reason, which grasps the Absolute as the pulsation-process externalizing itself in its finite productions.

Since the pulsation-process is not a form but the intrinsically negative activity by which forms are produced, there can be no intellectual intuition in the Greek sense of negative activity. At the same time, the intellectual intuition of Fichte and Schelling is useless, because it does not grasp the process qua process but achieves at most only a *feeling* of ultimate unity. Hegel's goal is a discursive account of the Absolute as the total activity of determinate forms. Unity in itself is an empty abstraction; Fichtean intuition provides us with a generalized feeling of the deficient characteristic of Platonic-Aristotelian intuition. Noetic intuition purports to capture the particular form (this qua this) in its immediacy, separateness, or being-for-self (*auto kath' hauto*). But "the particular, however, is just this, to relate itself to *another* outside itself." [8] Truth is never immediacy, never the direct apprehension of a formal element in abstraction from all others, but the mediation of its immediate self with its mediations. "The true is the Whole." [9] It is the result of the comprehensive interrelations of formal elements, and is "immediate" in the sense that actuality (*Wirklichkeit*) is the totality of mediations.

It is tempting to suggest that Hegel replaces Greek noetic intuition (*noēsis*) by discursive thinking (*dianoia*). Of course, as we have seen, he cites with approval Aristotle's cryptic discussion of *Noēsis tēs noēseōs*. But Aristotle's god does not speak or engage in logical explanations of the Whole; instead, it contemplates itself as the pure noetic activity which actualizes the world. To think itself is not also to think the world. Therefore, Aristotle's noetic thinking is more like Fichte's intellectual intuition than Hegel's science of wisdom. One might also object that Hegel does indeed allow for "the eternal intuition" by the Idea "of itself in the other; the concept which *has* carried *itself* out in its objectivity, the object which is *inner purposiveness,* essential subjectivity." [10] Intuition is present at the end of the development of the Idea, which sees itself as reflected into nature. In theological lan-

8. *Enzyklopädie,* p. 98 (par. 74); *Encyclopedia–Wallace,* p. 137.
9. *Phänomenologie,* p. 21; *Phenomenology,* p. 81.
10. *Enzyklopädie,* p. 184 (par. 214); *Encyclopedia–Wallace,* p. 365.

guage, God sees himself as reflected into the world, and so, as the identity-within-difference of himself and the world (as the immediate actuality of all mediations). Intuition is therefore present at the beginning (as the antecedent of representation and thinking) [11] and at the end of knowledge.[12] *But it is not a functioning component of the process of dialectico-speculative thinking itself.* Even as present within the fully developed Idea, intuition characterizes the Idea for itself, or as separated from and hence reflected within nature or the intuited Idea. "As intuition, however, the Idea is posed in one-sided determination of immediacy or negation through external reflection." [13]

We may summarize Hegel's treatment of intuition as follows: either it is empty of all determinate content, or it expresses the immediate and therefore incomplete element of form as a separate, nondialectical abstraction. In both cases it is associated with sensuous images rather than with intelligible structure. Noetic intuition provides at best a "picture" of a form, or of some aspect of a form, which cannot serve as the starting point for discursive analysis, except in the sense that the intuited form is *transformed* into its "other" or opposite. Hegelian dialectical thinking "develops" the form into the totality of formal structure and uncovers the logical oppositions or contradictions within this totality as the pulse-beat of the Absolute itself. In the discursive thinking of Plato and Aristotle, and so in the entire tradition culminating in Frege and the early Russell and Wittgenstein, the intuited form (or logical sign) preserves its identity, separateness, and stability throughout the process of analysis. In fact, it is the intuited form which gives stability to that process, or enables us to distinguish a successful from an unsuccessful analysis. It is the form about which we speak in our dianoetic or discursive analyses.

11. Ibid., pp. 361 ff.; *Encyclopedia Wallace–Miller,* pp. 192 ff.

12. K. Harlander, *Absolute Subjektivität und kategoriale Anschauung* (Meisenheim am Glan, Verlag Anton Hain, 1969), p. 110. This is a superior study. My objeection to Hegel is similar to that of Harlander, who starts from a Husserlian perspective, however. Cf. my review, "Alexandre Kojève, *Essai d'une histoire raisonnée de la philosophie païenne,*" *Man and World* 3, no. 1 (February 1970) : 120–25.

13. *Enzyklopädie,* p. 196 f. (par. 244); *Encyclopedia–Wallace,* p. 379.

Hegel rejects discursive analysis as grounded in the noetic intuition of separate, finite forms. Such an analysis leads to discontinuous, finite discourses, which are separated from each other because separated from the forms about which they discourse. In order to guarantee the correspondence of discourse to form, or to resolve the problem of guaranteeing that language "mirrors" ontological actuality rather than merely an appearance or human perspective, Hegel allows the *assimilation* of the form into discursive thought. *All* forms are so assimilated; there is no further distinction between *noēsis* and *dianoia*. There is no thinking without discourse.[14] The "silence" characteristic of intellectual intuition is rejected by Hegel as an inarticulate mysticism or subjective feeling, which cannot serve as a basis for logical truth. Discourse exhibits in its highest or speculative form the logical determinations of God or Absolute Spirit; it is in this sense also the truth of man's being.[15] Differently stated, logical discourse is the self-manifestation of God within the human spirit, or the complete explanation of the religious representation of Jesus Christ. Needless to say, the "logic" in question is not mathematical, since mathematical form, although no doubt universal, is abstract. It is neither the noumenal nor the phenomenal but something neutral, or common to both because indifferent to both.

The question nevertheless remains whether Hegelian logic is independent of, or functions apart from, a regulative intellectual intuition. If we do not see what we are talking about, how can we distinguish sense from nonsense? If formal structure is a linguistic convention, as is widely held today, then we return in part to the Idealism of Fichte and Schelling, except that nothing is said about the Absolute. Or one could say that we return to a quasi-Leibnizian doctrine of an infinite number of discoursing monads, only with no divine or comprehensive monadic structure to regulate discourse. In a final metaphor, the infinite sequence of finite discourses is an expression of infinite and discontinuous, but therefore mutually contradictory, instances of the will to power.

14. T. Bodammer, *Hegels Deutung der Sprache,* p. 60.
15. *Logik,* 1 : 9–10; *Logic,* pp. 31–32.

Hegel attempts to avoid all such consequences by his claim to have achieved total discourse or a complete account of the Whole. This claim to totality may hypnotize us, not simply because of its audacity but because of its compelling critique of the instability of incomplete discourse.[16] If we refute on logical grounds the possibility of a complete account of the Whole, we seem to doom ourselves to the silence of perpetual chatter, which may be schematized as "*P* and non-*P*." In this case, our logic is itself negated by the violation of the principle of contradiction. Given the simultaneous assertibility of *P* and non-*P* (in the same sense, sooner or later, because of the infinity of discursive chatter), the principles of finite logic disintegrate into the excitations of Hegelian logic. It would seem that the attempt to refute Hegel leads only to the confirmation of his own teaching.

Nevertheless, a complete account of the Whole, precisely as a discursive development, arises only from the weaving together of successfully completed finite stages. It is all very well to say that every stage *P* is no sooner asserted than contradicted by, or assimilated into, non-*P*. The fact remains that *P* must be described successfully as *P*, and not as *Q* or *R*, since non-*P* is the more comprehensive version of *P*, not of *Q* or *R*. We may grant that the assertion of *Q* or *R* leads *eventually* to *P*, but Hegel insists in every paragraph of his teaching that the order of assertion is not arbitrary. *P* and non-*P* are assimilated into *Q* not into *O* or *R*. *Q* and non-*Q* are assimilated into *R*, and so on until the completion of the logical alphabet, which then repeats itself in the circle of wisdom. The order of logical discourse follows, because it is ultimately identical with, the order of development or revelation of the Absolute. This would seem to mean that the successful assertion of *P* is guaranteed or certified by the coordinate moment or aspect of the development of the Absolute. But in my opinion, this is itself intelligible only if the successful assertion of *P* is rooted in the speaker's *vision* of the ontological coordi-

16. Hence the peculiarly hypnotic character of the interpretation of Hegel of A. Kojève, who insists beyond all other commentators on the element of complete discourse.

nate of *P*. The vision cannot be certified by the assertion or constituted by it, as is required through the assimilation of intuition into conceptual thinking, since we can only explain what has already occurred or become visible to us. As Hegel so frequently reminds us, philosophy is recollection of an already concluded experience. But a concluded experience is the manifestation of the Absolute. How can there be a conceptual recollection of a manifestation of the Absolute, if that manifestation is itself a *consequence* of its conceptual recollection? In sum, *Hegel claims that the actual is brought into being by discourse, and by a discourse which can occur only after the actual presents itself.*

So far as I can see, this is a contradiction which has no *Aufhebung*. Of course, as we have noticed on several previous occasions, Hegel would claim that, from the standpoint of eternity, the actual is fully developed and hence accessible to temporal discourse which, in explaining an aspect of the eternal, brings it into the development of time, or reconciles eternity and temporality to that extent. Time is God speaking in and to man. But we have also seen that this claim merely serves to complicate the situation. Hegel still cannot explain the accessibility of the actual to temporal discourse except, I believe, by intellectual intuition in the Greek sense of the term. If the actual is brought into time by the process of discourse itself, then philosophy is not recollection but *projection* or linguistic constructivism in the contemporary sense. The discursive ego cannot see what it has done until *after* it has acted or, in effect, spoken. The validity of what has been said is then factic, or arbitrary, and not rooted in a prior, let alone eternal, condition. In other words, Hegel is transposed into the Heidegger of *Being and Time*. The accessibility of the "eternal" is altogether in the form of temporal discourse. That is, *the eternal is altogether inaccessible:* it conceals itself by the very process which ostensibly reveals it. The eternal or the Absolute is separated from itself by the process of reflection in the Fichtean sense which Hegel believed himself to have overcome.

Hegel's rejection of intellectual intuition is related or similar to the later Wittgenstein's rejection of private language. In order to be tested by the universal or public criteria of reason, an intuition must be externalized in discourse. Discourse "is the existence (*Dasein*) of the pure self as self." [17] Needless to say, logical thinking is higher than mere discourse. Nevertheless, as T. Bodammer points out, "Only in pure self-determination is thinking actually free. But even this self-determination of thinking is on the other hand not possible, unless it expresses itself in linguistic signs." [18] Discourse is the genuine work of man, the medium in which the interiority of Spirit is united with the exteriority of objective nature. In slightly different terms, Spirit as universal manifests itself only in the individual, and discourse is the principle of individuation.[19] The transient character of existence is preserved in the universality of discourse, which grasps in the concept the otherwise separated and opposed moments of the universal and the particular.[20]

Thinking in the highest and most comprehensive sense is the Hegelian logic as a totality: the word of God rendered entirely accessible to man. But the logic expresses the sense of discourse; it is the total elaboration of the dialectical excitations of *partial* discourse. So far as the human thinker is concerned, the logic can only be thought one step at a time. What guarantees the validity of each step as it is taken? Certainly not the Whole, which is not visible or present until the *end* of discourse. As we have seen, Hegel comes very close to identifying the emergence of each stage of the Whole with the discursive thinking that "recollects" it in the concept. If each world-historical speaker utters the right discourse at the right moment, this can only be because he sees the form or shape of the concluded experience or revealed moment of the Whole, or else because man is entirely determined by an eternal necessity masquerading as history. In the latter case, however, the

17. *Phänomenologie,* p. 362; *Phenomenology,* p. 530. Cf. Bodammer, *Hegels Deutung der Sprache,* pp. 94 f.

18. Bodammer, *Hegels Deutung der Sprache,* p. 238; cf. p. 221.

19. *Phänomenologie,* pp. 362–72; *Phenomenology,* pp. 529–43.

20. Ibid., pp. 362 f.; *Phenomenology,* pp. 529 ff.

essential difference between history and eternity, or between Hegel and Spinoza, is destroyed. Self-consciousness is an illusion. Subjectivity is an appearance of substance, and dualism is restrained only by a return to acosmism or divine silence.

Let us now look at a different aspect of the same issue. Hegel's conception of work as negativity is central to his conception of individual and Whole. Just as the Absolute produces the Whole by the triadic negativity of position-presupposition-cancellation and return (*Aufhebung*), so the working individual is, as producing external actuality, "a *nothing* working itself out into *nothingness.*" [21] According to the classical Aristotelian teaching, "work" in the deepest sense takes place and is visible only as the presence of form. This conception leads to great difficulties, as we have seen, primarily concerning the analysis of "nothing," which is defined by Plato as "otherness" and by Aristotle as the absence of a determinate property in the presence of its contrary. The Platonic-Aristotelian definition of "nothing" reduces it to a syntactic property of predication: how we refer to what is actually present. "Nothing" cannot have ontological status because what is, is "something" or *ontina:* a thing or visible form. Hence "nothing" is intelligible only as negation, and is a consequence of the partial or perspectival character of human perception.

Hegel's analysis of "nothing" certainly sheds new light on the limitations of Greek doctrine. In my view, it is superior to the Heideggerian account in its effort to articulate *Nichts* or assimilate it into the Whole. The logical exposition of negative excitation is an attempt to render it ontologically intelligible without eliminating the difference between Being and Nothing. This exposition sets a standard which must either be surpassed or accepted as the best possible; I see no advantage in returning to the pre-Hegelian situation. Unfortunately, there is one point which Hegel does not seem to have explained. Let us grant his central assertion that every determination is a negation. We grant, in other words, that negation is not (simply) a syntactic operation external to the determinate form

21. Ibid., p. 287; *Phenomenology*, p. 421.

but part of its ontological structure. Let us admit further that the oscillation of position and negation intrinsic to ontological structure presupposes contradiction as a process by which things do not simply disappear but preserve their identity only through reflecting the Whole. The question still remains: how can we think determinately or positively the indeterminate or negative oscillations of form?

If form itself becomes thinkable as assimilated into the discursive account of the negative (nonformal) work by which forms are produced and interact to constitute a Whole, and if that work is nonformal, then the visible, determinate, positive, and self-identical must be conceived and explained in terms of the invisible, indeterminate, negative, or difference qua difference. One can understand the need to analyze form in terms of activity and activity as a function of presence and absence. What remains unintelligible is how presence can be explained as a crystallization of absence. Hegel seems to have lapsed back into the Christian doctrine of creation *ex nihilo,* despite his effort to assimilate the *nihil* into the logically accessible. I repeat: if form is produced by negative activity, then negative activity cannot be analyzed into formal constituents. Adapting a criticism of D. Henrich, we can say that the negation of negation leads to no development. The continuum of negative excitation remains negative, or empty of positive content. We have a sequence of moments of immediacy, called by Hegel "Being" and "Essence," but no genuine mediation of the two, no rise to a higher and more comprehensive level: no intelligible *Wirklichkeit* because no intelligible account of work.[22] Nor is it satisfactory to say that the continuum of negativity *already* has content (as Hegel in fact does, given the identity of Being and Nothing in Becoming). *For this claim either identifies the continuum of negative form and positive content with the Absolute, which contradicts its pure negative nature, or else it leaves separate and unexplained Absolute Spirit as the pure negative activity which produces the continuum.* As one might also express this dilemma, Hegel has attempted to explain the process of Be-

22. *Hegel im Kontext,* pp. 95 ff.

coming, but in such a way as to fail to explain how any *thing* comes to be. There remains a dualism between the immediacy of Being = Nothing, and Actuality, because the dialectical analysis of Essence gives priority to negative, nonformal excitation as the engine which drives us from the initial to the final immediacy. If this is a fair criticism, then one can understand more easily the extraordinary diversity in the best interpretations of Hegel. The "right-Hegelians" insist upon the separation of Absolute Spirit from the continuum of Becoming, whereas the "left-Hegelians" insist upon their identity. But in either case, the coherence of Hegel's teaching is dissolved.

In the dialectic of reflection, Hegel enriches our understanding of form and negativity because he uncovers what amounts to a new conception of form as the activity of formation. But his explanation of this new conception is defective because it is connected to a rejection of intellectual intuition. Greek intuition is excluded because it is associated with particular, static forms, whereas the formation activity is not itself a form, and neither particular nor static. Fichtean or Schellingian intuition is rejected because, as empty of determinate content, it provides no basis for a discursive account of unity or the Whole. Hegel is, however, unable to provide us with a substitute for these two kinds of intuition. He cannot explain *how* he is able to explain the formation process or to identify the Absolute in and as the dialectical oscillations of its productions. What we require is an account of intuition that sees both forms and their oscillations, or determinations and their negations, and so is the appropriate foundation for a logical account of the Whole as a One differentiating itself. The accessibility of negativity to discourse argues not simply for the identity of Being and Nothing, but for the visibility of the latter in the light of the former. I suppose this was Hegel's intention, since the *Logic* does not begin with *Nichts*. Nevertheless, for the reasons given, I am unable to see that Hegel carried out his intention successfully.

The ligatures of the Hegelian Whole are not invisible. Hegel's logic has too many valuable analyses of formation process for such an extreme criticism to be persuasive. But their visibility is shadowed by a failure to explain adequately, from a subjective as well as an objective standpoint, how they are visible. This means, I think, that the Whole is itself less than the Whole; the final stage of the science of wisdom has not yet been achieved. As the difficulty emerged within our study, the Whole is evidently both eternal and temporal, both complete and incomplete. The Whole is everywhere complete, yet an essential aspect of this completeness is its development *toward* completeness in human history. Perhaps we may restate this difficulty as consisting of two aspects. First, until such time as history is completed, there is a disjunction between human comprehension and the Absolute, which in effect negates that comprehension. Partial knowledge is for Hegel no knowledge at all. Hence arises the problem just examined: how can we utter the right partial speech at the right time, or guarantee the preservation of present incompleteness as a necessary element in a more comprehensive future stage?

Hegel tells us a good bit about negativity, yet he does not manage to explain how the negativity of the present moment serves as the engine whereby the concrete present is transformed into a still more concrete future. This is because his account of presence is finally (and impossibly) an account of absence. By the same token, since the completion of the Absolute depends upon the completion of history, yet must precede it, the Absolute is present within each moment of its own development in the "non-form" of its own absence.

The second aspect of our difficulty concerns the situation following the claimed completion of history by Hegel's science of wisdom or, in religious terms, the reconciliation between the Father and the Son in the Holy Ghost. The completion of history does not mean its cancellation, but its *Aufhebung* into eternity. In other words, even though divine, men continue to exist temporally within the circle of completed history. The presence of time in eternity is at once the presence of eternity in time. That is, God reveals himself in the discursive thinking of individual, finite, temporal humans. As Hegel says in the *Phenomenology,* the concept must unfold moment by moment, and is thus time. Spirit, as (incomplete) development, is thus within time: "Time appears as the fate and the necessity of Spirit, which is not complete in itself." [23] Spirit completes itself, and so time as well, by grasping itself in its pure concept, or as Hegel says, by transforming intuition into "conceived and conceiving intuition." This is of course an early formulation of a point which we have already studied in the later version of the *Encyclopedia.* But the early passage renders vivid the difficulty that Hegel never eliminated.

The Whole, or the identity between God and man, depends upon the identity of intuition and conception. But the assimilation of intuition into conception means the explanation of presence as particular by absence as universal. This is no doubt why some critics of Hegel believe that every positive assertion or formal analysis in his works is erased as quickly as it is uttered. Such a belief is exaggerated, yet not without substance. What we have is rather a dualism of formal analysis and the analysis of negative activity, but no mediation of the two. In the present context, the identification of God and man is at once a separation of the divine from the human. I say this because eternity both assimilates temporality in the *Aufhebung* of history and, since eternity is present only in human or temporal thought, is indistinguishable from temporality. It does no good to say that wisdom, or the complete thinking of eternity, is no longer temporal but "transcendental." If eternity is totality and not partial thought, then it is not the thinking of a sum of finite forms together with their finite relations, but a thinking of the total process or activity which produces finite forms and relations, and the thinking of this total process *as total.* Yet totality can only be thought by mortals in a temporal sequence of finite steps. If we achieve the Hegelian science of totality, we must cease to be human or become genuinely divine. Surely no human could negotiate such a process unassisted by the divine Spirit; but the proffering of such assistance amounts to the divinization of man from the outset, *prior to historical development.*

23. *Phänomenologie,* p. 558; *Phenomenology,* p. 800

The Whole must therefore be present in advance within its partial manifestations. Eternity must be present within temporality, prior to the development of temporality. And this contradicts Hegel's claim that eternity is achieved precisely by undergoing and completing the development of temporality. The completion of history is evidently either superfluous or impossible. It is superfluous if it has already occurred as a necessary moment of the Whole. But it is impossible if its completion depends upon the transformation of intuition into conception.

The Overcoming of Alienation

I should like to close this study with a general observation about *alienation.* I mentioned in a previous chapter that Hegel could be construed in no simple sense as a partisan of the ancients or moderns, since his entire teaching is intended to reconcile the best of both sides. Nevertheless, it is evident that this conciliatory intention is itself characteristically modern. In attempting to make man "at home" in this world, Hegel is led to deny the existential as well as conceptual detachment of eternity from temporality. Stated concisely, the "time" in which the sage dwells is the activity of eternity. This doctrine must not be confused with the classical notion, first enunciated by Plato, that mortal man achieves eternity by thinking or contemplating the eternal. The classical doctrine of the vision of eternity is at the same time a doctrine of *ecstasy* or transcendence of temporal existence. In other words, "alienation," within the early Greek and Christian traditions, is the highest possible human experience. If we disregard here the difference between the Greek and Christian versions of this doctrine, both in effect assert that man is "at home" in this world only by transcending it. The perfection of human nature lies in the transcendence, however momentary or intermittent, of human nature. But this is to say that man's nature is divided and self-contradictory.

In the Greek tradition, man achieves perfection by an extinction of practice in theory, whereas in the Christian tradition, perfection amounts to the assimilation of theory into practice. This is of course oversimplified, yet not, I think, misleadingly so. It serves to make vivid the sense in which Hegel's reconciliation of the Greek and Christian traditions culminates in the overcoming of alienation, which overcoming is understood as the union of theory and practice. What one may call the "Cartesian" dimension in modern philosophy, culminating in the doctrines of Nietzsche and Marx, amounts to the divinization of man, as based upon the effort to derive the spirit from the body. For a Hegelian (to say nothing of others), this doctrine results in the rendering absolute of practice. The activity of the body is given an "ideological" justification which, as itself derived from the body, fails to provide the necessary principle of stability, by which corporeal activities are explained and hierarchically ordered. Hegel recognizes the need to justify the body, as well as the impossibility of doing so on the basis of corporeal passions or work. He therefore interprets the body (that is, nature) as the externalization of spirit.

This externalization is "alienation" in the pejorative sense only for so long as spirit has not yet completely understood itself. Alienation can be overcome neither by assimilating the spirit to the body nor the body to the spirit. Instead, it is overcome in the recognition, anticipated by Spinoza, that the Absolute presents itself, through a common formation process, in the intelligibility of body *and* spirit. The *and* which connects the two is not a mere syntactic device but the sign of the "third" or Absolute Spirit. God or Absolute Spirit is incarnated, or takes on human form, in the Hegelian logic, that is, not in neutral or dead symbolic transformations, but in the living and self-conscious process of thought thinking itself or "mind minding itself."

I have already discussed the theoretical difficulties to which this teaching gives rise. But there is also a grave practical difficulty intrinsic to Hegel's union of theory and practice. As has often been objected, Hegel requires us to find "reason in history," or to reconcile ourselves to the concrete historical present as the presence of eternity. This doctrine can be interpreted in one of two ways. Either Hegel means that nineteenth-century

Prussia incarnates the divine *Logos,* or else he means that the sage is now able to reconcile himself fully to political life, which is in general, and not in its contingent Prussian form alone, the one and only medium of complete satisfaction. The first interpretation strikes most readers as absurd, although the Hegelian texts provide it with substantial support. However this may be, it is open to the immanent objection that, as Hegel's own remarks show, concrete history does not and cannot terminate in the Prussian monarchy. To say nothing else, this would mean the extinction of contingency, and so the destruction of the Whole. Governments rise and fall, and the Spirit of world-history moves from one nation to another, from one continent to another. There can be little doubt that if Hegel's Prussia embodies the union of theory and practice, then all sages after Hegel (that is, after the dissolution of the Prussian monarchy) will be subject to alienation, until and unless that monarchy can be reinstituted.

Let us turn therefore to the second interpretation. Accordingly, nineteenth-century Prussia embodies the politico-historical *illustration* of the union of theory and practice in the theoretical understanding of the sage that satisfaction lies within concrete political (and so historical) existence. On this interpretation, however, *the disjunction between theory and practice is preserved.* The sage's "reconciliation" to actuality is equivalent to the Platonic realization that the just city is historically impossible. A Hegelian may insist that the sage will find his satisfaction in comprehending perfectly the impossibility of political satisfaction. In my view, however, this is again a contradiction for which there is no *Aufhebung.* To state the contradiction in its sharpest form, the very existence of a sage is the most radical evidence of the difference between the few and the many. We return to the Platonic situation in which the philosopher descends into the cave, masked by Socratic irony. If the mask is dropped, for whatever reason, the philosopher is condemned to death by the *polis.* In our own time, the situation may take a form radically more desperate, as the condemnation to death of philosophy itself.

One way to appreciate the meaning of this Platonic teaching is thus by reflecting upon the post-Hegelian and especially (but not exclusively) the Marxist-inspired efforts to *enforce* the Hegelian doctrine of the union of theory and practice. It would be amusing, if it were not tragic, to show how contemporary efforts to establish "equality" enact the Platonic teaching that justice requires injustice against the philosophers (and so, of course, is no longer just). Since it is impossible to make all men sages, the contemporary thinker wills instead to make all sages men. The conception of "sage" is either jettisoned or redefined in such a way as to make "wisdom" universally accessible. Such a doctrine is sometimes, and in my view erroneously, referred to as a *secularized* version of Christianity. We would do well to remember that, in the Christian teaching, there is an eternal difference between man and God, to say nothing of the difference between angels and devils, between the saved and the damned. At most, Hegel's teaching offers the possibility for an end to alienation among the nonwise, thanks to a salutary political teaching. But the author of that teaching remains alienated. I must leave it to the reader to decide whether that alienation is to be understood in the ancient or the modern sense. In studying a dialectical thinker, it seems appropriate to end with a dilemma. We are often told that "to understand is to forgive everything." But the route to total forgiveness, when it is enforced by man rather than granted by God, seems to leave nothing to understand. Unfortunately, to insist upon the preservation of distinctions is to violate implicitly the wisest of Nietzsche's maxims: *keine Rache.*

Bibliography

Aristotle. *Aristote, Traité de l'âme*. Edited by G. Rodier. Paris, Ernest Leroux, 1900.

———. *Aristotle, De Anima*. Edited by R. D. Hicks. Amsterdam, Adolf M. Hakkert, 1963; 1st ed., 1907.

———. *Opera*. Oxford, Clarendon Press, 1956–64.

Bacon, Francis. *New Atlantis*. In *Works,* edited by Spedding, Ellis, and Heath. New York, Hurd and Houghton, 1864.

Baeumler, A. *Das Irrationalitätsproblem in der Ästhetik und Logik des 18. Jahrhunderts bis zur Kritik der Urteilskraft*. Darmstadt, Wissenschaftliche Buchgesellschaft, 1967.

Blumenberg, H. *Die Legitimität der Neuzeit*. Frankfurt, Suhrkamp Verlag, 1966.

Bodammer, T. *Hegels Deutung der Sprache*. Hamburg, Felix Meiner Verlag, 1969.

Brockard, H. *Subjekt, Versuch zur Ontologie bei Hegel*. Munich and Salzburg, Verlag Anton Pustet, 1970.

Burdach, K. *Reformation, Renaissance, Humanismus*. Darmstadt, Wissenschaftliche Buchgesellschaft, 1963; 1st ed., 1925.

Chiereghin, F. *Hegel e la metafisica classica*. Padua, CEDAM, 1966.

Cook, D. "Language and Consciousness in Hegel's Jena Writings." *Journal of the History of Philosophy* 10 (1972).

Coreth, E. *Das dialektische Sein in Hegels Logik*. Vienna, Verlag Herder, 1952.

Cornehl, P. *Die Zukunft der Versöhnung*. Göttingen, Vandenhoeck und Ruprecht, 1971.

Descartes, René. *Discours de la méthode*. Edited by E. Gilson. Paris, J. Vrin, 1947.

———. *Meditationes*. In *Oeuvres,* edited by Adam-Tannery. Vol. 7. Paris, J. Vrin, 1947–57.

———. *Les passions de l'âme*. Edited by Rodis-Lewis. Paris, J. Vrin, 1955.

———. *Principia*. in *Oeuvres,* edited by Adam-Tannery. Vol. 8. Paris, J. Vrin, 1947–57.

Dijksterhuis, E. J. *The Mechanization of the World Picture.* Oxford, Clarendon Press, 1961.

Dove, K. R. "Hegel's Phenomenological Method." *Review of Metaphysics* 23, no. 4 (June 1970).

Fackenheim, E. L. *The Religious Dimension in Hegel's Thought.* Bloomington, Indiana University Press, 1967.

Favrholdt, D. *An Interpretation and Critique of Wittgenstein's Tractatus.* Copenhagen, Munksgaard, 1967.

Fessard, G. *De l'actualité historique.* Paris, Desclee de Brouwer, 1960.

Fichte, J. G. *Erste und Zweite Einleitung in die Wissenschaftslehre.* Edited by F. Medicus. Hamburg, Felix Meiner Verlag, 1954.

———. *Grundlage der gesamten Wissenschaftslehre* (1794). Edited by F. Medicus. Hamburg, Felix Meiner Verlag, 1961.

———. *Science of Knowledge, with the First and Second Introductions.* Translated by Peter Heath and John Lachs. New York, Appleton-Century Crofts, 1970.

Findlay, J. *Hegel: A Re-examination.* London, George Allen and Unwin, 1964.

Flay, J. "Hegel's 'Inverted World.'" *Review of Metaphysics* 23, no. 4 (June 1970).

Fleischmann, E. *La philosophie politique de Hegel.* Paris, Plon, 1964.

Foster, M. B. *The Political Philosophies of Plato and Hegel.* 2d ed. Oxford, Clarendon Press, 1968.

Fulda, H. F. *Das Problem einer Einleitung in Hegels Wissenschaft der Logik.* Frankfurt, Vittorio Klostermann, 1965.

Gadamer, H. G. *Hegels Dialektik.* Tübingen, Mohr-Siebeck, 1971.

Girndt, H. *Die Differenz des Fichteschen und Hegelschen Systems in der Hegelschen "Differenzschrift."* Bonn, H. Bouvier, 1965.

Görland, I. *Die Kantkritik des jungen Hegel.* Frankfurt, Vittorio Klostermann, 1966.

Grégoire, F. *Études Hégéliennes.* Louvain, Publications Universitaires de Louvain, 1958.

Hahn, M. *Bürgerlicher Optimismus im Niedergang.* Munich, Fink Verlag, 1969.

Harlander, K. *Absolute Subjektivität und kategoriale Anschauung.* Meisenheim am Glan, Verlag Anton Hain, 1969.
Harris, H. *Hegel's Development : Toward the Sunlight.* Oxford, Clarendon Press, 1971.
Haym, R. *Hegel und seine Zeit.* Hildesheim, Olms Verlagbuchhandlung, 1962; 1st ed., Berlin, 1857.
Hegel, G. W. F. *Berliner Schriften.* Hamburg, Felix Meiner Verlag, 1956.
———. *Briefe.* Vols. 1–4. Hamburg, Felix Meiner Verlag, 1961.
———. *Einleitung in die Geschichte der Philosophie.* Hamburg, Felix Meiner Verlag, 1959.
———. *Enzyklopädie* (1830). Edited by Nicolin-Pöggeler. Hamburg, Felix Meiner Verlag, 1969 / *The Logic of Hegel* (Pt. 1 of the *Encyclopedia).* Translated by W. Wallace. Oxford, Clarendon Press, 1892 / *Hegel's Philosophy of Nature* (Pt. 2 of the *Encyclopedia*). Translated by A. V. Miller. Oxford, Clarendon Press, 1970 / *Hegel's Philosophy of Nature.* Translated and edited by M. J. Petry. London, George Allen and Unwin, 1970 / *Hegel's Philosophy of Mind* (Pt. 3 of the *Encyclopedia*). Translated by W. Wallace and A. V. Miller. Oxford, Clarendon Press, 1971.
———. *Grundlinien der Philosophie des Rechts.* Hamburg, Felix Meiner Verlag, 1955 / *Hegel's Philosophy of Right.* translated with notes by T. M. Knox. London and New York, Oxford University Press, 1969.
———. *Jenaer kritischen Schriften,* edited by Buchner-Pöggeler. In *Gesammelte Werke.* Vol. 4. Hamburg, Felix Meiner Verlag, 1968. Cited from this edition are: *Differenz des Fichte'schen und Schelling'schen Systems der Philosophie; Glauben und Wissen;* and "Verhältnis des Skeptizismus zur Philosophie, Darstellung seiner verschiedenen Modifikationen, und Vergleichung des Neuesten mit dem alter."
———. *Phänomenologie des Geistes.* Hamburg, Felix Meiner Verlag, 1952 / *Phenomenology of Mind.* Translated by J. B. Baillie. New York, Harper and Row, 1967.
———. *Die Vernunft in der Geschichte.* Hamburg, Felix Meiner Verlag, 1955.
———. *Vorlesungen über die Ästhetik.* Edited by F. Bassenge.

Frankfurt, Europäische Verlagsanstalt, 1955 / *G. W. F. Hegel: On Art, Religion, and Philosophy*. Edited by J. Glenn Gray. New York, Harper and Row, 1970.

———. *Vorlesungen über die Geschichte der Philosophie*. In *Sämtlichte Werke,* edited by H. Glockner. Vols. 17–19. Stuttgart, F. Frommanns Verlag, 1959 / *Hegel's Lectures on the History of Philosophy*. Translated by E. S. Haldane and F. H. Simson. London, Routledge and Kegan Paul, 1892–96.

———. *Vorlesungen über die Philosophie der Religion*. Hamburg, Felix Meiner Verlag, 1968.

———. *Vorlesungen über die Philosophie der Weltgeschichte*. Hamburg, Felix Meiner Verlag, 1968.

———. *Wissenschaft der Logik*. Leipzig, Felix Meiner Verlag, 1951 / *Hegel's Science of Logic*. Translated by A. V. Miller. London, George Allen and Unwin; New York, Humanities Press, 1969.

Heidegger, M. *Hegel's Concept of Experience*. New York, Harper and Row, 1970.

———. "Hegel und die Griechen." In *Die Gegenwart der Griechen im Neueren Denken*. Tübingen, J. C. B. Mohr, 1960.

———. *Schellings Abhandlung über das Wesen der menschlichen Freiheit* (1809). Tübingen, Max Niemeyer Verlag, 1971.

Henrich, D. *Fichtes ursprüngliche Einsicht*. Frankfurt, Vittorio Klostermann, 1967.

———. *Hegel im Kontext*. Frankfurt, Suhrkamp Verlag, 1971.

Huber, G. *Das Sein und das Absolute*. Basel, Verlag für Recht und Gesellschaft AG, 1955.

Hyppolite, J. *Genèse et structure de la phénoménologie de l'ésprit de Hegel*. Paris, Editions Montaigne, 1946.

Iljin, I. *Die Philosophie Hegels als kontemplative Gotteslehre*. Bern, Francke Verlag, 1946.

Janke, W. *Fichte*. Berlin, Walter de Gruyter, 1970.

Jones, R. F. *Ancients and Moderns*. Saint Louis, Washington University Press, 1961.

Kant, I. *Idee zu einer allgemeinen Geschichte in weltbürger-*

licher Abischt. In *Werke, Akademie Textausgabe*. Vol. 8, Berlin, Walter de Gruyter, 1968.

———. *Kritik der praktischen Vernunft*. Hamburg, Felix Meiner Verlag, 1952.

———. *Kritik der reinen Vernunft*. Hamburg, Felix Meiner Verlag, 1956.

———. *Kritik der Urteilskraft*. Hamburg, Felix Meiner Verlag, 1956.

———. "Von einem neuerdings erhobenen vornehmen Ton in der Philosophie." In *Werke, Akademie Textausgabe*. Berlin, Walter de Gruyter, 1968.

Kelly, G. A. *Idealism, Politics, and History*. Cambridge, Cambridge University Press, 1969.

Klein, J. *Greek Mathematical Thought and the Origin of Algebra*. Cambridge, Mass., MIT Press, 1968.

Kojève, A. *Essai d'une histoire raisonnée de la philosophie païenne*. Paris, Gallimard, 1968–73).

———. *Introduction à la lecture de Hegel*. Paris, Gallimard, 1947.

Koselleck, R. *Kritik und Krise*. Freiburg / Munich, Verlag Karl Alber, 1959.

Koyré, A. *From the Closed World to the Infinite Universe*. New York, Harper and Row, 1958.

Kremer, K. *Die neuplatonische Seinsphilosophie und ihre Wirkung auf Thomas von Aquin*. Leiden, E. J. Brill, 1966.

Krohn, W. *Die formale Logik in Hegels "Wissenschaft der Logik."* Munich, Carl Hanser Verlag, 1972.

Kuhn, H. "Die Vollendung der klassischen deutschen Ästhetik durch Hegel" (1931). In *Schriften zur Ästhetik*. Munich, Kosel Verlag, 1966.

Kümmel, F. *Platon und Hegel*. Tübingen, Max Niemeyer Verlag, 1968.

Labarrière, P-J. *Structures et mouvement dialectique dans la phénoménologie de l'ésprit de Hegel*. Paris, Aubier-Montaigne, 1968.

Leibniz, G. W. *Monadologie*. Preface, introduction, and commentary by J. C. Horn. Frankfurt, Europäische Verlagsanstalt, 1962.

———. *Specimen Dynamicum* in *Mathematische Schriften.* Vol. 6. Edited by C. I. Gerhardt. Hildesheim, Olms Verlagsbuchhandlung, 1965.

———. *Système nouveau* (1695). In *Die Philosophische Schriften.* Vol. 4. Edited by C. I. Gerhardt. Hildesheim, Olms Verlagsbuchhandlung, 1965.

Locke, J. *An Essay Concerning Human Understanding.* Edited by A. C. Fraser. New York, Dover Publications, 1959.

Löwith, K. *From Hegel to Nietzsche.* New York, Doubleday, 1967.

Lübbe, H. *Politische Philosophie in Deutschland.* Basel / Stuttgart, Benno Schwabe & Co. Verlag, 1963.

Lukács, G. *Der junge Hegel.* In *Werke.* Vol. 8. Neuwied and Berlin, Luchterhand, 1967.

———. *Geschichte und Klassenbewusstsein.* In *Frühschriften II.* Neuwied and Berlin, Luchterhand, 1968.

Marcuse, H. *Hegels Ontologie und die Theorie der Geschichtlichkeit.* 2d ed. Frankfurt, Vittorio Klostermann, 1968.

Marx, K. *Zur Kritik der Nationalökonomie—Ökonomisch-Philosophische Manuskripte.* In *Frühe Schriften.* Vol. 1. Edited by Lieber-Furth. Darmstadt, Wissenschaftliche Buchgesellschaft, 1962.

Maurer, R. K. *Hegel und das Ende der Geschichte.* Stuttgart, W. Kohlhammer Verlag, 1965.

Müller, G. *Sophokles, Antigone.* Heidelberg, Carl Winter Verlag 1967.

Mure, G. R. G. *An Introduction to Hegel.* London and New York, Oxford University Press, 1959.

———. *A Study of Hegel's Logic.* Oxford, Clarendon Press, 1948.

Nietzsche, F. *Werke.* Edited by K. Schlechta. Munich, Carl Hanser Verlag, 1955.

Oelmüller, W. *Die unbefriedigte Aufklärung.* Frankfurt, Suhrkamp Verlag, 1969.

Pascal, B. *Pensées* in *Oeuvres complètes.* Paris, NRF, 1954.

Peperzak, A. T. B. *Le jeune Hegel et la vision morale du monde.* The Hague, M. Nijhoff, 1960; rev. ed., 1969.

Plato. *Opera*. Edited by J. Burnet. Oxford, Clarendon Press, 1900–15.
Plotinus. *Enneads*. Translated by A. H. Armstrong. Cambridge, Mass., Harvard University Press, 1966.
Pöggeler, O. "Qu'est-ce que la 'Phénoménologie de l'Esprit'?" *Archives de Philosophie,* April–June 1966.
Popitz, H. *Der entfremdete Mensch.* 2d ed. Darmstadt, Wissenschaftliche Buchgesellschaft, 1967.
Pothast, U. *Über einzige Fragen der Selbstbeziehung.* Frankfurt, Vittorio Klostermann, 1971.
Proclus. *The Elements of Theology.* Translation, introduction, and commentary by E. R. Dodds. Oxford, Clarendon Press, 1963.
Purpus, W. *Zur Dialektik des Bewusstseins nach Hegel.* Berlin, Trowitsch & Sohn, 1908.
Riedel, M. *Studien zu Hegels Rechtsphilosophie.* Frankfurt, Suhrkamp Verlag, 1969.
———. *Theorie und Praxis im Denken Hegels.* Stuttgart, W. Kohlhammer Verlag, 1965.
Ritter, J. *Metaphysik und Politik.* Frankfurt, Suhrkamp Verlag, 1969.
Rohrmoser, G. *Subjektivität und Verdinglichung.* Gutersloh, Gerd Mohn, 1961.
Rohs, P. *Form und Grund.* In *Hegel Studien. Beiheft* 6. Bonn, H. Bouvier, 1969.
Rosen, S. "Alexandre Kojève, *Essai d'une histoire raisonnée de la philosophie païenne.*" *Man and World* 3, no. 1 (February 1970).
———. "A Central Ambiguity in Descartes." In *Cartesian Essays,* edited by B. Magnus and J. B. Wilbur. The Hague, M. Nijhoff, 1969.
———. *Nihilism.* New Haven, Yale University Press, 1969.
———. "Self-Consciousness and Self-Knowledge: The Relation between Plato and Hegel." *Hegel Studien* 9 (1974).
———. Sōphrosynē and Selbstbewusstsein." *Review of Metaphysics,* June 1973.
Rosenkranz, K. *Georg Wilhelm Friedrich Hegels Leben.*

Darmstadt, Wissenschaftliche Buchgesellschaft, 1963; 1st ed., 1844.
Rosenzweig, F. *Hegel und der Staat.* Berlin, R. Oldenburg, 1920.
Rotenstreich, N. "On the Ecstatic Sources of the Concept of Alienation." *Review of Metaphysics,* March 1963.
Rousseau, J. J. *Du Contrat Social.* Paris, Garnier, 1954.
———. *Émile.* Paris, Garnier, 1924.
Sarlemijn, A. *Hegelsche Dialektik.* Berlin, Walter de Gruyter, 1971.
Schelling, F. W. J. *Darstellung meines Systems der Philosophie* (1801). In *Schriften von 1801–1804.* Darmstadt, Wissenschaftliche Buchgesellschaft, 1968.
———. *System des transzendentalen Idealismus* (1800). Introduction by W. Schulz. Hamburg, Felix Meiner Verlag, 1957.
Schmitz, H. *Hegel als Denker der Individualität.* Meisenheim / Glan, Verlag Anton Hain, 1957.
Schulz, W. *Die Vollendung des deutschen Idealismus in der Spätphilosophie Schellings.* Stuttgart, W. Kohlhammer Verlag, 1955.
———. "Hegel und das Problem der Aufhebung der Metaphysik." In *Martin Heidegger zum siebzigsten Geburtstag.* Pfullingen, G. Neske Verlag, 1959.
Sebba, G. "Descartes and Pascal: A Retrospect." *Modern Language Notes* 87, no. 6 (November 1972).
Siep. L. *Hegel's Fichtekritik und die Wissenschaftslehre von 1804.* Freiburg and Munich, Verlag Karl Alber, 1970.
Spinoza, B. *Opera.* Edited by Van Vloten / Land. The Hague, M. Nijhoff, 1914.
Stenius, E. *Wittgenstein's Tractatus.* Oxford, Basil Blackwell, 1960.
Taminiaux, J. *La nostalgie de la Grèce à l'aube de l'idéalisme allemande.* The Hague, M. Nijhoff, 1967.
Theunissen, M. *Hegels Lehre vom absoluten Geist als theologisch–politischer Traktat.* Berlin, Walter de Gruyter, 1970.
———. "Die Verwirklichung der Vernunft. Zur Theorie-Praxis Diskussion im Anschluss an Hegel." *Philosophische Rundschau,* special supplement, 6 (1970).

Tilliette, X. *Schelling: Une philosophie en devenir.* Paris, J. Vrin, 1970.

Toms, E. *Being, Negation, and Logic.* Oxford, Basil Blackwell, 1962.

Wahl, J. *La Malheur de la conscience dans la philosophie de Hegel.* Paris, PUF, 1951.

Weiss, F. G. *Hegel's Critique of Aristotle's Philosophy of Mind.* The Hague, M. Nijhoff, 1969.

Wiehl, R. "Platos Ontologie in Hegels Logik des Seins." *Hegel Studien* 3 (1965).

Wittgenstein, L. *Tractatus logico-philosophicus.* In *Schriften* 1. Frankfurt, Suhrkamp Verlag, 1969.

Index

Since so many of the crucial terms in Hegel's science of wisdom are dialectically connected, an exhaustive index would be far too long to be useful. Some terms are partial synonyms, others entail the use of their dialectical counterparts, and still others necessarily recur on almost every page of this study. I have tried to provide the reader with a useful rather than an exhaustive index.